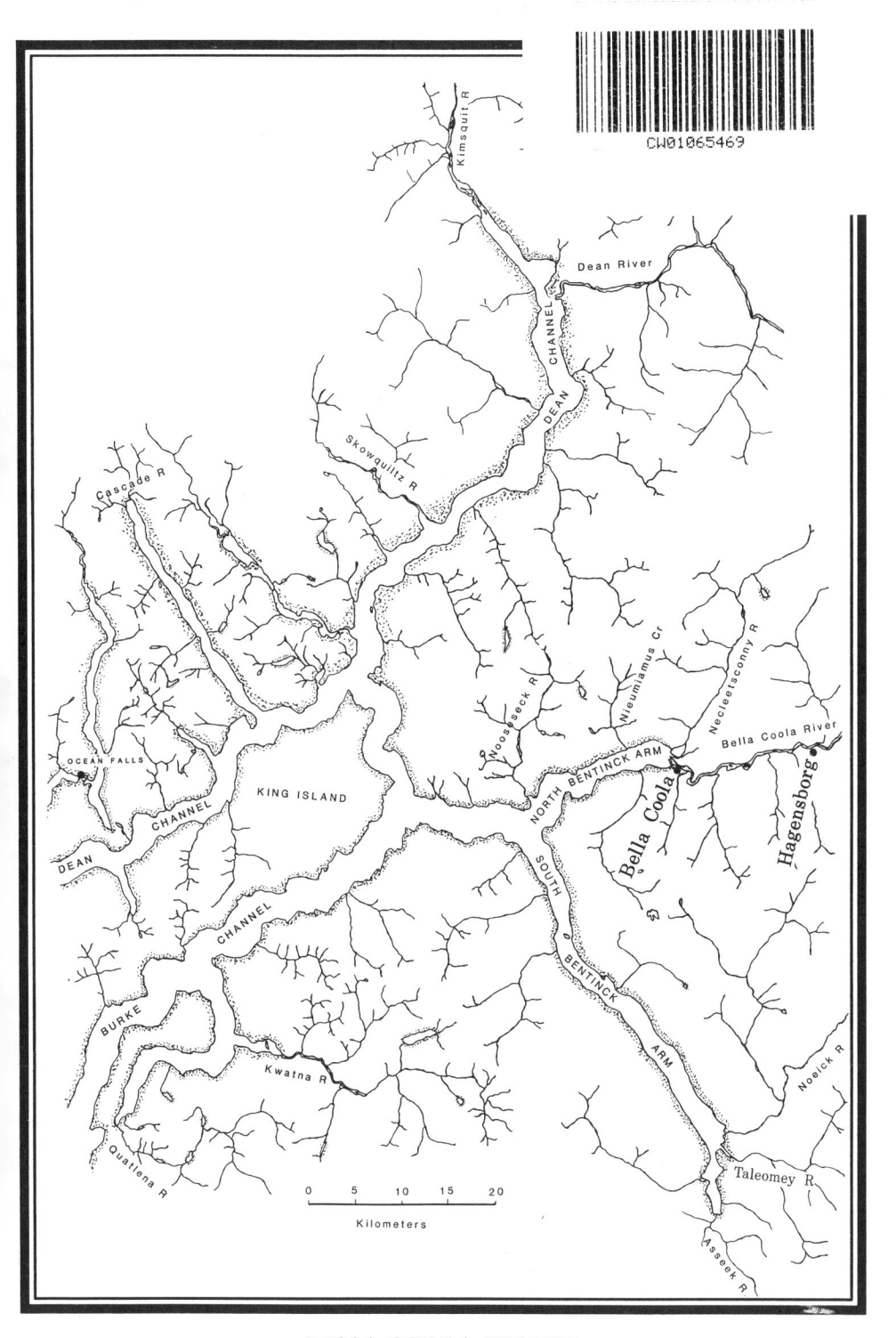

BELLA COOLA REGION

GRIZZLIES & WHITE GUYS

The Stories of Clayton Mack

Compiled and edited by
Harvey Thommasen

Foreword by Mark Hume

Maps and illustrations by Alistair Anderson

HARBOUR PUBLISHING
Madeira Park & Vancouver, British Columbia

Copyright © 1993 Harvey Thommasen
5 6 7 8 9 10 09 08 07 06 05

All rights reserved. No part of this publication may be reproduced, stored in a retrieval system or transmitted, in any form or by any means, without prior permission of the publisher or, in the case of photocopying or other reprographic copying, a licence from Access Copyright, the Canadian Copyright Licensing Agency, 1 Yonge Street, Suite 1900, Toronto, Ontario, M5E 1E5, www.accesscopyright.ca, 1-800-893-5777, info@accesscopyright.ca.

HARBOUR PUBLISHING
P.O. Box 219
Madeira Park, BC
V0N 2H0
www.harbourpublishing.com

Edited by Susan Mayse. Cover design by Roger Handling. Cover photograph courtesy Cliff Kopas. Maps and line illustrations by Alistair Anderson. Photographs pages 15 and 18 courtesy the Mack family. Photographs pages 26 and 29 courtesy Sage Birchwater. Photographs pages 16 (negatives #58531 and #56942), 23 (#62145 and #52007) and 25 (#50179) courtesy the Canadian Museum of Civilization. Photographs pages 42, 48, 59, 171, 184 and 230 courtesy Cliff Kopas.
Printed and bound in Canada

Harbour Publishing acknowledges financial support from the Government of Canada, through the Book Publishing Industry Development Program and the Canada Council for the Arts, and from the Province of British Columbia though the British Columbia Arts Council and the Book Publisher's Tax Credit through the Ministry of Provincial Revenue.

The Canada Council for the Arts / Le Conseil des Arts du Canada since 1957 / depuis 1957

BRITISH COLUMBIA ARTS COUNCIL
Supported by the Province of British Columbia

Canadian Cataloguing in Publication Data

Mack, Clayton, 1910–1993
   Grizzlies & white guys

   ISBN 1-55017-140-2

   1. Mack, Clayton, 1910–1993. 2. Hunting guides—British Columbia—Biography. 3. Bella Coola Indians—Biography. 4. Indians of North America—British Columbia—Biography. 5. Hunting—British Columbia—Anecdotes. I. Thommasen, Harvey Victor, 1957– II. Title.
E99.B39M33   1993   971.1'004979   C93-091645-X

This book is dedicated to my wife Carol,
who made it possible, and to my daughters
Keri and Amy.

H.T.

Acknowledgements

Many people have contributed to the contents of this book—thanks to them all. Special thanks to Audrey Haggkvist, Wayne Hay, Andre Mackenzie and Andrew Trites for their help on the word processor; Peter Piddington for his notes from the BC Archives; Glenn Krebs for his help on the RCMP-related stories; Al Purkiss, Pat Fletcher and Miguel Moreno for their insightful comments; Lillian Siwallace, Grace Hans, Karen Anderson, Ed Moody, Lorraine Tallio and Hazel Nappie for their help in the spelling of Nuxalk words; Larry Stranberg for advice on organizing a book; George Robson, Sage Birchwater, Lucie Mack and Obie Mack for their photographs and comments; Carol Thommasen and Tracey Gillespie for their help in editing the manuscript; and George Robson for his many helpful tips. Les Kopas very kindly allowed us to use his father's pictures. A very professional final edit was done by Susan Mayse.

Contents

Foreword *Mark Hume*	9
Preface *Harvey Thommasen*	10
My life	13
The guiding business	46
Hollywood	56
Close calls	72
Big shot hunters	92
The woman who wore blue lipstick	114
The sasquatch	123
Ways of the grizzly bear	140
The grizzly that slept in my bed	160
Molasses and the wolves	179
Old Chief Squinas	201
Fishing stories	211
Them Fish and Wildlife guys	220
Index	235

Foreword

MARK HUME, senior correspondent for *The Vancouver Sun* and author of *The Run of the River*

■□■□■□■□■□■□■□■□■□■□■□■□■□■□■□■□■□■

This book contains a remarkable collection of stories about a time and a way of life that has vanished. They are told by a natural storyteller, by a man who as a child was carried as a prop in native ceremonial dances, and who later found himself dining in Hollywood restaurants with California's most powerful people. Not surprisingly, there's a sense of showmanship to Clayton Mack's storytelling. But there is also a ring of truth to everything he says. His stories are like native ritual dances in that it's impossible to separate the magic from the realism, and after you have read him for awhile you realize that knowing where the line is isn't important.

Clayton Mack knew the coastal mountains like a grizzly bear. He knew people too. Sometimes I wonder if he wasn't born part bear, part Indian shaman. He was a dancer and a fighter and for a living he chose to help men who weren't half the hunter he was to kill bears.

His stories are wild and bawdy and funny and tragic. They reach back through history. From The Woman Who Wore Blue Lipstick to The Grizzly That Slept in My Bed, Clayton Mack will keep you spellbound. And at the end, you will wonder what was real and what was dream. The amazing thing is, it's all true. It's all true. ■

Preface

Clayton Mack was born on a hot summer day—August 7, 1910—across from Nieumiamus Creek, "the place of flies." He was born at a time when native Indians of the Pacific Northwest were struggling just to survive. So devastating was the impact of disease, alcohol and forced cultural change that many European settlers felt that soon natives would simply disappear from the scene. When Alexander Mackenzie visited the Bella Coola Indian territory in 1793, the population was estimated conservatively at twenty-seven hundred. By 1910 it had plummeted to three hundred. Despite numerous obstacles, the people of the Nuxalk Nation have survived.

This is the story of one Bella Coola Indian, Clayton Mack. His story is particularly interesting because his experiences span four distinct native cultures: Bella Coola (Nuxalk), Bella Bella/Rivers Inlet (Heiltsuk), Alert Bay (Kwak'wala) and Anahim Lake (Chilcotin-Carrier). Through his experiences in residential school, with white government bureaucracy, as a labourer in the logging, commercial fishing, and ranching businesses, and as a grizzly bear hunting guide, Clayton also developed interesting insights into the *q'umsciwa's* (white man's) world. Hard work and amazing versatility made Clayton Mack a success in his world of bucking broncs, vast tracts of unlogged watersheds, sailing fishboats, grizzly bear hunts and Hollywood movie stars.

Clayton Mack is best known for his grizzly bear hunting exploits. He was a legendary grizzly bear guide whose career coincided with a golden age of grizzly bear hunting on British Columbia's central coast. Clayton's early life experiences combined to make him a natural grizzly bear hunter. As a young boy he learned respect for grizzly bears from the native lore. His trapping experiences along the coast led him right into prime grizzly bear habitat. His time with the Chilcotin Indians in the Anahim Lake area sharpened his tracking skills. As a Home Guard Ranger Clayton had access to ten thousand rounds of ammunition, and his target practice allowed him to become an expert shot with rifle and handgun. As one of the first grizzly bear guides in the central coast, Clayton Mack led the rich and famous on trophy hunts that felled more than three hundred grizzly bears over fifty-three years. The hunting ground was a land of giant conifer forests—forests of trees over a thousand years old—where gigantic grizzlies, salmon, bald eagles, native Indians and the mythical sasquatch lived in apparent harmony.

Clayton witnessed many changes in the land he knew so well, changes which he did not like but could only helplessly observe. The Nuxalk people were willing to share their land with the white settlers, which brought more extensive changes than any of them imagined. In Clayton Mack's lifetime the majority of salmon-producing streams on the central coast have been logged; white foresters have systematically turned the ancient old growth forest into monoculture conifer plantations. The negative impacts of logging practices on wild salmonid stream stocks, wild bird populations and other animals are only now being understood. Commercial fishermen and sports fishers bicker and fight with fishery managers each year in their attempts to kill the greatest possible number of fish; the fishery managers respond with educated guesses of allowable harvest while crossing their fingers and praying wild stream salmon and steelhead populations will survive the onslaught of nets and lines standing in the way of the fish reaching their spawning beds. Many of the places where Clayton once peacefully trekked through groves of giant Douglas fir, spruce, hemlock and cedar are now massive clearcuts; the stream pools which once erupted with fish now contain a few nervous shadows attempting to hide from ever-present predators.

In May 1984 Clayton suffered a major stroke which left him wheelchair-bound. But until his death in April 1993 his mind remained bright, alert and full of stories. On any given day he could be seen in or around the hospital with plaid jacket and cowboy hat. Often he sat in his wheelchair in front of a topographical map of the central coast, perhaps recalling tales told by long dead elders, reliving experiences, riding lively horses in the Chilcotin country, crashing through ocean waves by Mesachie Nose in his forty-five-foot gill-netter, racing up Owikeno Lake rivers in river boats, setting traps on his traplines, climbing rocky cliffs in search of giant quartz crystals and gold nuggets, and tracking grizzly bears or the elusive sasquatch.

Clayton Mack was a natural storyteller. His stories are simple, direct, authentic and often witty. They reflect an oral tradition which is rapidly disappearing among native people swamped by information overload from radio, television, newspapers and videos, and they present a perspective until now unknown to the majority. I hope you will enjoy them, and appreciate the truth, insight, humour and—in some cases—frustration, confusion and anger of Clayton Mack.

HARVEY THOMMASEN

My life

I am the last one, and my brother Orden, that's all. Two left out of seven brothers and sisters. Just me and Orden left now. Two more to go!

Noosgulch is where my mother's family came from. Her name was Mary Samson. Her father was a big chief in Noosgulch Village. My mother told me that long ago God, Jesus Christ, put her people on the top of Noosgulch Mountain—called Mount Nusatsum now—and they go down to the bottom of the mountain. That mountain belongs to my mother's family. Her people build a village at the bottom of the mountain, and lived there for years and years until the white men came. Noosgulch Mountain is the biggest mountain in the Bella Coola Valley. Noosgulch Village was the biggest Indian village up-valley in the olden days.

When I was a kid, I listen to my mother tell me a lot of stories about the old days. Sound like lot of the old Indian stories same as in the Bible. That big flood happen here too. But not just one boat was made here. Lot of people make boats, lots of boats. Like war canoes. And the people go in them. They paddle to Noosgulch Mountain because it's high and they pull their canoes up, climb up the rock and wait for the flood to go down. Some people paddle to Bella Bella, other people paddle to Queen Charlotte Islands.

My dad's name was Willie Mack. My dad, he don't got no Bella Coola mountains that I know of. Because he was a half-breed, I guess. Half Bella Coola Indian, half Hudson's Bay English man. I don't know where the name Mack came from, Fort Rupert name, I think.

My dad's grandfather's name was *Ulalitsuk,* which is a Chinook word for berry homebrew. He like to make homebrew. His Bella Coola Indian name was *N'anikda.* N'anikda told my dad that there was a time when the Bella Coola Indian people get smallpox, and die like flies. Every day they die. People would dig big deep graves, crawl in and die, and hope next person come would bury them before they crawl in and die too.

N'anikda had a daughter, that is my dad's mother. Her name was *Q'uit.* One day N'anikda have to get out of Bella Coola and get a job in Victoria. N'anikda told his daughter, "Get ready, we going out. Go to Victoria." So they got ready, packed up the canoe and took off. They got as far as Port Hardy, and that girl get spots on her face. The old man think, "My daughter get smallpox again." N'anikda didn't want to spread smallpox to Victoria. They went by a little island close to Port Hardy, and they turn in there. N'anikda decided he's gonna have to leave Q'uit, his daughter, on that little island. But no way he can kill her. So N'anikda packed wood, light a fire for her. Left her there, then he keep on going to Victoria. He was sure she was gonna die from smallpox. Some people from Fort Rupert came through there and they found that girl. She didn't have smallpox again. Q'uit was okay. A Fort Rupert chief took that girl. He took her as his own daughter. Anyway, the chief look after this girl and she grow up.

Then a white man named John Clayton came to Fort Rupert and start a store there. He had stores in many villages from Vancouver to Prince Rupert. Hudson's Bay Company

My life

stores. He wanted this girl, the chief's daughter. He want to keep Q'uit with him in the store. She did live with him. And they got a kid, that's my dad. His name was Willie Mack. So my dad was born in Fort Rupert. Born sometime around 1875. John Clayton later moved Q'uit, and my dad to Bella Coola. Q'uit came back to Bella Coola, the place where she belong to. N'anikda was so glad to see his daughter was alive. And he loved the boy—my dad—so much. That's the story I heard. That John Clayton was my father's dad. My dad was pretty white. He had one boy who was pretty white, Samson. One of my brothers. I also heard a story John Clayton had another Bella Coola Indian woman after my grandmother. He had two girls with that other Indian woman. Related to Schooner family, I think. The two girls took off to the States. They didn't like to stay with the old man, I guess.

When John Clayton first came to Bella Coola, he put up something like a store at Clayton Falls. That's how it got its name: Clayton Falls Creek. He built a wharf in there too. Something like a cannery wharf, a wharf built on pilings. Big flat-deck wharf. Lot of boats came in to his store. Later he moved the store up here, on the townsite by the Bella Coola River. Then there was land trouble with John Clayton. He get

Clayton's grandfather, John Clayton

Clayton Mack's parents, Mary Samson and Willie Mack

the Bella Coola chiefs to let him borrow the land from Clayton Falls Creek to the edge of townsite. He said he would use the land and put the people to work. At that time there were Indian houses all over the townsite. Clayton wanted to borrow that land, just to use it and put the Indians to work. He promised he gonna help the Indian people out.

So the chiefs said, "Let him have it. Gives us jobs, anyway, and clears the land." The Indian people chop the woods down by hand, pull the stumps and hand-plough the land for John Clayton. So the townsite used to be a big open field, all the way toward the tideflats. John Clayton would plant potatoes, and all kind of different vegetables. Right around where the hospital and school are now. Then John Clayton got cattle. He got a bull. I don't know what kind of bull he had. It killed an Indian man. Pinned him right against the fence, against something solid, and cut his belly right open. After that the Indian people not care too much for John Clayton.

My grandmother Q'uit died. I never did see her. I think she died in her old age, that's all I know. I try to find out before but no one know. After my grandmother died my father lived with N'anikda, Old Berry Homebrew. They made a big chief woman out of my grandmother in Fort Rupert, and they make a big chief out of the boy, my dad. They had a big potlatch for

My life

them. Mungo Martin, Tommy Hunt families. Fort Rupert is outside Port Hardy. They didn't make my dad a chief here for a while. Fort Rupert people make him chief first, then Bella Coola people made chief out of him again. Bella Bella even made him a chief. My dad was chief over lot of coast—Fort Rupert, Bella Bella, and Bella Coola. I know my dad knew Fort Rupert pretty good. He took us there once.

My mother, Mary Samson, was one of the last to live in Noosgulch Village. She move down to the Bella Coola Village when she was old enough to live with a man, old enough to get married. They kind of forced her to marry a guy here. The fathers compare each others, big chiefs both of them, so these rich peoples make their kids marry. My mother wasn't in love with him at all. They didn't get along. So she quit him. But she did have one kid with that guy, Thomas Walkus's mother. Mary Samson married to my dad after. Then they had seven kids. Eliza the oldest, Donald next, Minnie, Samson, Orden, then me, and Alfred's the youngest. Two years behind each others. Two years apart all the way, like.

Donald get killed in a logging camp, he was about twenty-one years old. Eliza got TB and died when about twenty-five years old. Minnie get pneumonia and died when she was about twenty years old. Samson died when about sixty or sixty-five from a heart attack. Alfred he was about fifty years old, I guess, when he got heart attack and then died.

John Clayton already died when I was born. I didn't see him. When I was old enough to remember, I knew John Clayton's second wife, a white woman. He went to England to get that woman. John Clayton's wife, the English woman, she's the one that give me my English name Clayton. Because my dad's father was Clayton, I guess. She named me after him. That English woman's name was Elizabeth Orden. They call one of my brothers Orden, maybe after her.

With his white woman from England, John Clayton had two white boys and two white girls. I used to see my dad with the two Clayton boys. I see them together all the time; work together, like. Them Clayton boys liked us kids. My dad used to take me over to John Clayton's store when I was a little boy. I don't buy nothing at all. They just give it to me. I look at the shoes. "You want shoes?"

"Yeah," I said.

Put it on me. "Okay, you can go home. You have new shoes now," they say to me.

When I was young I like to go with my father. Wherever he goes, I go with him. He was a carpenter, boat builder and house builder. He build three houses for us across the river. Anything goes wrong, he's right there to repair it. My mother used to work in the B.C. Packers fish cannery in the net loft. Make nets, salvage nets, hang nets. She filled salmon cans too.

One day I asked my mum, "Where was I born?"

Willie Mack and his family during the 1910s

My life

She said, "You were born right here at the cannery, on a hot summer day. August 7, 1910."

I work at the cannery, myself, I work for a Chinaman. I earned thirty cents an hour to wash fish. I was about nine years old. I worked in there for about two years, about five hours a day, up to seven days a week. Work wasn't too hard, we used a brush. A machine cut the head off, the guts came out, and we would brush where the guts used to be and wash it out. In the fall time we'd go home. In the early spring we'd go back again.

My dad, he got a contract to cut two or three hundred cords of wood for the cannery. The cannery would cook fish with that wood. My dad was paid five dollars a cord, a four-feet-wide and eight-feet-long pile of cut wood. He would start around February and quit in May. One year I told my dad I wanted to help cut wood. He cut an eight-foot hand saw in half, filed it for me, and I used it to cut wood. No power saw in those days. With this little half saw I went to the tideflats, cut the butts off the alder trees, and at high tide I would tow them down to the wharf where we would split them. There was a platform at the top of the wharf. My dad used to help me haul the wood to the top of the platform. From February to May I cut six cords of wood, thirty dollars. I was doing all right for a kid. I buy myself running shoes, nice pants, nice shirt. I was about eleven years old at this time. That was hard work, cutting that wood.

Wintertime we would go to school in day school, they called it. Three hours in the morning and three hours in the afternoon. I start school when I was pretty young. I go for about two years. Phyllis Gibson was the teacher. Preacher's daughter. Teached us in English. She speak English to us all the time. I learn little bit of English from her. After a while I learn a little bit what she mean. At home I speak my own language, Nuxalk language. My mother teach us Nuxalk language and she teach us how to speak Chinook language too. She can't speak English but she speak Chinook real good. My dad, too, he speak

Chinook language. Chinook language was something like English language in them days. Everyone know that language on the coast. My dad, when he meet guys from Bella Bella or Alert Bay or Rivers Inlet they all speak Chinook language. My mum and dad were both pretty good at Chinook. My mum, she sing songs in Chinook too. So I learn Nuxalk, then I learn Chinook, then I learn English. I didn't really learn English at that day school, I learn it most when I work for and work with white people. Nowadays none of my kids speak my language. They just laugh at me when I speak our Nuxalk language. They say, "What they hell you talkin' about?" They don't know Chinook too. Only language they know is English. That's all they know.

My dad died when I was pretty young yet. July 8, 1923. He died when he was only about forty-six years old. That's all. Busted appendix in the summertime. He had a big boil on the back of his neck too. Doctors didn't know why he was so sick. Later doctor found out it was his appendix. After my dad died we were pretty poor. There was eight of us altogether: my mother, five boys and two girls. I go trap muskrat then, down by the tideflat. I sell the muskrat for fifty cents a piece, buy a little bit of bread and other food.

I spend a lot of time campin' out in the woods with old guys like Joshua Moody and Alexander Clellamin after my dad died. Mostly with Alexander Clellamin. Alexander Clellamin lived not too far away from our house, and he took me when I was about thirteen years old or so and teach me how to hunt, teach me how to trap muskrat, mink and marten. He was part Indian from up-country. Half-breed. Half Chilcotin Indian, half Stuie Indian. He would take me way out in the ocean, and we'd trap those mink and marten in the forests. Near Restoration Bay.

It was pretty tough going, out there in the ocean. I'd paddle and row with oars against the wind and big waves, paddle and row so hard that my hands would bleed sometimes. Hungry, too, not much to eat. The old man would dig clams

My life

and feed me those clams raw, not cooked. Makes you a tough man! I got used to it after a while, eat raw clams not cooked. But I still like to make a fire on the beach sometimes, and roast and barbecue clams on the campfire. Sometimes he get sea eggs, sea urchins, and feed me that too. After a while, I get tough, I don't care what I eat. We jig for cod fish, cook them and boil it. Shoot a deer and fry it or boil it. I would go out with him for a couple of months at a time. Come back home for a short while and go out again.

I would still go to day school little bit, but not much. We used to run away from that school at recess time. We would go up to the little river behind the school, where the fish go up there, and we gaff-hook them fish and take them home and smoke them. This school was in the old town, on the other side.

One day the Indian agent grabbed me by the hair and dragged me, pulled me up to my mother. He going to send me to poor kid's school in Alert Bay. Any poor kid around, they put them in that school. He tell me, "You got to go to school and learn something." He took me and my brother, Alfred, in the boat and send me down to Alert Bay. Alert Bay is on an island, only a few miles across and seven miles around. I was about fifteen years old.

But when I got there everybody gone home, still gone for holiday. One guy there, he asked me if I know how to handle horses and cows.

"Oh, yeah, I can handle them," I said.

The principal, he says, "Good, you stay here, you not going home, we will pay you one dollar a day to look after the horses and cows."

So I feed the horses, clean the barn, feed the cows and later even milk the cows. I get up at four o'clock in the morning sometimes and go look for them cows. I had ten cows. I'd get up, round them up, put them in the barn, feed them bran and then milk them. Then I have to get the milk ready for the

Chinaman to pick up. Let them cows out for the day. In the summer it was really hard work. When the school closed in summer they gave me the girls' cows too! The girls had about eight milk cows. So I did, looked after the whole works for two years. I also helped look after the farm, help with the potatoes, and helped cut the hay. I tried to go to school but there was not enough time. I worked most of the time. I went to Alert Bay for school and instead they put me in a job!

After the second summer, when the principal came back from his vacation, he gave me three choices. "Do you want to go home, do you want to stay another year, or we could send you to Vancouver for short course training school?" He said, "We could send you to special school to teach you like hell and you, you learn quick and go through high school then you could go home after that."

I said, "I want to go home right now."

"All right, you can go home," he said. I was thinking about my mother who was all by herself and getting old. And I always wanted to be a cowboy. When I got home here, I check my mum was okay, then I plan to go up-country right away. With the money I earned at Alert Bay, one dollar a day, I buy myself a suit, nice shoes, nice shirt. I was about seventeen years old now. I had an old horse called Fred. After I buy them clothes I put a saddle on Fred and I went up-country to Anahim Lake. At Anahim Lake I traded Fred for a wild horse. This wild horse used to be a race horse before—mean bugger. I got him from an Indian guy up-country. I learned about riding wild horses, bucking horses, from riding this horse.

Only four white people up there, Anahim Lake, when I get there. Bowser and his wife, Shilling and his wife. Lester Dorsey came about a year after me and bought Schilling out.

When I first went up, I hanged around with Old Chief Squinas and his son Thomas Squinas. Tommy's dad was old and couldn't do much any more. He ask me to stay with him. So I stayed with Old Chief Squinas for two or three winters. He

Old Chief Squinas and Thomas Squinas

could speak my language, and I learn a bit of their language from him. I'd feed his horses, haul hay for him, and cut wood for him. He had a few head of cattle and lots of horses. I helped look after what he's got. I learned how to ride bucking horse and steer when I was up there too. In the end a moose got Old Chief Squinas, punched him all over his body. Lived about a month, that's all, then he died.

The third winter I worked for Lester Dorsey too. Cutting fence logs. No power saws in those days. We had to chop those logs by hand, double-bladed axe. We had to chop a hundred logs a day. We had to chop like hell to make that much. But we helped each other, three guys in a crew, three hundred logs a day. Each guy earn three dollars a day. Dorsey used to own a big ranch in that country. He's got some boys—Steve Dorsey, Mike, Freddie, Dave. Dave's up-country now, he took over the ranch.

After Old Chief Squinas died, I stayed at his place for just a short while. One day in winter, I saw three womans chopping a hole in the ice on the Dean River. I walked down there and looked. And I meet my first wife, Doll Capoose. They call her Doll because she was so pretty when she was a baby. When we met, I was about nineteen years old and she was about the same age. She was with her big sister Josephine and her mother. They were sure tough girls, them girls. Josephine was born underneath a jack pine in the Itcha Mountains. Josephine's mum was Rosalie Sandyman. She was from up-country, Indian woman from Quesnel, I guess.

I asked them, "What you doing?"

"We gonna set a net underneath that ice, we got nothing to eat."

"How you gonna do that?" I asked.

They got about a twenty-five-foot stick. Tie the end of a net to the end of the stick. They measured out from here to the next hole in the ice, about twenty-five feet. They stick the stick underneath, she grab a rope attached to the end of the stick. Pull the net underneath the ice, to the next hole. I helped them. That water was sure cold. We got to stick our hands in the ice water to get that net. They talked like hell to me. They can't stop talking! Then they said they were gonna pull that net out in the morning.

"What time?" I asked them.

"About seven in the morning we gonna pull that net out. That's when we will take the fish out of the net."

"Okay, I'll be down here at that time," I said.

I came back and helped them pull that net. Not too many good fish. About ten rainbow trout. But about a hundred squaw fish. Nobody want that squaw fish—too many bones. They took the rainbow trout and the squaw fish out of the net.

"What you gonna do with all them squaw fish?" I asked.

"Cut them squaw fish open and smoke them for the dogs."

They were gonna feed them squaw fish to the dogs. They don't waste any fish. They wanted me to go with them. "Come with us."

"Where you stay?" I asked.

"At Behind Meadow."

They live in a small little house at Behind Meadow. Four of them in one small little house. One boy about twelve years old lived in there, too, with the three womans. I moved over there with them, about ten miles down below Anahim Lake, toward Anahim Peak. We talked about moving out of that small little cabin. There was another small cabin by the river. The guy who own it go to Vancouver. So we moved over there. Then I built a longhouse for them, about sixty feet long, right against that little cabin where we stay. We had lots of room in that new house.

Doll, Josephine and their mother didn't live with Old Man Capoose. He lived near in his own place. He don't want them in his own place. Old Man Capoose, Anton Capoose, got another woman in Vancouver, so he don't look after his wife or two kids. Make them work for him all summer, put up the hay. Wintertime, he don't look after them, don't feed them, don't let them live in his house. Instead they live in a small house, cold and hungry all the time. In the summer they get back to Capoose's place, live in his smoke house. They hungry all the time. Instead of take care of his family, he buy a fur coat for his other wife in Vancouver, eight thousand dollar coat.

Old Anton Capoose owned over a hundred head of cattle, about sixty or seventy head of horses, about sixty head of

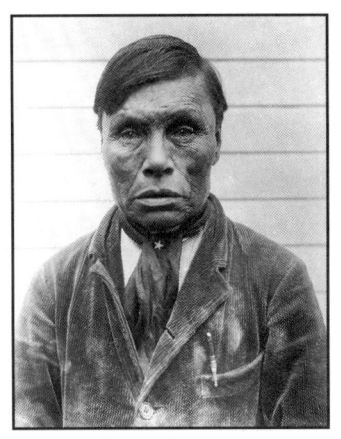

Anton Capoose

sheep—over two hundred head of animals. And my wife she own about fifty head cattle, twenty-five head of horses. Her sister Josephine owned about the same number of cattle and horses. At one time, altogether, there were over a hundred horses, over two hundred cattle and over fifty sheep, for the whole works, the family. They were good horses. Old Anton Capoose paid eighteen hundred dollars for a thoroughbred stallion. He got mares and breed them with that stallion and got nice colts. Nice horses, all right, big and strong and tall. Long-legged buggers! I used to break them, ride them.

  Old Anton Capoose was a smart guy. In the beginning, he would trap in the wintertime and come to Bella Coola and sell those furs. Then he would buy grub and pack it back up there to Anahim Lake. After a while he had forty head of pack horses. In Anahim Lake he'd trade that grub—sugar, flour, dried peaches, dried apples, canned fruit, coffee, tea—for more furs. He'd get maybe five or six thousand dollars worth of furs. Then he'd take the furs all the way to Vancouver and sell that fur himself. He'd buy lots of grub, clothes, and come back up on the Union

Capoose pack train going up the Precipice Trail

Steamship. He'd buy good second-hand stuff too. He had a little store, kind of a warehouse in Bella Coola, where he'd store all that stuff. In the fall he'd pack it all up-country to Anahim Lake and he'd sell it in the wintertime and trade for fur again. The white people buy a lot of stuff off him too. Next year Old Capoose do the same thing.

His daughters Josephine and Doll would be there waiting for him at Stuie. Waiting with forty head of pack horses. Waiting for that two or three truckloads of stuff. The girls have pack horses there to pack that stuff up to their place by Abuntlet Lake. Capoose and his girls would take that forty head of pack horses and go through Puntzi Lake, and all the way to Anahim Reserve near Alexis Creek. They sell stuff all the way. Sugar, flour and other stuff to every rancher too. Josephine was right there with him. She was in charge of that forty head of pack horses. Each pack horse carry about two hundred pounds of stuff. All Anton Capoose had was his two girls to help pack that stuff. In the wintertime they go up to Ulkatcho Village to sell that stuff. Use sleigh to go up there.

Capoose said to me one time, "I know just as good as a white man. My skin just a little black, that's all. My head just like a white man. I can read and write, but my skin just a little bit dark, that's all."

A white woman found out about this old Indian man who was making a lot of money. Capoose was getting to be old now, too, but still he couldn't say no when she came after him. He fell in love with her. He started to buy diamond rings for that woman, fur coats—thousand dollar coats. He bought her all kinds of stuff. She'd write letters to him. When he'd go to Vancouver he would see her. I used to read her letters. I remember the day that Old Man Capoose brought her up to see his house. He just had a little house. No insulation, no bath tub, no running water, just a little wood kitchen stove and a bed all made out of split jack pine. He got no toilet, doesn't even got an outhouse. She got to go out in the bushes to take a shit!

I was there when that white woman came, so was Old Man Capoose's Indian wife and his two kids, Doll and her sister Josephine. We were all lookin' at her when she came. Old Man Capoose's Indian wife she didn't get mad, she just said, "That poor woman. She can't live in this country."

Josephine saw that woman and said, "What kind of woman is that, Clayton?"

That white woman, she got a dress, silver fox scarf, mink coat, diamond rings, diamond bracelets, sharp skinny high heels and a diamond necklace. I told Josephine, "Maybe that woman come from Hollywood."

Josephine said, "Maybe that's the silver fox I trap last year. The fox I sell for four dollars and my dad buy again for a thousand dollars!"

My wife Doll, she don't say anything, she don't know what to think of that white woman.

That Hollywood woman walk around. Look at everything up and down. The house, the barn, the lake. She didn't talk too much. Only to Old Man Capoose. She wouldn't talk to us. Stayed a couple nights, then she took off. Old Man Capoose keep in touch with her. Every time he goes to Vancouver he sees her and buys her things. I think he see that white woman for over twenty years altogether. He usually go down to Vancouver once or twice a year to see his white woman wife. Go live with her for one week and come back. Come back broke! So Old Man Capoose had two wives, an Indian woman at home and a white woman in Vancouver.

Capoose's Indian wife, that old lady, when she first found out about that white woman she go down to see Maxie Heckman. She was mad and want to get even with her husband. She came down in the summertime when the fish go up the Bella Coola River. And she stay with old Maxie Heckman, a German guy who used to live up Atnarko. Maxie get the fish for her and he get two kids from her. That's Josephine and my first wife Doll Capoose. Nice looking girls, too, when they were young. So their dad was Anton Capoose,

Josephine Capoose, Louis Squinas and Doll Capoose

but their real father was Maxie Heckman. Josephine was the one told me that Maxie Heckman was their real dad.

I married Doll. It was around 1929. I took her down to Bella Coola. Got married at the United Church. Went back home to the ranch. The priest, Father Thomas, he raise hell with me. Try to fine me. "You married a Catholic woman in a United Church. It's not on the books," he said. "I fine you ten bucks." Supposed to marry in Catholic Church.

"I got no money to give you ten dollars," I told him. "But I'll get married three or four times if you want. I'll get her now and we'll get married again Catholic way. I'll marry her twenty times if you want." So I married twice with Doll, in a Catholic and in a United Church.

Up-country, we lived in that longhouse I built. Then I built another house, a real home. Three rooms on the bottom. Me and my wife and Josephine, three of us, helped look after old Anton Capoose's ranch. We did almost all of the work. Cut up to three hundred ton of hay a year. Old Man Capoose never helped, never do nothing. He was all right to me, he better because I help him lots. When the sun come up, just come out of the mountain, I started to cut hay. Just when the sun get behind the mountains, going down, then I quit. No wrist watch in them days. Old Man Capoose never paid me cent. But Doll, Josephine and the old lady look after me pretty good. Cook for me. We eat moose, deer, fish. No garden. I buy grub down here in Bella Coola. I got money to buy grub by going out gill-net fishing in summertime.

Clayton Mack on a horse

Every year, I come down to Bella Coola and start gill-net fishing May to early August. Doll would come down here too in fishing season. Sometimes she go gill-net fishing with me. Mostly she stay in our house in Bella Coola across the river, on the other side. All that I make gill-net fishing, I buy grub. One year I made three hundred dollars, that's all I made. Next year after, I make about twelve hundred dollars. Lots of grub that year. We had twenty head of horses, pack horses. We pack that grub up to Anahim Lake. I always plan to start cutting hay by my birthday in August. Seventh day of August, "Okay, time to quit gill-net fishing, let's go back up to Anahim Lake to cut hay."

Up in Anahim Lake country some families have a lot of kids. In hay time they have nothing to eat. I would say to them, "You guys got no money to buy grub? I got lots of grub. Give us help in the hay field. You can eat all you want. Take some of the grub, cook it, camp here."

One guy, Jamos—he dead now, someone shot him in the chest—he come every year and I feed him, give him some grub. Another guy, Felix, come from Ulkatcho every year. Felix work real hard. He start cutting hay before daylight. I paid him three dollars a day during hay season. Altogether, we would cut up to three hundred ton of hay. Hay season start in August and last just about to the end of October. We worked real hard for three months every year.

Old Capoose never bought the land. It was Indian land. Capoose fenced off his own ranch. The cabin I built was inside his fence. In the olden days the government surveyed the land for the Indians. The Indians were scattered all over in that Anahim Lake country. Old Capoose claimed his area because he cleared the land, fenced it off, cut the hay and kept it up. The Indian agent knew Capoose, Capoose was a well-known guy, with a lot of money and good horses.

I live with them for about two or three years when Old Man Capoose died. Capoose was pretty old when he died, about seventy-five years old, I guess. Old age. Died in the summertime. I was down in Bella Coola when he died. I think he was robbed too, when he died. We knew he had money, all right, I talked to my wife and Josephine. Yeah, he had money in the bank. I went through his papers, but we never knew how much money. Gone, too.

After old Capoose died, the Indian agent told me to carry on like that: look after the ranch, cattle, horses, sheep. Promised to pay me a dollar a day. I wanted five dollars a day. I told him it is a lot of work to look after that place. In the winter, fifty below zero, I have to take out two sleigh loads of hay to cattle, and take another load of hay to the barn to feed the calves, sheep and horses. I told the Indian agent I pay Felix three dollars a day to help me in hay season. I told the Indian agent that I even paid some of the other Ulkatcho Indians who helped me to put up hay at Capoose's place. I told the Indian agent I even gave some of them horses, packsaddles, different clothes when they help with the hay. But the Indian agent just say, "No, five dollars a day is too much. I will just pay you one dollar." I look after that ranch for two to three years after Capoose died.

Then one day, the Indian agent took away the land, took everything on Old Man Capoose's land, and sell it. Took the whole works and sell them. I thought he would cut the cattle three ways, to Capoose's wife and two daughters. Instead we got nothing, I got nothing too. I look after that cattle, horses and sheep for free all that time. I couldn't do anything, nobody to talk to, you know. What did he do with the money? The Indian agent, he's supposed to look after us. I helped Old Man Capoose for two years while he was alive and never got paid. After he died, the four of us—Josephine, Doll, Old Lady Capoose and myself—ran the whole thing for two or three years. Lot of work. That ranch was four mile wide and ten miles long. We cut hay and feed the cattle all that time and got nothing. We got nothing. The Indian agent didn't even pay me the dollar a day he promised me. He lied to me.

The Indian agent's real name was Foughner, but the Bella Coola Indians just called him Crooked Jaw. Called him Crooked Jaw because he had a long crooked jaw, and because he lies to us. He was the Indian agent for many years. The Indian agent didn't go up to Anahim Lake to take away Capoose's land. Instead, he sent up Teddy. Teddy was the police constable, and Crooked Jaw tell him to sell everything.

I try to tell Teddy, "You are sellin' our cattle too."

They sold all the cattle and all the land and horses. Not only did the Indian agent sell Capoose's land, the horses, the cattle, and Capoose's stuff but he sold Josephine's, Doll's and my cattle too. Both I and Doll, we are partner up there. Josephine had her own cattle and horses too. I guess we made a big mistake, use Capoose's brand on the cattle and horses. We didn't have our own brand. The girls just use their dad's brand, we thought that would be okay. Everyone in the country knew Old Man Capoose was the dad of Josephine and Doll. After the Indian agent sell everything we got to get our own cattle brand. I told Doll and Josephine we better get our own brand.

Mostly it went to Andy Christensen. Andy Christensen bought the whole works. I remember that he got a kid to bid for him. That kid was only about seven years old, I guess. Just a kid doin' all the bidding for Andy. They would drive a cow out into a small corral. "How much?" That kid would bid five dollars to sixteen dollars for the cattle. The highest he paid was sixteen dollars for a cow that was gonna have a calf. Nobody bid against them, nobody else there, nobody got any money, I guess. I didn't have any money left to bid for them cows or horses or sheep. I spend all my money to pay the people to help us put up the hay. Them cows were worth a lot more than five to sixteen dollars a head. In those days you sell cattle to Williams Lake, get three hundred dollars a head. Paying ten bucks for a three hundred dollar cow! I couldn't believe it. Christensen bought over a hundred cattle at that auction for just five to sixteen dollars a head. In the summertime Old Man Capoose used to drive forty head cattle down to the tideflat. Every week he butcher two cow for the fish canneries: one for B.C. Packers, one for Tallio cannery. He sure got more than ten dollars each, he must have got three to four hundred dollars a cow. Fishermans paid a lot of money for a steak in them days.

I never heard who got the horses and sheep. I was mad but I can't do nothing. Police constable right there. Teddy from Bella Coola. They were still there when I left. I went to get my horses, I wouldn't let them touch my horses. They must have left some sheep for the old lady, but no cows or horses. Doll wasn't there, she must have been in Bella Coola. In Bella Coola with Eliza. That's our kid. Eliza was born April 10, 1934.

From the gate at Cless Pocket, north to Poison Lakes and Anahim Peak, that used to be Capoose land. Nice meadows in there—Cless Pocket, Behind Meadow, Blaney Meadow. Christensen got a big part of Capoose's land. He claim Behind Meadow and Cless Pocket. Good grass in there. He didn't get all the land, they let us hold onto the land right close to the cabin by Abuntlet Lake.

I remember that when Old Man Capoose still alive, Andy Christensen and Vinny Clayton go around sizing things up. Waiting for Capoose to die, I guess. I was related to those guys. Vinny was my half uncle, and Andy Christensen married his sister. Them guys were up there lookin' at the meadows, I guess to see if it's rough place or good place to cut hay. They could see that it was a good place to cut hay so they gonna claim it. Right after Capoose died, that Andy Christensen built a house on the Behind Meadow, back toward the Itcha Mountains. Right in the middle of Capoose land. Right away he got the best hay meadows. As soon as the hay was ready, they cut hay right away in those meadows. He hired a lot of Indians from Anahim Lake to cut the hay to put up the hay quick so we can't get in there. Cut Josephine, Doll, me and the old lady off right away. Wouldn't let us touch it. Claimed he owned the whole works.

The Indian agent tried to sell Sam Sulin's land too. He send up Teddy the police constable to kick Sam Sulin off the land. He was living near Morrison Meadow. So Teddy went up there and tell Sam to get out of there, "Get out of that house, Sam. That house belong to the government now. It's not your house any more."

Sam was mad. His grandfather built that log cabin he was living in, and his father live there too, and then Sam took over from his dad. Sam even built a big fence around that place. He was a fence contractor, builds real good fences. Sam Sulin got real mad when he hear that the Indian agent wants his land. Sam knew that they took Capoose's land already. Sam grab an axe, and he threw that axe at Teddy. Teddy was sitting on his horse. That axe hit the seat of the saddle; if he aim little higher would have cut Teddy's backbone in half. Teddy arrest him, put him in Williams Lake jail. Sam sits in jail for a while. When they had court Teddy told the judge, "Sam Sulin tried to kill a police constable. Better lock him up for a long time." Teddy wanted Sam to get locked up in jail. But Sam tell the Indian interpreter why he throw the axe at him. Why he tried to kill the constable. Sam tell the judge that he born there, that his father was born there and died there, and that his grandfather build that house and die there too. Sam told the judge that he took over that place from his father and that he fenced it off. Judge say to Sam Sulin, "I fine you ten dollars because you tried to kill that Indian constable. Go back to your house stay there till you die. Stay there till you die of old age because that's your home."

But Sam was too scared to go back to his house near Morrison Meadow, afraid of the guys who take it over. Afraid he's gonna have to sit in jail again if he fights for his land. Instead Sam Sulin moved to a place just this side of Nimpo Lake. In that old, high house by the highway.

I always wonder if there wasn't crooked work all the way around. Three of them partners in it: Andy Christensen, Teddy the Indian constable, and Crooked Jaw the Indian agent. Nobody to talk to in those days. I didn't know about lawyers. Indian agent supposed to look after us. What did they do with all that money from the cattle, horses, and sheep? How did they get Capoose's land? They wouldn't tell me when I ask. I still don't know. I guess I will never know. I heard that Andy sold the land quite a while ago for 300,000 dollars. I don't know if that's really true but that's what I heard. That land has been turned over quite a few times now. I'm not sure who owns it now.

I never did tell Andy Christensen that I was mad at him. He and his wife, Dorothy, were too nice to me. I kind of think his wife knew we were relations. Dorothy Christensen was one of John Clayton's daughters. She always speak nice to me when I visits. Gives me coffee and cake when I go over there. I knew that Andy Christensen pretty good. He was a good guy. Speaks real friendly to all the Indian guys up there. Jokes all the time. I get along with him real good. He hires a lot of Indian guys to cut his hay. And I packed stuff for him on horse pack train too. When he wants a guy who has good pack horses to pack big stuff or important stuff he hire me. I pack some big stuff up for him, like heater stoves, and I pack things like money and rum. He needs money to buy furs. After Capoose died Andy Christensen pack train most of the stuff between Bella Coola to Anahim Lake. Packs mostly food to Anahim Lake, and packs mostly furs back to Bella Coola. Kind of took over Capoose's job.

I did bid on one thing at the auction. Capoose had land up-valley, where park headquarters is. Ninety-four acres, old small cabin and lot of fir trees. I bid three hundred dollars and I get it. But every year they tax me—school tax, property tax—so I sold it. I keep it for about two years. One woman, Jane King, she after me every day pret' near to sell it. Connie King's wife. She lived in Bella Coola then. I sold it to her for same price I got it, three hundred dollars. I hear she sell it for fifty thousand dollars to the government after I sell it to her. Maybe she knew it, knew the government wanted to buy it, that's why she after me so much to sell. There was a lot of timber in there too. She logged that timber, then she sold the land to the government. The government make a kind of a watch land for the Tweedsmuir Park after that, call it park headquarters. That's where the park rangers who look after Tweedsmuir Park live now.

About two years after they sold everything my wife died. She died of galloping TB. She died in early summer. July 12, 1936. She was pretty sick. I remember she was coughing, dry coughing all time. I got screwed up too. Wait too long to come to Bella Coola to see doctor in hospital. There was this travelling doctor who come up-country. Pack horses with all kinds of medicine. I asked him, "My wife's pretty sick. Coughs. Dry cough. Got any medicine for her?"

"I got the medicine right here," he said. "Try that."

I pay five bucks a bottle for it. I buy two bottles. Look like tea water. Maybe it was just tea. Takes two teaspoons full. But she get worse-like. Cough more, can't get rid of the TB. So I told her, "Let's go to Bella Coola, see the doctor."

Eliza, our girl, was just a kid. Not walking much yet. We pack her down in a basket. I worry about packing Eliza down in basket on my horse because my horse was a bit wild. I always used wild horses, lively horses. I like that, you know, horse jumping around. But I couldn't help carry the basket, horse might buck it off. So we got the old lady to come down with us to the hospital too. The old lady packed Eliza down in a basket.

Once we got going, I told Doll, "I'm gonna go ahead. Set up camp at Precipice. Just take your time." I lead that pack horses down the Precipice. Set up the tent. I get the tent up, build a fire, and started cooking. I make pancake, bannock-like pancakes. I make a big plate of pancakes. Then I heard a big noise, *bang!* Thunder. By God, next time it was right close. I could see the lightning was close. Wind started to blow hard. I think about Doll, wonder how they are making out. So I run back on the horse trail. I see them coming. I went to run back again to the camp. The tent was gone. Blew away. Thunder rumble again. Real close now. I run in the creek, stand in the water. Then a lightning bolt hit a tree just behind me. Bust the tree end right off, like it was shot by a big bullet.

I got my axe, chop a tree down where that tent was. Made a lean-to and find my tent and put it up again. I tell my wife, "I cooked some bannock—well, something between a hotcake and a bannock."

"Holy smoke," she said. "Look at that black dog there, he ate all that bannock."

I don't know where he come from. Nobody live around there. Lost, I guess. Wasn't a wolf, it was a dog. Medium-sized black dog. He ate all the bannock!

Took us quite a while to get down to Bella Coola. Five days from Anahim Lake. I took Doll to the hospital. She was there about one month. My wife was in hospital when she died. I was out fishing the day she died. They found later Eliza, the baby, had a spot on her lung. The doctor see that spot on the X-ray. I don't think they worry about TB with me. I sleep with Doll, too, but I never get TB. I don't know why I never get TB. My mother look after Eliza for quite a long time after Doll died. Then we sent her to home school, Alert Bay home school.

Old Lady Capoose went back up-country. I tried to help Old Lady Capoose and Josephine a bit after that. I tried to help them with putting up the hay after Doll died. Old Lady Capoose died of old age a few years later.

Josephine stayed on at Capoose's ranch near Abuntlet Lake. Had a few cattle. Josephine didn't get anything after Old Capoose died. Lost it all. Josephine start all over. Get more cattle. Build up the herd. Sell so many cattle every year. Then she lived together with Louis Squinas. Not married. They just lived together for quite a few years. One day Louis sell a lot of her cattle. "I get thirty thousand dollars in the bank after Louis sell that cattle," that's what Josephine told me. "I got a lot of money in the bank," she said to me one day, "but I can't read how much I got left in the bank after Louis takes money out of there." Josephine told Louis, "You better quit that or else you go." But Louis never quit. So Josephine took off on him. She came down to Bella Coola. Later she went to Atnarko and married Bert Robson. So Louis claim everything up there at Josephine's ranch. Josephine lose everything again. Poor woman. She worked so hard all her life.

Josephine could do everything. Good trapper. Good shot with a gun. First year I meet Josephine was 1929, I think it was. First rodeo in Anahim Lake. That's when I first see her. Good horse rider. She ride buckin' horse and she win first prize in woman's riding. Good cowboy. Break in a lot of wild horses. Only woman I see that can break them wild, real bad horses. Capoose horses. Big horses too. Real tough horses. She break them and ride them just like that.

Her trapline was all the way from her ranch at Anahim Lake to Atnarko. Up on the mountains on top, Little Rainbows, and south to Heckman Pass. Every year she trap till she was old. Tell us a lot of good grizzly bear stories. "Grizzly bear, he spring my trap. He eat the bait. Sometimes I get a mink and he eat that mink," she say to us. I used to play with her. I go hunt deer up Atnarko. If I see one of her traps, I cut some of the long hair off a horse tail and I put it in the trap. And I scratch around like somebody's head been caught in there. She know it was me right away. When I see her, she point at me. "Sometime you gonna get your finger caught in my trap, Clayton," she said.

I remember a grizzly bear start to come around Josephine's place one year. Josephine start thinking, "I'm gonna feed that grizzly bear the same way I feed them deer." She got some smoked fish. That grizzly bear took the smoked fish from her hand all right, but it wasn't enough for him. He pound his feet on the ground and swing his head back and forth. Josephine took off back to the cabin. She run fast. That grizzly bear right behind her. Bert Robson was watching her all the time. Bert had a big gun in the cabin. He got the gun. Josephine run right in the cabin. That bear was halfways through the door and Bert shot him. Shot him right in the head. That grizzly bear was halfways through the door, dead. Halfway inside.

Oh, she could hunt too. The best I ever met who knows good meat. One day we were looking at some moose. "That other moose there, no good," she said. "Meat tough. Take that other one." Deer too. She could tell which moose or deer had the best meat. After she kill that deer or moose she saves all the meat to eat, and she tan the hides to sell them or make moccasins. She could make real good gloves and moccasins. Sell them cheap too.

Old Maxie Heckman had a plum tree not too far from his house. Pretty good plums grow on that plum tree. Sweet. Real good plums. And Josephine would come down every year and make jam out of the plums that grow on that plum tree. When she moved down to Atnarko, there was a short walk to get to that plum tree from her cabin. One day she walked down there to get some plums. There was a black bear up in the tree. A big black bear. Josephine went back home and she get her saddle horse. Get her lasso rope. You know, she was a pretty good roper too. She went back there and that black bear didn't want her around there. He snap his teeth at her. She roped that black bear and pulled him right out of the tree. Black bear drop on the ground. And he turn around and try to get away. The black bear has nice hook claws on them, they just sink their claws in the ground and they pull. That black bear did that. He pull that horse sideways. That saddle just about come off. And Josephine had to let the rope go. Let that black bear go. Had the rope little half-tied on that saddle horn. She took the rope off and that black bear's gone. Gone with her rope. And she went home.

She didn't want to lose that rope. Special rope for her. Josephine used it for roping calfs in spring when they brand them. She walked back to her cabin to get her gun and then she walked back to the plum tree to get that rope. The black bear was up in the tree again. Rope was on the ground. Bear got it off. Josephine was happy. She didn't have to shoot the bear. She just ran and grab that rope and drag it home to the house.

Josephine had seventy-two deer, wild deers. She feed them. Every four days them deers clean out a sack of oats. She could feed them by her hand, like that, you know. They eat it right off her hand. She had a big pocket and fill it with oats all the time. Her favourite deer was called Billie. Big buck. Had a big set of horns on him. Mule deer. She put oats in a little bowl and put it on table. She got a plate for him. Open her door, "Okay, come on in, Billie." That deer come right in and he eat with her at the table! If she don't call him in, he would go to the window and look in. Look at you eating through the window. I tried to feed him from my hand the way Josephine does. I smell different, he took off like that.

After I left Anahim Lake, I came back to Bella Coola and do lots of different jobs. I trapline, logging, fish, guiding. Most I did in my life was fishing and grizzly bear guiding.

I married again, to Cora, my second wife. November 23, 1937. She was a Bella Bella woman. I met Cora a couple of years after Doll died. I was about twenty-eight years old. I met her in Bella Bella. I was in a foot race, won, and all the girls go after me! I married Cora, stayed in Bella Bella for about one year, but didn't like it there. I fished, trapped in the wintertime there. I moved back to Bella Coola with Cora. I had three kids from Cora: Wanda, Doris and Dusty. Cora help raise Eliza too.

I trap with Cora's father for a few years after I get married. That guy was a pretty good trapper. Trap Poison Cove, Mussel Inlet and north, and trap on Calvert Island and south. I trapped all along the coast. We start trapping November. End of De-

Josephine's favourite deer, Billie

cember, I think, I come back. Trap for mink mostly. Lot of fur there in them days. I didn't have my own trapline. I use herring fishermen's traplines. There was good herring fishing in them days. A lot of herring fishermen got traplines too. But they don't use their trapline because they make good money herring fishing. So they lend their traplines to us. "You use my line, trap my line," they say to us. After a few years I didn't trap too much. Trap a bit with Herb Edgar up Kwatna, and I also trapped a bit in Dean and South Bentinck. Quit long time ago.

For over fifty-two years I spend four months a year in the woods. Two months in the spring—May, June—and two months in the fall—September, October. Sometimes even three months in the fall—September, October, November. I come home, get grub, go out again.

My wife Cora, she think I'm crazy, she say, "Why can't you get enough camping, Clayton? You gone two months every spring, gone out all summer fishing, and then you want to go out camping again all fall."

I tell her, "I like to be alone in the woods. No one to tell me what to do out there. I'm gonna go rest for a while, camp out in the woods."

I owned a logging camp for a while. I bought a little A-frame. I bought George Draney out when they call him to go to the army. Had about a eight-man crew. I met some big shots from Crown Zellerbach. They want to hunt big game animals, and I used to take them hunting up-country. Tommy Walker's guiding territory. He owned Stuie Lodge for years. Tommy knew I know that country pretty good and he hired me then to work for him too. That's how I start guiding with Tommy Walker.

I had my logging company for about eight years. Something like that, anyway. Logged any place on the coast. In the summertimes. All over. I had a good deal from Crown Zellerbach Company. They would give me anything I want. Reed Branford run the logging camps from Ocean Falls. He told me, "Any log claim you want out in the Inlet, close to the water, float your A-frame there and get them logs. If you want grub, come to Ocean Falls and I'll give you all the grub for your crew too."

They had a pulp mill and lumber mill in Ocean Falls in them days. Was good business but I took my brothers to partner up with me. It was the worse thing I did in my life. They started drinking. We used to stay in Ocean Falls, make friends with some Ocean Falls boys. They get bottles, get drunk like hell and don't keep track of the time we supposed to work. Turn alcoholic, like, drinking every day pret' near. It didn't work out. After I quit my logging company, I did some handlogging. I think I did that handlogging until the sixties.

I fish every year since I was about seventeen years old. Gill-netters mainly. For salmon. Only fish for herring a little bit. We used sailboat when I first started. About twenty-five-foot-long boats. Sail across, gain a little bit, go across again, zigzag all the way out to Green Bay from Bella Coola. Sometimes tugboat used to tow us out too. Wind blow too hard in, they have to tow us out to go fishing. Maybe twenty boats on one towline. Look nice, you know. All the masts in a row behind that tugboat. Tugboat start out around twelve o'clock after lunch. Tow us out to where we want to go. Lot of fun. Just let go of the rope, pull the sail up and go where you want to go. When it's real windy we fish in Labouchere, not much wind there. When not too windy I fish around Green Bay. Farthest out in sailboat I go was Kwatna. Fished maybe eight years with sailboats. After sailboats I had about three different boats. Gas boats. Used company boats too. If you a good fisherman they rent you boats, nets, all you want. If you a good fisherman they give you a good deal too.

My last boat was a nice gill-netter. About forty-five foot long. Had a drum on it. Nice motor. It blow up on me. I load up tank with too much gas. Sprung a leak. Gas run all in the bilge, right to the bow. Just when I try and press the button to start the motor, *boom!* Threw me up. Them guys said I look like a rag way up in the air. I fall down right in the hatch. Right beside a bottle of whisky. I borrowed a boat from the company, finished the season, then I quit. A few years later I got the stroke.

The guiding business

Grizzly bear guiding was good business. I make a good living grizzly bear guiding. Get a new pickup truck every two years. Make a lot of good friends from all over. Americans and Germans. They give me lots of free gifts. Lots of things. Knives, guns, flares, rain gear, gumboots, clothes. I had about twenty rifles given to me, altogether, all my time guiding.

I see over three hundred grizzly bears get killed. I only shot the ones that tried to kill me or the wounded ones, that's all. A few were wounded and got away but I find most of the wounded ones. That's my job, when a hunter wounds the bear, I go by myself and look for that wounded bear. I chase one wounded bear for three days. Caught up to him on top of the mountain. Still alive and strong. But he was gut-shot wounded. Sometimes I feel sorry for them grizzly bears. They got no gun to shoot back, not like in the army. So they got to hide when they are wounded. They will dig a hole in the middle of the trail about three feet deep and lie in it—you can just see the eyes and the ears, or they hide behind a tree or roots, and they wait for you to come. When you follow that wounded bear's blood trail, and you get there they make one big jump and try and knock you down. If you wound a sow with kids, them kids will lick that blood coming from that bullet hole. And you won't see much blood after when tracking. The big kids, about three or four years old, are mean. If you wound their mother them big kids will run in a circle around you, bark almost like a dog, sometimes up to two hours. If you go after him or head him off, he will charge you.

I like to think there's still quite a few grizzly bear around. But I know grizzly bear numbers going down quite a bit in some of the rivers. I think we losing a lot of bears to that gallbladder business. Them poachers and local guys shoot grizzly bears, cut them open and take out gallbladder. Sell it. And they cut off the claws. Sell that too. They killing too many bears just for the gallbladder and claws. Will be no more bears for the guides. Fish and Wildlife gonna stop the bear hunting.

Best rivers for grizzly bear are Kimsquit, Kwatna, Washwash, Machmell, Chuckwalla, Kilbella, head of Moses Inlet, Tzeo, Inziana and Sheemahant. All real good. Kimsquit River is number one. Owikeno Lake has lots of grizzly bears too. Look up any creek that runs into Owikeno Lake, and you will find grizzly bears. Dean River, Bella Coola River, Skowquiltz River, Koeye River, Taleomey River, Noeick River, Asseek River has grizzly bear, too, but not as much. There are some grizzly bear up Cascade Inlet, Swallop Creek, Eucott Bay, Nascall and around Nootum, but not too many. No grizzly bear on King Island or on the coast by Bella Bella.

In my life I guided about three hundred bears, maybe more. I guided for almost fifty years. About twenty Boone and Crockett grizzly bear too—biggest bears in the world. That's how I get a good name as a grizzly bear guide. I had a Boone and Crockett book, the book that lists all the world trophy bears. Lend it to a white guy but he never return it back.

My first time guiding was for Tommy Walker. It was in the summertime. Kind of early in the summer, yet. I was guiding

Clayton Mack at Kwatna, 1940

The guiding business

fishermans. Some of them fishermans come from England, some come from the United States. I took them to Tanya Lakes, way back of the Rainbow Mountains. One, two, three days it take to get there. Horseback. There's a creek there, at the lake, runs out of the Rainbow Mountains into Tanya Lake. Bright steelheads spawn in there. Real silver. Big ones. Thirty-pounders. We eat steelhead every day. After a while we get tired of eating steelhead. No smokehouse there, so we had to eat fresh steelhead, we couldn't smoke and save any to take back home. There were spring salmons to fifty pounds too. That was my first guiding job with Tommy Walker.

Then, around October, it was open season for grizzly bear. I took fishermans from Stuie Lodge out to hunt grizzly bears. Sometimes Stuie is pretty poor to hunt grizzly bear. Some years nothing. Tommy Walker would tell people, "Lot of bears down there." I'd take the hunters down there, nothing! No bear. No tracks. Nothing. I tell Tommy that, "No bear down there."

But I knew where to get a grizzly bear. I know where there was lot of bears: Kwatna. I trapped there before and knew there was lots of grizzly bears there. But I got no boat. We would have to hire a boat to go down to Kwatna River. Tommy don't want to pay for no boat. So he keep telling me there's a lot of bears down by the Atnarko River below Stuie. Below his lodge.

"No, Tommy," I said. "You go look." He go down there, but I know he never looked. After a while I get tired of that bullshit. I get tired of lying to the hunters. So I told Tommy one morning, "I'm not going down to the Atnarko River again. Why do you keep telling those guys a lie? Why do you keep telling them there is lot of grizzly bear down there?" I quit and gonna go home. I had my car there. I packed my sleeping bag and threw it in the car. Gonna go home to Bella Coola. I told that hunter, "If you can't get nothing here, maybe we can get a boat, get somebody to take us down to Kwatna. Get your bear in the first day," I told him. That hunter, he told Tommy what I said. And Tommy gave me shit for that. I get fired and I quit the same time! I think that hunter told Tommy off, after Tommy fire me.

The hunter came to me again before I left. He said, "You go to Bella Coola and get a boat. I'll pack all the stuff here."

"Okay," I said, "we go to Kwatna." So, we got in my car and took off. I look around on the weekend for a boat. I got Joe Saunders's boat, he charge us ten dollars a day for two days, only twenty bucks. I was happy. We went on the weekend. When we got to Kwatna, I told Joe Saunders, "There's a good place up there. Tie up on the pilings up there."

There is a bluff right at the mouth of the Kwatna River. There was two big grizzly bears walking around there. The hunter started shooting. He missed. I don't know how many shots he shot. He missed, and missed, and missed. I look at his gun, his peep sight come off! He couldn't hit nothing—no sights. We went up the Kwatna River in a canoe, about two hours upriver, to a side valley there. Saw one big grizzly bear. *Bang,* the hunter get him. We came down in the canoe. The policeman with us also, he came along because he just wanted to see the country. The policeman was from Bella Coola. Talk about bears in that country, in them days! We saw six bears in one day.

That hunter give me fifty dollars tip, he call it. "But don't tell anyone," he said. "You go by yourself, go independent. Not with Tommy Walker, don't go with him any more. Quit him. Go on your own." That's how I got started.

Tommy Walker hired me again to hunt moose, deer and bear the next fall. There was a lot of bear around Stuie that year. I took some hunters up to Belarko. The horses were drinking water, and the hunters were resting on a log. I went up, crossed the Atnarko River and saw four grizzly bears. I went back and whistled, and they came up. They came up quick. Season not open yet for grizzly bear, it was the day before open season. I told them that.

I had a small gun, a .30-.30. It was during the last world

war, and the government allow me ten gun shells, that's all. Ten .30-.30 shells, that is all they allowed me to use for the whole season as a guide! The government wanted to save all the bullets in Canada for killin' men overseas during the last world war.

Even though I told them hunters it was the day before season, they said, "Aw, that's nothing, we'll come back and skin them grizzly bears in two days."

They emptied their guns shootin' at them grizzly bears. Soon they had no more shells, so one of them grabbed my gun and emptied it out too. They killed the whole works, killed four grizzly bears, right there. These hunters were from California. They shot all my shells. I got no shells left for the rest of the guiding season, and grizzly bear season not even started yet! "You guys have to buy me shells now," I said. But I was worried. I knew it was hard to buy the shells, you need to fill out special papers. I did get shells later from them hunters, they buy gun shells when they get back to the United States and mailed them to me.

One of the bears they shot was trying to swim across, they hit it in the head, he sank and drown in the water. The other three dead grizzly bears were on the bank. I tried to swim in the water and find that drowned bear. "I'm going to try and save that bugger," I said. I went up the river a little bit and I swim out, current take me down and I saw it—big black thing underwater. I dive under, grab hold of his leg. I half dive, half swim and pull it to the beach. I roll it up, I got him. Went up and swam across the Atnarko River and we all went home. That's how come they like me so much, them guys, after that.

I took them up moose hunting a few days later. I show them five moose, four bulls and a cow. Tommy Walker was yelling, "Don't shoot 'em, don't kill them moose. I got no way to pack them out of here." We were in the mountains. One of the Americans shot at a bull anyway. The bull moose fell down, stun him I guess, but got up and ran away. That American hunter, he don't want any moose meat, all he want is that moose's horns, that all he want. Poor bull moose.

After that, them hunters really like me. When they leave, they come down to Bella Coola to catch the Union Steamship. They going to get on that boat and go home. They see the policeman on the float. "Is that the policeman?" one of the hunters asked. "Yes," I said. One of them said, "Let's go get hold of him." The whole four of them got the policeman between them. They told him, "We want you to get Clayton Mack the best class guide licence. We want to come back next year and we want him to guide us. We don't want to go to Stuie any more." In them days, there was no game warden, the police looked after everything like that. The policeman said he would do that, give me a guide licence. Soon after they give me a guide licence, Tommy Walker left the country.

Once I got a guide licence, I could hire anybody I want. The year after, around May another bunch came in for a grizzly bear spring hunt. From Oklahoma. A grizzly bear nearly get me that first time. He hit me on the foot, tried to grab me. This was up Kwatna. We shot that grizzly bear on the tideflat, and he went up the mountain. One of the hunters was a millionaire, oil guy, Oklahoma oilman. This was the guy who shot the grizzly bear. I went and followed that bear's track and caught up to him and he charged us. So I shot, hit his front leg; kind of slow him down but he came, came again.

The hunter said, "Don't shoot. Let me finish him off."

"Okay, go ahead, but shoot quick," I said.

He start shooting and the bear keep coming. The bear went down. I got a stick and poked him in the lip, poked that grizzly bear in the mouth. He bite that stick, chop it in half like an axe. And he still breathing. Every time he turn his head I can see the steam, like, coming out of his nose.

"Quick, shoot him, finish him off. Shoot right in the neck behind the head," I said.

Bang! He shot him.

"I think he's dead," I said. "I think he's finished now." And I kick that bear in the ass end, kick it with my gumboots. He turned around and slapped me right on the toe, broke my toe. Then he fell down dead. Tough animal, that grizzly bear.

That Oklahoma multimillionaire came back nine years in a row with me. He died of sugar diabetes. He paid me good. More than what he should have paid me. He would come in with big boats, big yachts. I got him a grizzly bear every year too. I don't know what he did with all them grizzly bear skins. He was the first guy to get a Boone and Crockett bear, biggest bear in the world.

Out on the coast are blacktail deer. Most are small, biggest go to only about a hundred and fifty pounds. These deer like to live down low. They come out and eat that grass or seaweed along the edge of the beach. They must like that seaweed. Them deer are feeding right at the edge of the timber. Not too hard to hunt them. Just row or take boat with small little outboard motor right close to the timber at high tide and you will see them blacktail deer. Shoot them right from the boat.

The mule deer are the big ones. Some are real big. The biggest I know they got up-country weighed four hundred pounds. Get 'em from Stuie on up.

I had five hunters one time. Took them mule deer huntin' up on top of the Mosher Creek. Right on top. We hunt moose, hunt deer. A whole bunch of us. Guides, cooks and hunters. Four guides, five hunters and two cooks. Three young hunters and two old hunters. None of the guides wanted to take the old hunters. They just wanted to take the younger hunters. I told them old men, both over seventy years old, to stay in the camp and that I would stay in the camp with them the first day.

The three younger hunters bet who is gonna get the biggest deer. They bet amongst themselves. Their guides bet too. All the younger hunters and all the younger guides bet who is gonna get the biggest deer. And these poor old guys got to sit around at the campfire. I make coffee for them. And I went and check up on the horses in the meadow, back about half a mile I walk. I count how many head of horses are there. The horses were all there. While I was looking I see two sets of deer horns in the middle of the horses. Deer! I could see the horns moving. Them two deer were together, right close together. I went back to the cabin and told those two old guys, "There's two deers laying down in the meadow where them horses are. Let's go and get them." And then we went back.

I lead these two old guys, each one over seventy years old, and I tell them, "You guys shoot. If you miss I'll shoot, I'll give you a hand. We win that money, you guys will win that money for killing the biggest buck." First guy, he shoot but he miss and the deer start to run but I shot him right through the neck and down that deer went. The other guy he shoot, he miss too and the deer run. I shot that deer right in the neck too. We get both them right there! I went and get us one of the horses and drag them two deer right back into the camp. We weren't too far from the camp. Good going. We hang them deer up in a tree right by the camp. Nice deer, real nice ones. Same size, about three hundred pounds each with big racks on them.

Them younger hunters and young guides come back that night. One of them hunters catch on. Kind of a smart alec guy. He caught on quick that I shot that deer. He see that both of them deer were shot through the neck.

"Them two old guys can't shoot like that," he said to me. "You shot them deer."

"No, I didn't," I said.

The old guys get that money for shooting the biggest bucks. I don't know how much they made out of it. That smart alec guy after me all the time. Say I shot them deer. A few days later I caught that smart alec guy shooting a little baby deer. They couldn't find a big deer, so they shot a little deer. Him and Tommy Walker. And he want me to go ahead and tie that little deer to my saddle, and drag it behind my saddle horse. That deer was the size of a little coyote, the size of a little dog, and I got to drag it behind my saddle horse. When I get down to Tommy Walker's lodge, Stuie Lodge, I hide that little deer. I don't want anybody to see it. I put it in the food cellar. Hang it up inside the food cellar.

That smart alec guy keep after me about them two big deers. He tried to get me to drink lot of homebrew so that I will get drunk and tell that I shoot them big deers. Try and get me drunk, so I tell the truth that I shot them two deers.

I said, "Look, I caught you guys shooting a little, little deer. That baby deer looks like a little coyote. I sneak it underneath inside the food cellar right now, hang up in there so no one else will see it. If you don't leave me alone, I'm going to take that deer and hang it up outside the Stuie Lodge." I said, "Everyone will see what kind of hunter you really are."

"No, no don't do that," he said. He pulled his wallet out and he pulled out Canadian money, eighty bucks. "Here is eighty dollars Canadian money. Don't say nothing about that little deer," he said. And he never bothered me again after that! Money doesn't seem to mean anything to some of them hunters.

Hollywood

I am a pretty good tracker. I can track you, track you down if you go up any mountain. I can find you. I can tell how old your track is out in the woods. In the sand or in the snow I can tell how long ago you were there. I learned how to track animals when I was up-country. Lot of guys show me how to track up there. Old Man Squinas, Tommy Squinas, and another guy named Tommy Cahoose. Real good trackers!

I took two multimillionaires into Kimsquit. Walter Butcher and Walter Shutts. It was a fall hunt. They wanted to kill the biggest grizzly bear in the world. "I'll try," I said. I see old tracks, about sixteen inches long. We measure it. Sixteen inch.

"Holy smoke, that's what I'm looking for," he said.

"That track about a month old," I told him. "It starting to wash off now." And we went on up. We saw that grizzly bear's track again. It was getting fresh. "Maybe four days ago," I said. "He came through here maybe four days ago." It was getting late in the evening. We go on again. Saw his track again. See another grizzly bear's track too. "Them two bears fightin' like hell here," I say. "The other grizzly bear went in the woods. That big one keep on going up the riverbed. Not too long ago." We didn't have to go very far before we caught up to him.

That big grizzly bear was laying down underneath one log.

Part of the log was under the ground, the other part sticking out in the air. He was laying down underneath that log. I didn't see that bear right away. Walter Shutts saw it first.

"Is that him underneath that log?" he ask.

I look underneath that log stickin' up in the air. "Yeah, that's him," I said. "Try and hit him in the lungs," I said to Walter Butcher. I told Walter Shutts, "Try and shoot him in the heart and I'll try and get him in the kidney." The whole works of us shoot at the same time. Three guns goin'. *Bang! Bang! Bang!* That big grizzly try and come out, but drop in the water. When we get there he was dead already. Hit the water, head in the water and drown same time. We try and pull him out, couldn't do it. Big grizzly bear. We came back next day and skinned it.

That Walter Shutts say he never see a guy who can track like that. They put that in the paper in California, I guess, and a lot of guys see that. Read that Walter Shutts say I'm best tracker in the world he ever seen. On front page. Put my name on it. Bella Coola guide. I got a lot of letters from guys who want to hunt after that. The *American Sportsman* television program people also read about me. They write me a letter. Ask if they can go on a grizzly bear hunt and go fishing with me. I write back, "Okay, I'll take you out." It was in the sixties, I think.

The *American Sportsman* people came to Bella Coola with a big boat. Big minesweeper! But it not a minesweeper now, they turned it into a passenger boat. Big boat, maybe two hundred feet long. They come and pick me up in Bella Coola. Around the end of September. Their skipper don't know the coast, he let me take the wheel. We went into Kwatna first.

Joe Brooks, one of the best fly-fishermen in the world, was on that boat. I took him out for ten days fishing for coho. Joe Brooks told me that some guys think he can never get a coho with a fly. He get into an argument with a lot of guys that coho don't take flies. He wants me to take him out where I think he can get one. We went up Kwatna River about ten miles. Joe didn't get anything for quite a while. Few hours.

I told him, "Sink it a little bit, about four inch or six inches deep. Down a little bit." And he did. "What kind of fly you got on there?" I asked.

"Polar bear hair," he said.

By God, he get one. Later he switched to a grey brownish coyote-tail fly. That work pretty good too. He get two or three coho on a fly the first day. They had a lot of fun. Altogether they caught about twenty coho in ten days on a fly. Keep one, I think, cook it in the boat. Just let the rest all go, let the whole works go! They took ten thousand feet of film.

After we go to Kwatna River, we came back to Bella Coola. Get more grub and water. Next we gonna go to Kimsquit and hunt grizzly bear for eight days. Rick Jason was going to be the hunter. Rick Jason is an actor. Tall and tough but a real nice guy. When we ready to go to Kimsquit, we pick up Rick Jason up at the airport and then we take off. We got a grizzly bear first day. Seven hours after Rick Jason left his house in Hollywood, I get him a grizzly bear. Fish and Wildlife allow them only one grizzly bear. So after the first day we just look around at the country, lookin' for big game animals. We saw moose, deer, wolves. When we saw one big moose, Rick Jason aim at it. "Can I pull the trigger?" he asked the movie director. The head guy with the movie camera said, "No, you can't do it." So they let that moose go, let it run away. When we were up there I did see one moose fight with five wolves, but they didn't get to take a movie picture of it. They shoot nine thousand feet of film up Kimsquit.

Rick Jason really like his vodka when he's out makin' that *American Sportsman* movie. Money don't mean nothing to him. That vodka cost about ten bucks a bottle. And that airfare cost two hundred dollars. When that bottle's empty, he got on the telephone and he call Wilderness Airline in Bella Coola, "Bring me another bottle again!" Wilderness Airline people go down to the liquor store and buy another bottle of vodka, then they fly it to the boat for two hundred dollars.

"What, you crazy?" I said.

He open the bag and look inside. "Oh, look," he says, "I get a big lemon too! Wilderness Airline got to make money too," he said.

Everyday a bottle come in. I told him, "Buy a whole case." But no, he'd drink that bottle in one day and phone for another bottle again next day.

I had two reels of film of the *American Sportsman* movie that I was in. A guy from Florida stole it. He want to borrow that film, take it to Florida. Later, I try and phone him, "Send

Clayton at the wharf with a grizzly, 1965

my film back." He said that he send the film to a guy in Hawaii. I call the guy in Hawaii but he never got it. I think the guy in Florida keep it. I used to have two good photo albums too. I lost one in Vancouver in hospital; I lost the other one in Williams Lake Hospital. People there at them hospitals, they fight to see it. "Can I borrow this?" they ask. "Okay," I say. Then I never see them again. Too bad they had to steal them.

Just cause I was a good guide, one of those Hollywood guys give me a free trip to Hollywood for ten days. It was in the fifties, I think. I satisfy him quick, get a grizzly bear. Biggest bear in the world. He was happy and he took me with him. They pay my trip over there.

    I stay with that deputy attorney, head guy of the police force in Hollywood. Ten days. Alton Myhrvold was his name. When I was down there, Governor Brown heard about the grizzly bear we got, and come and meet me. That deputy attorney guy I live with, him and Governor Brown they work together. Governor Brown is hunter. He wanted to go hunting up here but I wouldn't take him out. He wanted to take a girl—a secretary to write about the trip—a typewriter, movie camera guy, movie outfit, everything. Nah, too much. Not a woman on a trip like that. Wet in the fall, got to cross creeks with gumboots. My cabin not made for womans, not made for high class womans from Hollywood.

    After I meet Governor Brown he say, "Twelve o'clock tomorrow, I'll be on the top of that little mountain. There's a cafe there. You come there twelve o'clock we'll eat together." And I go up there. You can see the whole North Hollywood, and where all the rich people live in South Hollywood. Governor Brown, he own that cafe, I think. I eat with him almost every day, same cafe, and I tell him stories about grizzly bear and sasquatch. He think I am a liar, he think I bullshit him all the time. He's pretty smart guy.

    "Tell me the story of what happen," he say. I start to tell

him. "Wait, quit," he says. He would break the story off. That's what he does to the criminals, I guess, he's a lawyer. "Twelve o'clock tomorrow, come back we'll eat together again." And I go up there. "Okay, we got to finish that story you tell me." He broke the chain of story the day before. I say, "I don't like that broken chain, I have hard time to find where to splice the story together." He just laugh.

Sometimes I visit him at his house in Hollywood. About four times, I guess. He paid eighty thousand dollars for his lot and built his brand new house on it. He had a brand new house when I was there. You can see the whole Hollywood, you can see the North and South Hollywood from his house. I think Governor Brown is still alive. He told me to buy the lot beside his house. "Worth about a hundred thousand dollars," he said. "You build a house there."

"Bullshit," I said. "I don't got no hundred thousand dollars to buy a lot." I met his son too, Jerry Brown, he was Governor of California too. He took over a few years later. Jerry Brown already growing up then, but still talks like a kid. Like a teenager. He likes me. Likes to talk to me about how many times I get close calls with grizzly bears. Jerry don't got no wife then, but the old man had a wife. That Governor Brown got a nice wife, real nice woman.

There was a guy who made real good friends with me. Ned Gilbert. He owned the store they call Fairbanks. Right underneath that big writing HOLLYWOOD on the mountain. There is a store right at the foot of that mountain. He sell everything in that store. He had no home. He lived in a motel. Real fancy motel. He sell cars too with a guy named Wayne. One day Ned Gilbert took me to a place where people act. Where they look for new actors. Short acting, half an hour and it's all over. Near an old stopping place. The old road to Mexico went right through there. Barrooms there where they drink whisky in the cowboy days. You sit down in seats. The camera right behind you. The guy in front pick anybody up out of the crowd, picks who he likes from that crowd. He's the producer. I was sitting down with my cowboy hat on.

The producer said, "You, you cowboy come on up here."

Ned Gilbert pushed me, "Go ahead, go." And I went.

"We going to make a short movie," that's what he said. Half an hour movie. "You go in the door, in that room there. There's a beer parlour there, sellin' a lot of beer. You rob that," he said. He give me a handgun, toy gun, I guess. "Kick the door in and ask him for all the money," he said.

So I kick that door down, point my handgun, "All the money, put it in the paper bag." They give me all the money. We took off, got out of there.

Out in the street, the producer told me, "There's a beer garden over there. You stop there and take a drink." I went there and sit down on a chair which rolls around. Bartender ask me what I want.

"Vodka and coke," I said. I drink that and say, "One more."

And he gave me another one. Then I pretend to be sick. Start heaving up. Slide off the seat, hit my stomach on that stool that goes around. I try to puke still. Then, I get up. There's a wall in there. Spectators all in there watching me. I went to that wall and open my trousers to pee!

"Cut, cut," he said.

After I almost pee on the wall, they want me to be an actor for them. Take over for Dan George in a movie. They say, "You see how Dan George acts, well you can do the same thing," he said.

"No, I can't act like Dan George," I said. "He doesn't like white people, you know."

American Sportsman also want me to act in a movie. They want to take me to South Africa. They started after me about it when we were still in Kimsquit. Want me to track down a bunch of water buffaloes. They supposed to be worse than a grizzly bear. You track them and those water buffaloes come around behind us. "They always do that," he said. I didn't go. I wasn't ready. I should have gone to Africa. My wife didn't want me to go.

That was my first trip to Hollywood. I went back about a year later after a grizzly bear almost get me.

I was hunting in Owikeno Lake with three brothers. American boys. We came across the lake and I saw grizzly bear walking on the tide flats. At the Tzeo River, in that Washwash River country.

I said to the oldest brother, "There's a grizzly bear over there walking this way, looks like a lion." I never see a grizzly bear like that before. Only thing different between that grizzly bear and a lion is that the grizzly got no tail. Got a fluffy collar, long hair on the neck—just like a lion.

"Any good?" he ask me.

"Damn right," I said. "Take him."

He lay his gun right on the roots of the stump and he shot it. He get him.

It was still early yet, more hours yet to hunt. My brother was with me, my boy was with me, and my son-in-law. Three of them in the boat. I told them, "You skin that bear, we'll go around and circle and come right back. By the time you finish, we'll be back, and we'll all go across back to the cabin."

I took this kid, the youngest of the brothers. I was walking ahead of him and I saw a grizzly bear coming. A big one. Big grizzly bear! I stopped right away as soon as I saw it. "See that big grizzly bear coming?" I said. I stopped, never moved, just stand still. And there was a little baby grizzly coming behind her. I said, "Jack, it's a sow grizzly bear. Female. We don't shoot them. She's got a little baby. We can't shoot 'em. If we shoot the mother the wolves will kill the baby. They'll eat it up. That baby grizzly going to be sick for a long time, if he has no mother. Don't shoot her," I said. "Let 'em go."

So I stood in front of that grizzly bear and said, "Go on,

beat it. Go on, bug off," I said. "I got a big gun, you don't want to get killed." The bear stopped and looked at me. She was about thirty feet away. She took off, took her little kid up a bank right into the heavy timber.

I said, "Let's go around, go circle around, hit the other creek. Get away from that cranky son-of-a-gun." Just as we started walking down to cut across to another creek we heard a stick breaking in the woods. "She's here already," I said. "She's on her way to the top of that bank. She try and run away too." I turned around to go back. I didn't know that it was a different bear, that one we heard on top of the bank breaking sticks.

Just as I started walking down the Washwash River, right where she turn around and went in the woods, that big grizzly bear sow, she came out of the woods. Full gallop. Not with her cub this time. She take that cub and hide it in the woods and come back herself. She started snorting, I grab a rock and throw it right in front of her. It hit the water. She stood up on her hind feet. And I keep yelling at her, "Go on." That hunter was pointing his gun all the time. "It's all right," I said. "Don't shoot. Let me do the work," I said.

The bear keep coming toward me. She was gettin' pretty close now. I kneel down and I use my boy's gun. It's a big gun, .300 Winchester magnum. Big shells in it. I shot between the front legs. Hit the ground so the rocks will spray up into her stomach and make her run away. So I shot but the son-of-a-gun never, she never run away. Just keep coming. And I try and load again. If she makes one jump she'll reach me I thought. This time I going to shoot it in the head. I aim right between the eyes, like. *Bang!* I missed. I just burn the side of her head, one side. That bear come right after me. Jump, run and hit me on the side, left side. Threw me about twenty feet. She didn't slap me. I think she used her head. Run and hook me with her head like a cow, like a bull cow. That bear throw me quite a ways. I landed right on my back.

I had too much stuff on my neck; I had binoculars, a

Hollywood

camera, walkie-talkie and the big rifle. Too much in the way, like, I couldn't recover quick. I try to reload but she got me. She came, came right on top of me. I lay there, never move. Just keep still. She step on my one shoulder little bit with one foot, and she step on the other shoulder with the other foot. Put her nose right in my face. Kind of smell me, snorting, like. Saliva coming out of her mouth. I can smell that old rotten fish breath!

That hunter was kneeling down aiming at the bear. He shoot, *bang!* I hear that gun. She never bite me, I thought she was going to bite me right in the face. Funny, it don't bite. I don't know why it didn't bite. Then the blood came down. That young hunter, he shot right high in the neck, right on top of the neck. Cut the skin. And the blood drip all over my face and my chest. I can turn my head a little bit to watch that young hunter. He was aiming again. "Try and hit him in the ribs," I told him. "Shoot him right through the ribs, right through the lungs." He shot again, *bang!* and more blood came. Then the bear lay right on top of me. All that weight drop on top of me. Weigh about six hundred pounds. She just lay there, I couldn't move. She lay right on top of me, dead now. Blood just pouring out.

"Now, Jack, how you going to get me out?" I asked. "This son-of-a-gun weigh about a thousand pounds," I said. That young hunter try and move that bear off me but he can't do it. "Leave it for a little while maybe," I said.

He asked me if I can stand it.

"Yeah, I can stand it. You can run to the boys if you can't move it," I said. "Do you know where they are?"

"No, I don't know where they are," he said.

"Then leave this grizzly bear on me for ten minutes, maybe. Maybe it will get stiffened up, easier to roll it off then," I said. After a while I can feel it, that the bear startin' to get lighter. I get used to it maybe, get used to the weight on me. "Okay, push it, roll it to the right side," I said. By God, it rolled off. I get out of there quick. Blood all over my face.

We went to the boys skinning that other bear. "Bear got you, huh?" they ask.

"No, just lay on top of me, that's all," I said. Good story for them guys. We left, next day they went back and skinned that bear that got me.

I buggered up my backbone. Pulled the joints in my backbone and pinched the nerves, or something like that. Stayed in camp for three days. Three days, I was laying down outside in the tent. I couldn't move. My back was no good any more. I could walk only little bit. I get a can to pee in, but I can't go outside and I can't walk. They made a stretcher for me out of plywood. We phoned through a fishery camp to Vancouver and they get an airplane to come pick me up. Fly me to the old hospital here in Bella Coola. I was in the Bella Coola Hospital for one month.

A friend of mine from North Hollywood phone my wife. I was in hospital. My wife told him, "Clayton, he just about get it this time, he's in the hospital right now."

"Just hang on to him till I get there," he said. He own his

own jet plane, small one, I think. They fly in this way and try and land in Bella Coola. Strip too short, they couldn't land. They went back to Vancouver. They phoned here and ask for someone to drive me to Williams Lake. I got to Williams Lake. Then they fly me to Vancouver, then to California. He meet me and take me into to the hospital down there. Santa Barbara hospital, where I stay for another month.

I told my Hollywood friend, "I got no money."

"Never mind about the money," he said. "I'll take care of everything."

There were so many doctors in that hospital. Forty-four doctors in there, in that Santa Barbara hospital. All specialists too. I stay there one month. I get X-rayed from head to toe. They took me in their office and ask me questions about grizzly bears and sasquatch. Found out I had broken bones all over. They see it on X-ray and ask, "How did that happen?"

"Most of them old broken bones happen from buckin' horse," I told him. From rodeos in the old days. I used to ride in rodeos quite a bit.

When I get out of hospital I stay in Hollywood for about another month. First, they give me a motel room, room seven, right close to hospital. I get a hotplate in there. I cook, make coffee. Pretty big in there. Got bed in there too, and a chesterfield. Rich Hollywood people, big shots, they all want to make friends with me when they see my *American Sportsman* movie, and heard I was in a Hollywood hospital. Like Rick Jason, Robert Mitchum. I see some more but I don't remember their names. The one I really wanted to see was Elizabeth Taylor. The guys there they don't want me to see her. But they come and bring me cigarettes. They want me to tell them what happened to me.

They asked, "Were you mauled by the grizzly bear?"

"No, she just hit me. Then she just lay on me," I said.

Then they want to hear the story more, come back with more guys. Some girls too. After a while they bring bottles in there, we all start drinking whisky! In my motel room which belong to hospital. They all want to invite me for supper, for parties, drinking parties.

They invited me to see this guy, the last white hunter, they call him. His first name is Jack, he was the last big white hunter in South Africa. He make eight million dollars guiding. He was a guide like me, I guess that's why they want me to see him. We go to Beverly Hills to his house. He had a big motel house. You stop outside a green light and the black people, they meet you there. The watchmans look after your car. Two black people take the key away from the car and they drive that car some place, and they come back and tell us where to go. They have a television, something like a television, outside in a little shed. He turn it on, and you can see the people we going to meet in there. We go through iron gates to that motel house. Them black people they control the whole building. Just push a button, gate open up inside and you go through that. After you get by, they close the gate behind you. All iron, iron fences. It was just like that last white hunter lived in a jail.

And then you go to iron bars again, another gate. And them black guys watch you and press another button that open up the next big gate again and you go through. When you get by, they close that gate again. *Bang!* Closed again. Millionaires in jail, it is just like going into a jail! We go in there and meet Jack. He don't feed me. All they do is drink this whisky. We just drink. Then we go back home.

I wouldn't want to live in that country. One day, my friends take me out. They take me downtown. I look at big buildings all around me, great big buildings. Big mountains, like. I look way up there. "How the hell you make the money to build all the big buildings? How do people make a living here?" I asked. "No big trees to log here, no big game animals to hunt here, no salmon for fishermans to catch."

"I'll show you," one guy said. He drive me to one big building. Bars all around it, too, just like that millionaire

Hollywood

jail-home. "Come on, let's go look," he said. We went inside. The guy who owned that, he wave for us and call us in. This guy had a smoke pipe, diamonds all around that smoke pipe. He show us a big glass case in there. Just full of gold and diamonds. That's where the money comes from to build all them big buildings in Hollywood. The money comes from that gold and diamonds. They buy them in Africa someplace, cut it in small pieces. Make an earring out of it, or diamond necklace. Hundreds and hundreds of thousands of dollars worth of gold and diamonds in that building.

One guy I met made gasoline for jets and planes. He invited me over to his place. Had a lot of kids, about fifteen kids, that guy. His wife, she was married to another guy before, he was married to another woman before too. Then they married each others. Two families together, like, and then they make their own kids. He wanted me to go and meet the guys who run Club Safari. I said, "All right, I like to see the country anyway."

At night-time they come and pick me up. We travel a hundred miles an hour in a little car. Go like hell. Night-time too. Multimillionaires can do that, you know. Near the gearshift he opened a little compartment and pulled out a handgun. I look at that gun and give it back. "Never know when you might need to shoot someone, never know who is gonna try to stop us," he says.

We went in that Club Safari place. Mostly doctors and millionaires go there. I sit down at the bar. All different kind of bottles of alcohol there. You name a drink, they bring it to you. I look up at the ceiling, there was a big stuffed snake up there. Skin, that's all. Almost goes right around the room.

"That's from a hunt," he said. South America, south of Mexico.

I told him, "Look, you can take me out to hunt a grizzly bear but no snakes. I just don't like snakes." And they laugh like hell. Those snakes are one to two feet through. Biggest snakes in the world. People get ideas where to hunt in the world from going to this Club Safari place. I didn't know that until I see that place.

When I get better, I leave the motel and stayed with the deputy attorney. Sometimes I asked him what kind of work he does. He was head guy of the police force in Hollywood. Deputy city attorney. In them days, one of the worst thing they don't like in Hollywood is the homosexuals. Homosexuals they call them. There was a guy who had a movie outfit. He take movies about boys and girls with no clothes on. He shows a movie to girls and boys in a room, shows them what to do with no clothes on, and those boys and girls got to do the same thing to each others. Then he takes a movie of them. The deputy attorney order the policeman to break into that moviemaker's house. The guy who makes them kind of movies. The deputy attorney tell the police to get the whole works. They call me to go join them. See what's going on. "Okay, I'll go," I said.

When we get to the moviemaker's house, the policemen get a big wood, big pole, almost the size of a telephone pole with a punching bag, like, on the end of it. All padded at the end. Maybe eight policemans hold onto that pole and they run it right into that door. And that door flies open. The whole works go in there. Them girls and boys still laying on the floor, moviemaking still going on! We were inside looking at them. They were all in a circle on the floor. Naked, every one of 'em. Two to each mattress, man and a woman. Some in the bedroom too. That's why they want me to go with them. They ask me to go check in the bedrooms with another policeman. I was in the police force! But I'm not a policeman! I just wanted to see what was going on. They arrest the movie camera guy, he get a big fine but they didn't arrest any of the other girls and boys. Didn't find any homosexuals, I guess.

The police ask me, "How did you like doing that job?"

I said, "No, I wouldn't like to do that for a living."

After a while I want to go home. I didn't like it after a while. No mountains, no snow-capped mountains there at all. The guy I stay with, he fight all the time, fight with his wife. I get tired of that. I got to get out of there. Maybe I causin' the trouble.

While I was there, a man from Bakersfield, California, came to visit. I told him, "I want to go home to Bella Coola. This guy, him and his wife fight every day and night."

The guy from Bakersfield said, "Pack your stuff, you comin' with me. You stay with me at my home. I've got a brand new house."

"Okay," I said. I packed my suitcase and we took off. He keep me there three days in Bakersfield.

I told him again, "I want to go home now."

"How you going to get home?" he asked.

"Drive me to Los Angeles airport and I get a plane."

He said, "No, you not going to go on a plane," he said. "You go out in the car lot, and pick out the car you want. I'll fix it up. You drive it home," he said. This guy own a big car lot, and a big car garage. Thousands of cars, new ones and second-hand ones. He had his own plane, too. I didn't do it, I didn't want to drive home. Maybe I get lost, end up in Alaska. Go the wrong way, end up in South America where them big snakes live. "I'll make a map, draw it so you can follow the road right to Bella Coola," he said.

I didn't drive, I had a return ticket on the plane. I went home on the plane instead. When I see them snow-capped mountains in Washington State, I sure feel good. When I see them big snow-capped mountains in Washington State, I know I'm finally getting close to Bella Coola.

Close calls

I was home, in the house. My wife answer the phone. "There's a guy name Walmark who want to talk to you," she said. So I talk to him on the phone. I know the guy, I seen him before. He came here once before that. He said he had two guys who want to hunt grizzly bear in Kimsquit. "It's okay," I said. "Sure, come in."

They came in, fly in an airplane to Bella Coola. They get in my pickup. They get out a gun case. Nice gun case. They open it, there was a nice little gun in there. They said they didn't know how accurate it was or if it was any good for grizzly bear. I asked him, "What calibre is it?" Remington .350 magnum. Short rifle. That gun kick like hell. Uses shells that aren't very long, but they big around—thick. Them guys want me to use it, they want me to tell them how good it is for grizzly bear, and write down where I hit them grizzly bear. Then they want me to send them a report, tell them how good the gun is.

"Okay," I said. I asked him how much that gun was. "About seven hundred dollars in the store," he said. But it was special made for me. Short barrel, my name on shoulder mount, "First class guide—Clayton Mack."

I took them to Kimsquit. George Anderson, my son-in-law, came with me as my assistant guide. We took two hunters out the first day, got two grizzly bears. George got one, I got one. And then I took this guy, he was the youngest of the bunch. I took him quite a ways up the river. Lot of grizzly bear up there. Lot of fish spawning up there. And he shot at one grizzly bear. Gut-shot it, I guess, shot it through the stomach. We try and look for him, we see the blood all right, but we couldn't find him. George, he doesn't like guys like that, who gut-shoot the bears. He don't like to take them out. I try to tell George, "You take him out."

"No, you take him out," he said. "That bear was very close and he gut-shot him. Make the bear mad."

So we decided I would take that young guy out the next day. We finish skinnin' them two grizzly bears we got and then took the skins down to the boat. Spread them and salt them down.

We still got to get one more bear for this young guy. I took him up by myself the next day. I went up the Kimsquit River about a mile. There is a side stream, breaks in from the main river. Right close to the mountain. Trees are all small there, biggest about a foot through. I walked through some trees and came to a riverbed. A little water in there. A few fish in there, few dog salmons. I saw a bear go into the timber, I saw him walking. This young hunter was pretty clumsy. Noisy, clumsy, fall down and get his gun barrel stuck in the mud. You have to take that mud out of the barrel or else it blow open. He don't seem to care. I tell him to be careful, he's going to ruin his gun. They told me later, "He has too much money, he doesn't give a damn what he does to his gun. Got so much money, he don't care." He was so clumsy I was worried he might get hurt.

There was a logjam. I put him in there. "You stay right here, I'll go back down and chase the bear up toward you. When he comes out of the woods there shoot him," I said. I went down, walk down the river. I thought I was quite a bit below the bear now. That grizzly, he's behind me now I thought. So I went in the timber and started yelling like you chase cattle, *Ai, ai, ai!* I walk up, I don't see any sign of fresh bear track. Lot of old tracks. I was about a hundred yards to the guys, when I heard something behind me. *Woof, woof, woof.* Every jump she make, she made that noise.

I look back and saw a pretty good sized grizzly bear coming toward me. I had this brand new gun. I stop and stand still. She keep coming, I didn't shoot right away. She stop about twenty, twenty-five feet away, and she stand up on her hind feet. About eight feet tall. Then she walk toward me on her hind feet. Look like she was gonna try and grab me up. I lift the gun up, try and shoot her in the chest. That gun slip. Barrel slide up her chest, and go off. Shot her under her chin, above her neck. She fell down, touched me a little bit on my leg. Dead. Big gun. I look at it. It was a sow, a female.

I stand there, and I hear sticks breaking, noises where this bear came from. Sound like a person blowin' their nose. He snorting. I look back, by God, I see another grizzly bear coming. Running toward me. This time I run. I run as fast as I can. There was a riverbed—ditch, like—about six feet deep. I jump down into it, I slide down on the bank, like, and hit the bottom. No water, dry riverbed.

I look up. It was a young grizzly bear, about four year old, I guess. Stand right there, right on top of his mother. He put his foot on her and he look at me. Pret' near as big as the mother. Pretty big, too. I look beside me, there was a hole under the ground. It was a bank, overhanging bank. Flood, I guess, washed out quite a bit under the bank.

I look up and see that bear start circling around toward me. Joe Edgar told me that's a bad sign. Mean's he's a real bad bear. I shot the mother, you see, so he was mad at me. He wants to come after me. I thought, "He's gonna jump down." Gun loaded. I go under the bank. I hear the bear on the overhang, over my head. That bugger come right on top. That overhang roof about ten inch thick. I was afraid the overhang bank would break, and bury me alive. The bear could smell me underneath there. I stayed in there looking up. Like a roof over me. I waited, if he comes down I shoot. But he didn't, he was still on top of me, on the overhang.

He smell me, try and put his head down little bit once. Then he reach, try and put his hand down to feel for me. Then he came down with both front legs, try and feel for me underneath there. I see yellow jackets then, comin' out of his hair. They buzz all over me. The air was yellow with yellow jacket bees. I was scared to move too much. If I run that grizzly bear will get me, if I stay, I get stung. Then he came down, slide down, in an awkward way, like. He came down with his head down and then I see his jaw. I see his whole head is over toward me now. I shot him right between his jaw. I just about touch him, then I pull the trigger of that short .350 magnum rifle. *Bang!* He keep still there, I think I got him.

Talk about yellow jackets! Buzzing and flying all over. I

came out of there, walked a little bit and climbed up the bank. I got on top of the bank and walked back toward the bear. I put my foot on the bear, spread the hair apart. He was just yellow inside the hairs. I guess he been raiding a yellow jacket nest. They like that, to eat the nest of yellow jackets. Lot of honey in that, and young yellow jackets.

I was standing there looking at all those yellow jackets in that bear when I heard something again, coming. I think, "Another bear coming. Must of had two young ones—two full grown young bears." I started to yell at him, "Go on beat it, I don't want to kill you." I went down little bit back to that clumsy guy. He asked, "What did you shoot?"

"Two grizzly bears," I said. "They try and get me. Come on, let's go look at 'em." He came over with me. That other third bear was still there. Sitting beside the mother. I heard my walkie-talkie, somebody talking on the walkie-talkie. They heard me shooting from the boat. They asking who shooting. I said, "A bear try and go after me." My son-in-law told me, "Better get out of there." We went down for the night.

We eat, had breakfast. Then went back up with the jet boat to skin them bears. We skin the mother, no yellow jackets on it. Just the young one. We try and skin the young one but you can't touch it. Not for the yellow jackets under the hair. They come fly in your face. So we drag that grizzly bear to the boat, sink him in the water to drown the yellow jacket, then we can skin him. I never seen anything like it. Just yellow inside the skin.

I had another close call. It was at the mouth of the Skowquiltz River. I was all by myself that year. No assistant guide to help me. No one want to come with me that year. Usually, they fight to go with me. That year no one ask me. I had two hunters. I thought I could handle them. It was a spring hunt, end of May now, green grass startin' to get long.

It was in the early evening when we took off to look for

bear. The two guys were from the States. Real tall guys, six feet two and six feet four. I'm short you know, the grass was just about the same height as I am—five foot seven inch. I couldn't see ahead of me, through the grass, and I was ahead of those two hunters. We get to the slough where there is no grass, just mudflats. Then I heard something snorting on the sidehill.

"We lost that bear," I said. "He's gone."

Then they started to talk against me. "What the hell matter with the guide? You can't see?"

"No," I said, "I can see pretty good but the grass too tall. What wrong with you guys, you guys tall enough to see over the grass to see that bear. Maybe he'll be there tomorrow. We'll come back tomorrow."

Early in the morning we took off again. No bear, he's still gone.

"There is sometimes grizzly bear on the other side of the bay," I said.

One of them guys was real pushy. "Go and get out on a little rowboat, and row across to the other side of the bay. Look around at that place you talkin' about. Any bear there, you come back right away and call us to go kill that bear."

I'd been up since four o'clock in the morning. Not enough sleep. Only a couple of hours' sleep that night, that's all. But I did go across. Across the bay are some great big logs. They fall down from the edge of the timber. Them big trees fall toward a dry riverbed in there. Some logs build up there on one side of that dry riverbed. There is a meadow just above that big logjam. I rest with my back against one of the biggest logs, and watch for bear to come out in the meadow. I'm gonna lay there till the bear come out. That logjam is good cover for me, bear come out but they can't see me there amongst all the logs. I was pretty sleepy. Keep dozing off. It was around six o'clock in the morning. Then all at once that big log move. I feel that log pushing against my back.

"What the hell?" I thought. I didn't get up. Just looked around slow. I look at the butt end of that log. A big grizzly bear standin' there on the butt end of that log. He'd jump on the butt end of that log, and the top end would spring up and push against my back. "You son-of-a-gun, don't come this way, you bugger," I thought. I had a small gun, .30-.30. That bear started to come toward me. Real slow-like it walks toward me. It was a big grizzly bear. And it keep on coming toward me. About halfway down that log, he jumped down off the log, walked up the creekbed and then climbed the bank up to the meadow. He walk up the hill away from me. When walking he keep biting the grass like a horse. He eatin' on his way back into the timber.

He was about fifty yards away when he turn around. "By God, that bugger coming back this way," I thought. "I got to hide." Behind that log, was a ditch. Deep ditch, about four-and-a-half feet deep. "That's the place to go in," I thought. And I slide myself in there. I stand in the ditch, keep my gun on top and look toward the bear with my head above the ground level. He still coming. I never move. I stand real still, eyes open. Hard to do it, though. I want to scream. He must have smell me after a while. The wind was blowing toward him, I could feel the wind against the back of my neck. He start snorting, put his head up, open his mouth too.

After a while he stop, eat a little bit of grass again. I load the gun slow, lever action, and have it ready. Small gun, .30-.30, and I was worried because I didn't really want to use that gun to try and kill that grizzly bear. Then he come toward me again. He keep coming my way. Takin' his time. He smell again and start snorting. Was only about ten feet away by this time. Wind start blowing hard, he smell me again, and stand up looking toward me. I stand real still. He go down on all four feet again and he keep coming toward me. He stand up again, go down, keep coming and then stand up again. Third time. He was right by me. Toes pointing toward me, on each side,

Close calls

my head was right between his feet. He smell me pretty strong. Keep looking down over me.

I look at his feet when he stand in that mud. Water come between his toes. From all his weight pressing on the ground. Standing on his two hind feet, I see that mud and water come out between his toes, both feet like that. I keep still, don't want to move. I can't move. I too scared to move. He was almost touching my head with his hind legs. He stood on his hind legs quite a long time. I could look up and see his balls hanging down! "I wonder what he do if I touch them?" I thought to myself. I was close enough to grab them grizzly bear balls! Someone would have laughed to watch me there. The bear went down, took off, and run like hell. I took off and run like hell the other way. I fell down over the log where I was laying before. Hit my head on it. I fell back. I lost my gun too. For a few seconds I thought another bear had hit me on the head. I look behind me and don't see any grizzly bear, I look back and see that grizzly bear was still running away from me.

One of the best huntin' trips I ever guide was with two guys from California. A policeman and a cotton field guy. Two young guys. They write to me, they want two grizzly bears, but they only want big bear, real big grizzly bears. After they write to me they phone me. Want to make sure I can get them big bears. "I think I can help you," I said. They asked me what date. September is best I think. Good run of sockeye at Rivers Inlet, Washwash River, in September. And so those two guys came in one September. I had George Anderson as my guide. He's a pretty good guide.

I was all ready for them before they get here. I get all the grub, gas for the motors, and packed it all up on Wilderness Airlines plane. And they came. "Okay, we go right now. We got the plane here, we fly to Washwash right away," I said. We pack their stuff on the plane, got on and took off. Sometime around two o'clock in the afternoon, I think, we left Bella Coola. The plane landed on a sand beach. I get out and grab the rope, I tie the plane up. I look around on the sand beach, I saw big bear track. About sixteen-inch foot print. I just stand there and wait for those boys to come up. And they came up.

"One of you boys wanted a big bear. Here's one headed to the Inziana River. That grizzly bear was right here less than an hour ago," I said. I called them to look at it.

The policeman said, "I want that. That's what I'm looking for."

That cotton field guy, his name was Boo-Boo, he chew tobacco all the time. Boo-Boo said, "I want one, too, just like that."

"Well, pack up your stuff, pack it in the cabin and we'll have something to eat and go get 'em. We'll fix the beds up, have a little bit to eat, and then we go on evening hunt," I said.

I said to George Anderson, "George, you got to walk all the way to that Inziana River to catch up to this big track. And I'll go across with Boo-Boo in the small canoe to the Washwash River." We had walkie-talkies. George took one, I had one.

I paddle that canoe like hell to go across to the Washwash River with Boo-Boo. We get across and we walk up the river, the Washwash River. And I saw a grizzly bear coming down. About a year-old grizzly bear. Coming right straight for us. He go in the bushes, short bushes and I don't see him any more. I wonder if it go to its mother in them bushes.

I heard a bang. "By God," I said. "Sound like they catch up to that big bear already." I heard two more shots. I pick up that walkie-talkie, "You get him?"

"Yeah, we get him right in the water," George said. "He's right down in deep water."

"Both of you take off your belts," I told them. "Make a rope out of it and tie him up. Don't let it drift down to the lake. We don't want to lose a Boone and Crockett bear—we don't want to lose one of the biggest bear in the world."

And Boo-Boo he ask, "He get 'im?"

"Yeah, he get that big bear," I said.
"I got to get one too like that," he said.
"We'll try," I said.

Right at once that year-old grizzly bear's mother stand up. Came way above them bushes. She snort and snort, spittin' old red sockeye fish out its mouth when it make that noise. And I look at Boo-Boo, he look at me, and that chewing tobacco drooling out his mouth too. Slimy stuff coming out of his mouth in a string, like. Just like that fish coming out of that bear's mouth. Just the same, both of them! That mother grizzly bear was only about ten feet away. About ten feet high, I guess. Big sow grizzly bear.

I told Boo-Boo, "Wait, don't shoot." I was all ready, too, to shoot if I had to. Them grizzly bears headed off into the big timber. Took off quick. Three of them. Mother and two young ones, both about a year old. "Okay, Boo-Boo, let's go."

We went on. Right away we see three more bears again, different ones. And then we see more and more bears. I counted eleven bears before we saw another real big one. One of them eleven try to get tough with us. He stand up and sniff and snort. "He looking for trouble," I said. And Boo-Boo aim right away. "No, don't shoot him. Not the one we looking for." Was about twenty feet away. I throw rocks at it. One rock hit him right in the nose. I could tell he feel that. Boo-Boo was throwing rocks too. Hit it right in the chest. Seemed like it almost sound like a drum. We were throwin' big rocks. Finally that grizzly bear took off.

About a hundred yards from where we throwin' rocks at that grizzly bear we saw that real big grizzly bear. He was fishing. When he know we were there he started to run like hell away from us. I said, "Go ahead, Boo-Boo, take him. That's the grizzly bear you been looking for."

Bang! He was a good shot, too. Got him right through the lungs. That big grizzly bear run only about fifty feet and fall down. We left the bear and head back to camp. Gonna skin it the next day. The skin of that bear was only two inches smaller than the one George get with the policeman. We got two big boars, the policeman get one and the cotton guy get one too. Same size bears. And we get both of them Boone and Crockett bears in the same hour.

When Boo-Boo and me get to the camp them two boys want to go home right away. Same day.

"We'll phone in tomorrow," I say.

They told me, "We both just got married and we come out hunting." That's how come they want to go back home quick.

But I say, "We got a big job to do yet, got to skin two big bears. Salt them down. You don't want to go home today. You get your bears, and that's good, but you want to go fishing too." So they stayed that night. We had pork chop for dinner. After, I dug a little hole on the edge of Owikeno Lake and I put garbage in there from the dinner table. Pork chop bones. I covered them up.

Boo-Boo asked, "What are you gonna do with that?"

"Oh, we'll feed them bears," I said. "Poor buggers get hungry too. Leave the bones there, those bears will come out and eat it." I was just bullshitting him, you know, I didn't really believe that.

Next day we go skin the bears, take the heads off and pack that head and skin back to our camp. After that, them boys go fishing. At the mouth of the Washwash River and a little upstream. There's an old fish trap there. Good fishing there. Big trouts in there. Rainbows, look like, and all different kinds of trouts. That Washwash River is pretty clear. Can look down from a stump and see some big trouts right in the river.

After a while, I see them boys come back in the canoe paddling like hell.

"Trout for supper?" I ask.

"No, we got to get out of there," they said. "There is six bears in there fishing. Six of them grizzly bear are runnin' around chasin' the fish." Then they came in and had coffee.

"Did you take your camera, take pictures of that six bears?" I ask.

"Yeah, we took some, I don't know if the pictures will turn out," he said. He had a good little movie camera. Super 8.

I go back and skin that grizzly bear head outside the cabin. About forty feet to the cabin. And Boo-Boo was splitting wood. He was about thirty feet to the cabin. George was cooking supper, I think. I hear a noise. George, my son-in-law, was making a hissing noise trying to get my attention. I look back and look at him. He pointing over there. I look and see two grizzly bears coming. Them bears smell that pork chops. Coming toward us. They jump over that canoe. One grizzly bear stepped on the canoe edge and they flip that canoe upside down.

And Boo-Boo was watching. A mouthful of chewing tobacco, snoose, dripping and hanging from his mouth. "They turn that boat upside down," he said.

"Yeah," I said and I went back to skinning that bear head. Boo-Boo go back to chopping the wood.

Then George, he make that hissing noise again. I look again. A great big grizzly bear right here, about ten feet away from me. Maybe less than ten feet away. That big mother bear keep coming. I just keep still. I get too scared, I guess. If I run maybe she get me, I thought. She started to smell me, smell my nose. Sniffing me. Her whiskers touch me right in the face. Grizzly bear got long whiskers. I never move, I keep real still. Her eyes four inches away. I look at her eyes, she look at my eyes too. Face to face. Smelling me all the time. Then them yearling grizzly bears start crunching on that pork chop bones. She look down to her yearling pups. I look too. They were eating them pork chop bones. Make a lot of noise crunching them bones. I reach for my cowboy hat, and then I hit her hard as I could right on the side of her face. I hit her real hard. She jump back, and I run for the cabin as fast as I can. I made it to the cabin too.

That policeman film the whole thing on his Super 8 movie camera. But I never hear how it turned out.

The first arrow hunter I took out was Mastrangel. I took him out about thirty years ago. He wrote me a letter, said he was one of the champions of the world who can shoot an arrow. He outshoots the best arrow hunters in the world. I said, "All right, I'll take you out." I took him out to Kwatna River.

First day out we saw a grizzly bear, right on top of a log. Little one. Mastrangel shot him with the arrow, but he didn't kill him. Arrow went right through that small grizzly bear. The grizzly bear took off. I see the blood, lot of blood, but I lost it. Too much water. He walk in the water so I couldn't track him.

I take that hunter on up. On way up I saw a real big one. Great big grizzly bear. Stood up on his hind feet. About ten feet tall. About forty feet away. I told Mastrangel, "Try and get him right through the heart. Right through his heart." He shoot and hit a tree. I can see the feather in that tree. He missed that bear. Pulled back another arrow again. But same way again, he missed, shot a tree. Then he missed again. Three arrows missed. Bear went down and took off. I followed him, no blood. We went on. We ran into another one, another big grizzly bear.

Mastrangel, he didn't try and shoot that one. Pulled the arrow back, all right, but he never let it go. I was glad too, in case he wounded that big grizzly and we can't find the bear. We let that bear go.

Mastrangel changed his bow to fifty-five-pound pull from sixty-five-pound pull. That fifty-five-pound pull is lighter pull, slower arrow, but he can aim good with that, he told me. So I made a big circle to go down to another stream. I get on top of a log, and I see another big grizzly bear. He was lookin' up at me. I said to that hunter, "Try and get him in the big blood vein in his neck." By God, he hit him right where I said. Blood just shot out, just like that. Blood everywhere. That grizzly bear took off. I had a gun, too, I should have shot him. Bear took off across from us and climb up on the bank on the other side. Mastrangel shot again and hit that bear right in the hindquarter. I can see that arrow feathers in the hindquarter. The grizzly bear get on top of the bank, look back and the hunter hit him again with another arrow, third shot. Hit him right in the jaw. The arrow broad-head just went in, just go in the bone in the jaw. Didn't damage him, bear just took off again with arrows in his bum, in his neck, and in his jawbone. That bear took off again. We followed him. Blood, lot of blood. He made a big circle back to same place we started from, then he lay down. It was getting late too.

Finally I caught up to that big grizzly bear. "Try and hit him in the kidney this time," I said. "Way up high on the hip, top of the hip." By God, he hit him in the kidney. He got him, that grizzly not move much. But his jaw was wide open. I told Mastrangel, "You shoot him right through there, right at the roof of the mouth. Just a thin bone to the brains there. That arrow will go right through there and hit the brains, you'll kill him just like that." He shot right between the jaw, and that arrow went right into that grizzly bear's brain. The bear just stiffen up like that, it kill him quick. It was a big bear, a real big one. It was a record, biggest bear on arrow.

This hunter was part of forty guys who hunt all over for grizzly bear. Want to see who can kill the biggest grizzly bear with bow and arrow. Some went to Alaska, some to Northwest Territories, Yukon, and this guy to Kwatna. Third day we get our bear. The ones who went to Alaska, forty days they never seen a bear. I got the Mastrangel one right away. Front page of a newspaper in the States somewhere. Mastrangel give me his bow and arrows after that. I give it to my kids, I never try and hunt with it.

I had another arrow hunter after that, then I quit with them. The second guy got his bear too. I took three guys to the west arm of Kwatna, this one arrow hunter and two rifle hunters. Grizzly bears were eating crab-apples when I see them. We anchored out on the mouth of the Kwatna River. I look through the window of my boat, I saw a bear standing up on his hind legs eating crab-apples in tree. Small tree, not big one.

I told one of them rifle hunter, I call him out, "There is two grizzly bears up there eating crab-apples." He not like that arrow hunter, this rifle hunter. This rifle hunter, he said, "Get rid of that arrow hunter, get rid of him. Let him get that bear and we'll get rid of him soon so we don't have more trouble." He didn't like to hunt with someone who hunts with bow and arrow. So I took the arrow hunter up. There was a high bank, like, near the crab-apple trees.

I rowed the boat right into there. Had just a short way to climb up. He shoot right from the top of a bank. Not very far away. Gut-shot that grizzly bear. Cut the skin in the belly, and his guts came out. He try stuffing back his intestine, but kept pulling out. The bear started to go up to heavy timber, but when he walks he steps on his intestines and they keep coming out like a long rope. I try to say to that arrow hunter, "Shoot, give him another." He tried to, but he missed him.

That bear went in an island of timber. He went inside there. I circle around that island of timber ready to see his tracks. He still in there, he didn't come out of there, he still in there. So I circle back around, and went in. The arrow hunter right behind me. I see that bear laying on his back, he was holding his stomach like a human being would do. His guts all trying to come out, so he hold it close. I say to that arrow hunter, "Shoot him right underneath his chin so that arrow will go right into his brains."

His broad-heads were razor blades, dangerous, you know. I had my gun, .30-.30. He let his arrow go, hit that grizzly bear right in the knee cap! That bear come charging, just like that. Not very big one. But damn fast he come. This hunter then turn and run by me, he was running away! When he run past me he cut my hand with the broad-head of an arrow. I lowered my .30-.30 down, I just hold it down to the height of that bear's head. The bear run right into that barrel and the gun went off. *Bang!* Right on the head. This hunter turn around and come back around again. And the bear somersault and hit the hunter on the legs. That arrow hunter fell right on top of the grizzly bear! That arrow hunter stand up and he grab hold of me, he grab me. Going to hit me, I guess, because I shot that grizzly bear. I kill it with my .30-.30.

The two other guys grab hold of that arrow hunter and lead him out of there. "Come on get out of here," they said. They give him shit for try to hit me. He wanted to kill that bear with arrows, but why did he run away?

I told him, "Look, I got a wife and I got three kids from my wife. That grizzly would have killed me. Who's gonna feed my kids? You, too, you maybe have got wife. That bear could have killed you too."

After that he was happy, put his arm around my neck once in a while. "You're a good man," he said.

That arrow hunter, he want to kill a wolf too. My nephew told me he saw two wolf on tideflat. So I told that arrow hunter, "Let's go." We went down to the tideflat. And I tell my nephew, "You stay here and watch. Grizzly bears sometimes go across that river right there." He stay there. When we sneakin' up to those wolfs, I heard a shot, *bang!* It was close to night-time, already getting dark.

I told that arrow hunter, "Let's go back. Never know what those guys trying to do." Guide got to look after everybody. Play it safe. I walk up and see one of the rifle hunters holding his gun. "What he shoot?" I ask.

"Grizzly bear," he said. "Four or five of them go across, and we shot one. Percy's looking for blood."

I said, "You guys get out of here. Let's get out of here now."

At this time of night, stumps look like grizzly bear. Black stumps all over. You don't know if it's a grizzly bear or stump. Next thing you know, one of them stumps will jump on you.

In the morning I went back again. Look for the blood. I could tell that the rifle hunter who shot that bear wounded him. I found the blood. I could tell that grizzly bear went straight up the mountain. I followed it. It turned around and went back down to the river again. That wounded grizzly bear did that. I see something moving down there by the river. I was up on the hill looking down. I see the tops of the bushes moving. So I went down. There was a big cedar, split open, and that grizzly bear went in there, I guess, that night. A wolf smell the blood and he follow that blood trail. I see the wolf tracks. That wolf, he scare the grizzly bear out of the cedar, the grizzly bear started to go again. I follow his track again, pick it up again and keep on going.

The hunters all follow me, right close behind me. That arrow hunter had a movie camera, big movie camera. My nephew had a good gun. The guy who shot the bear the day before, he came with us too. I walk ahead, when I stop they bump me from behind. I said, "You guys, ten feet this side and ten feet that side, let me walk in the middle. When that bear see us, he don't know which one he going to take." I keep on going.

By God, I see that bear. He was looking at us already. He

was ready already, ready to jump. I stopped. He right there. I could have shot him myself. About a hundred feet away. I show him to that arrow hunter. "He's right there." He put that camera right beside him, on top of a log. He get behind that log and start to take pictures. My nephew come behind me. I walk up to a big tree and look at him, that big bear. I look. Then he came. That bear come right now. Comin' at us real fast.

I pull my gun back, step behind the tree so he's gonna have to come around the side of the tree to get me. I switch around so I can shoot to other side of tree when he comes. I stand up on the mossy roots but the moss peel off and I fell down backwards. I fall right down. The gun went off on me. I just miss my legs. I try and put that gun down and reload it. But that bear ran right into the barrel and he poked that stock right into my ribs. Broke two ribs. He step on my foot too. Had me right against the tree. My nephew see that, he took off and started to run away. Good thing too. That bear went after him! He chase my nephew. There was one big cedar tree, windfall, just in front of my nephew. Where the roots used to be there was a big hole. That kid run and fell right into that hole. The bear jumped clean right over the windfall root hole. I can see a flame, like, a big flame of fire in my head. I guess I hit my head against a tree. I see that bear running and that kid droppin' into that hole.

I try and look for my gun, couldn't find my gun. I guess it got in between that bear's legs and it spin off my hands. I look, and I see that bear watching me. I look back at that arrow hunter. He had that string, way back to the corner of his mouth. But he won't let the arrow go.

All I want is to get my gun back. There were short bushes a few feet away and I crawl into those short bushes. Lay on my side. You know, I was hurt. I couldn't talk, couldn't take a big breath. My ribs hurt so damn bad. That gun poked me, the stock, broke my right ribs. I lay down for awhile. I heard my nephew. Sound like a little puppy, crying like a puppy left outside for the first night. I look. By God, I saw my gun on the ground. Like a hundred yard foot race, I get my right leg in the right place. I gonna jump for my gun. I dived for my gun, grabbed it. I loaded it and walk to my nephew.

The grizzly bear was back in his hole, gettin' ready to charge again. Told my nephew to get up and run home—he was about two feet away from the bear—he got up and ran right past the bear. I walked up to that bear, to four feet away, I swear at him, then I fired three quick shots and killed that bear. We find out he had been gut-shot the night before.

I wouldn't take arrow hunters after that guy. Before he left I told him, "Indians used to have arrows in the olden days. We used arrows long time ago. Then the white man come in with nice guns. We Indians throw those arrows away and we use guns now. Why you want to use arrows anyway?"

I even got a letter from some guys who want to kill grizzly bear with one of those things which come around after you throw them—called boomerang. Couple of guys want to hunt with aluminum boomerangs! I wrote back, "Arrows bad enough—I'm not gonna have anything to do with hunting grizzly bear with aluminum boomerangs."

Big shot hunters

Most of my hunters come from United States, but quite a few come from Germany too. I liked them German hunters. Easy to satisfy them German hunters. Just shoot a black bear, they are happy. Shoot a medium-sized grizzly bear, them Germans are real happy. But most of them Americans, they only want to shoot Boone and Crockett bears—biggest grizzly bear in the world. Not happy with anything else.

I got a letter from this German guy one year. Mr. Pat Graff. He was head of Audi car company. The letter was all in German writing. I couldn't read it. So I went in the Co-op Cafe. I asked one lady if she could read German. She named another woman who could tell me what it said. She said, "Go ask Hanna Ounpuu."

I showed it to Hanna Ounpuu. She told me he want to go hunting grizzly bear for ten days. She asked, "How you gonna understand him?"

"Use our fingers I guess," I said.

"I can understand German," she said. "I'll go with you, be interpreter for him, tell you what he wants."

"Tough going, that hunting," I said. "I don't like to take a woman into the woods."

I also know one guy, Bernie, from Williams Lake, who

speaks German. He's a real estate guy. Friend of mine. I think about him and I went to Williams Lake. I took that letter with me. He said he would come but he wanted big money to be an interpreter. I told him I couldn't pay him but he could keep a grizzly bear skin if I get one when he's there. That was gonna be his pay, a grizzly bear skin. "A lot of guys pay big money for a grizzly bear skin," I told him.

Bernie wasn't a hunter, he didn't have a hunting license, he wasn't gonna be a guide assistant, but I said he could be the interpreter and help with the cookin'. So he said, "Okay, I'll be your interpreter." I check with the game warden if it's okay to get Bernie as an interpreter. I don't want them to think Bernie is poaching. They said it was all right for me to bring Bernie. I told Bernie he could come. He asked me, "How many bottles you take out there?"

"None," I said. "If the German drinks he has to bring his own drink."

Bernie said, "I got some bottles to bring. Is that all right?"

"That's all right with me," I said.

The German guy came in the fall, and we all went to my cabin on Owikeno Lake. When we get in the cabin I told Bernie where to sleep, and I put the German's stuff in there and I fix his bed. "You gonna sleep in there tonight," I said. "We go hunting right away, before it gets dark we go hunt." Before we went out Bernie poured himself a drink right away. I told him, "I don't allow anybody to drink when we go out hunting. Guys who get drunk make noise and they don't look after their rifle right."

The German understand me, he heard what I said. He get mad and fight Bernie right away, yell at him in German. Really yell loud at each others. That German guy, he must understand a bit of English. I think Bernie drink more than once. I think he sneak another drink before we go out.

I told them guys, "We not really hunting yet. We just see if there is any good grizzly bear sign. Sign of bear tracks, where they feed, so we can go there in the morning and really hunt." So we went looking for sign. Went across the Owikeno Lake to Washwash River and walked up the stream. I duck underneath one log. There was some water below, about one foot of water. I duck my head to go underneath that big log. I had my cowboy hat on. Bernie had a cowboy hat too. The German guy come right behind me next. He didn't have no cowboy hat. He just bend his head down too and duck under that log. We stop and look back at Bernie, he's coming behind us. He bend down to duck under that log, slipped and dived right in the water. His hat came off and start to drift down the little creek. "Get your hat," I said. And Bernie run and get his hat. I poked that German guy, "You see how that whisky works. That whisky make him fall down."

He talked to Bernie in German, and they yell again at each others right there again. I think that German guy told Bernie that he drinks too much.

"My business, that's my business. Mind your own business," said Bernie.

"We got one more place to look," I told them. We circled around, never seen no sign of bear but a lot of tracks. We saw one big track and the German guy say in German, "Wow, that's all I want to see." About sixteen-inch long track.

He said, "We go home."

"Okay," I said. I told him, "We'll come back early in the morning before daylight. We'll walk over with a flashlight and we sit down here. When the bear come out you shoot him."

I get up quite early and tell the German guy, "Let's go. If you drink coffee, if you want a little bit of toast, I'll make toast for you," I said.

"Okay," he said.

That's all we plan to eat till nine o'clock when we come back. We cross again to the Washwash River. No wind. We walk up. We sit down at the top of the bank. Same place as the night before. It was downhill little bit. And that bear came across a tideflat, came across right in front of us. About forty feet away from us. This German guy had a fancy rifle, two triggers on it. German guns always have that two triggers. I saw that bear coming. "There, Pat, he's right here now," I said. He lift that gun up straight up, he's gonna come down and shoot I guess. Barrel was still pointing way up when the gun went off, *bang!* He missed that bear. He said something in German. Then he did the same thing again, *bang!* That bear take off. He's gone. I could have shot that bear myself, but I don't want to, let the German kill it.

Then he told me, "You go home, I'm going to sit down here for awhile."

"How I know when you come down?" I said, "You can't walk home, cross river and lake, you'll need boat." He understand a little English.

"I shoot, I shoot," he said.

"Okay, you shoot, I come and pick you up," I said. And I took off back to the cabin.

Bernie was standing there, at the camp, smiling all by himself.

"How's the coffee?" I asked.

"I didn't make any," he says.

Bang! That German hunter was down already, I got to go and pick him up. So I get in the boat and I went across. He jump in the boat and I highball it back to our camp. We get up and walk in the cabin. Bernie had another glass of hard liquor, he was drinking whisky again.

"Coffee all ready, Bernie?" I said.

"No, I forgot to make some," he said.

"Never mind," I said, "I'll make some." I got a propane stove, pretty good stove. Gets hot quick. I made coffee right now. Bernie was sitting pretty close to me now. I poured three cups of coffee.

I pat on his shoulder, "How many lumps of sugar you take, Bernie?"

"Two," he said. I put two lumps sugar in his coffee.

I asked this German guy, "Pat, how many lumps of sugar you take in your coffee?"

"Nein," he said loudly.

I thought he was mad. I count nine lumps sugar, and put them in his coffee. Overflowed the coffee. Too much sugar, filled the cup right up. I gave it to that German hunter. Pat took a drink. He spit out the coffee in his mouth. He speak German a little bit.

I asked Bernie, "What did he say?"

"He said you try to kill him with sugar!" he said. *Nein* means none, he don't want any. That's what Bernie told me.

"Why didn't you tell me that before?" I said.

We got the German hunter his bear after a few days up the Washwash River. We saw three grizzly bears together. A big sow with her two full-grown kids. I told the German, "Stay put. I'm gonna go around to the side." But when I start to go away that German start to get scared, he say, "Clayton, come back." Bernie was quite a way behind and the sow grizzly bear see him and went at him. The German and I start to shoot at that bear. Bernie shot at the bear too. Bernie had a good gun, 7 mm, and when he hit the bear it went down. When we skin that bear it had six or seven bullet holes in it. The day before Bernie killed a small grizzly bear and he even shot a wolf. Even though that big sow had six or seven bullet holes in it, and even though Bernie had already killed a grizzly bear and wolf, he try and claim that big grizzly bear sow skin too. I try and tell Bernie, "You give the German hunter that big skin. You already have a little grizzly bear skin and the wolf skin. I'll take you out again someday. We live in this country all the time. He come all the way from Germany. Give him the big grizzly bear skin." Bernie said, "No." Bernie wanted the whole works.

The German hunter find that out, and they had another big fight. Yelling at each other in German language. Yell at each others all the way back to Bella Coola. When we get to the dock,

Big shot hunters

back home in Bella Coola, I get Hanna Ounpuu to come down. When she hear what was happenin', Hanna blow up. I told Bernie, "You better get out of Bella Coola before Hanna shoots you, she's really mad at you. You don't have a hunting license or grizzly bear tag and you still want all the skins." So Bernie let that German hunter have the little grizzly bear skin.

After, I think Hanna Ounpuu would have been a better interpreter for that German hunter! I had a lot of German hunters after that who don't speak English, but I don't need an interpreter. We get along fine even though we can't speak to each others. I sure never ask Bernie to be my German interpreter again after that.

I remember one American hunter, he talks lots all the time. Big shot. He said he was a pilot, he flies long flights in a big plane. Kind of hard to tell him anything. He came with two other guys. Three of them. I forget their names. They were all from the United States. Big American guys. Two weigh over two hundred pounds, one guy weigh over three hundred pounds. Two were all right, but the biggest guy was kind of hard to talk to.

I took them to my cabin in Owikeno Lake to get their grizzly bears. Took one of the guys up the Sheemahant River, he shot a grizzly bear that same day. It's quite a long hunt, that Sheemahant River hunt. We got to go about ten miles up the river with a jet boat. That is as far as we can go in that boat. About ten miles up. Lot of grizzly bears in that country. One year we count about fifty-two grizzly bear in three trips. That was before they logged it out. After that one guy got his grizzly bear up the Sheemahant River, that big shot guy just want to go up there to hunt. I had real problem with him. He can't shoot and hit the bears; he shoot at them all right, but he miss. Miss all the time.

I had an assistant guide from Vancouver with me. Real nice guy. Jim Mullin, his name was. When this big shot hunter wake up in the morning, he yells at Jim, "Jim, I'll be up in about twenty minutes from now. You better get some water from the lake and warm it up before I get up. Warm it up on the stove. I don't want to wash my face in the cold water."

One morning, one of the other guys heard him saying that to Jim, "Warm up the water." He get mad and say to that big shot, "Why don't you get up on your feet, you lazy bugger. You wonder why you are so damn fat. You don't want to do nothing. Go down to the lake and wash your face like what we do." He was a big, fat guy all right. That big shot doesn't like to walk, too. He was a lazy hunter. He don't want to hunt grizzly bears up in the woods. He just want to sit down in the boat and look for bears. Hunt from the boat.

I told him one day, "I seen a big track up there in the woods. Great big track. Let's get him."

"No," he said, "I want to go up to the Sheemahant River today."

My boy, Dusty, was at the camp. He had just come from Bella Coola, and when he got near the camp he look down from the airplane. He saw that there was a big grizzly bear right near our camp. He said, "Dad, I saw that big bear that made that big track." Tzeo River. "How far back where you saw it?" I asked. "Just a little ways," he says.

I told this lazy hunter, "You go up with Dusty tomorrow and get that big bear."

"I don't want to go there," he said. "I don't want to walk up there. I want to go up the Sheemahant River again."

So Dusty went up the Tzeo River with one of the other guys, early the next morning. They only have to walk up not even a hundred yards before they saw that big bear, a Boone and Crockett bear, and they killed it. That lazy hunter was still in bed when we heard the three gun shots. *Bang! Bang! Bang!* That lazy hunter was sleeping in that day.

Not too long after, I hear that big jet boat motor coming our way. Fifty-horse motor. Going wide open. Makes a lot of noise. That's why I didn't like to hunt from the boat like that lazy hunter always wanted to do. It's quieter to walk. Dusty run that boat right up the beach. I grab hold of the rope. Tie it up. Tie the boat up.

"You see him?" I ask.

"Yeah, we got him," he said.

"That big one?"

"Yeah, we got that big one," he said. "But he still in the water. His feet sticking up out of the water. We have to go back and skin him."

"We'll have our breakfast and then we'll go up there," I said.

That lazy hunter still lay down in the tent. He don't want to get up or go up there and help with skinning that bear. I ask Dusty, "How many of us can we get in the boat to skin that bear?"

"We'll need the whole works—all of us. It's a great big bear, about a thousand pounds," he said. "I look at his hind feet. It's about sixteen inch long. One of the biggest grizzly bears around this country."

"It's a Boone and Crockett bear," I said. "It's way up high in the book." So we went to get that grizzly bear.

We had to roll it up on the bank first; tipped the boat over a little bit and then rolled that big bear in. We took the whole thing. We didn't skin it. Take too long to skin it there. We couldn't skin it there because that lazy hunter keep asking me when we gonna go get him a bear. When we gonna go back up the Sheemahant River? He wanted to go hunting right now. He was mad because he didn't have a bear yet.

"Too late to hunt now," I say. "Middle of the day pretty soon. Bears all laying down now." It was too late in the day to hunt. Grizzly bears feed twice a day, I tell him. They come out early in the morning and feed, rest, then come out again late, toward the evening. "Sometime around one o'clock or two o'clock we will take off. Take two hours to get up the Sheemahant River. We will wait about two hours, then we will come down the river when the bears start to feed again," I told that lazy hunter.

That lazy hunter didn't want to go up alone. He wanted them other hunters to come up and see him kill a bear. I had a hell of a time with him. He not want to go alone with me. I told him, "Just me and you together." My Vancouver assistant guide, Jim Mullin, said, "Clayton, I better come with you too. I'm sure you'll get a bear and you'll need help." This lazy hunter keep calling to those other two guys, "You two guys come too." Those two other guys didn't need to come, they already had their bears. I said, "No we can't do that. We burn gas going up that river. With two guys we can plane that boat. But five of us—three hunters, Jim and I—is too much load, it's just too heavy. There is some fast waters, waterfalls up that Sheemahant River too. I can't run all you guys up through the fast waters. We gonna run out of gas before we get back to camp." This lazy hunter said, "We'll walk around that fast water and we can phone for gas tomorrow, we'll phone to Bella Coola to bring us some more gas." I get tired of arguing with him. "Okay," I said. "We'll go up there. We waste time just talking here, not hunting, not do nothing."

When we get up there to that fast water of the Sheemahant River the hunters got out. Jim take them, took them to walk around the fast water. I took the jet boat through the fast water. After I get through the fast water, then them hunters and Jim get back in the boat again. We keep going up, go up as far as we can go. We didn't see any bears on the way up. We usually see bears on the way up this river. We waited a while. "Four o'clock, about time to go down," I said. I told them, "You got to keep quiet. I'm gonna just idle the motor all the way down. Go down the river low. You guys hunting bears, you gotta stop talking and look on the banks all the way down for grizzly bears. I can't do everything. I got to steer the boat all the way down. There's a lot of deadheads on the way down." Those guys start talking all the time. Talk about girlfriends.

I tell them, "Keep quiet. Those bears can hear pretty good. They can't see so good but they can hear pretty good."

That river was pretty dangerous. Lot of stumps and deadheads under the water. I put Jim at the front of the boat to look.

"A deadhead under the water," he would say, and then I know I got to go around it. Then this lazy hunter start talking about womans again, talk about all his girlfriends. Talk about how he gonna stay overnight in Washington with one of his girlfriends. We were going down the river fast, we were in fast water, and we hit a deadhead. Bumped it. Boat lifted up and twisted, like. Almost flip over. I blow up, I give them hell. "Talk about girls when we get to the Cedar Inn Hotel in Bella Coola. We are hunting grizzly bear now. We not hunting girls now." Then I saw two bears running up a bank. One big one, silver-tip. Had a white collar on him. "When you talk about girls when you hunt, that gives us bad luck. Look at those bears going now. You could have got that nice big one," I said.

Then we went over another bit of swift water, waterfall, like, there. I see two bears coming down toward the river. They were way up high on the sidehill. And Jim pointed, "Yeah, I see them too." When we got into some slower water, a whirlpool, like, I stopped that motor, just paddle the boat then. Them bear don't hear nothing now. And that big one there, he slow down and stop. Pretty good size grizzly bear. He stop and look at us, and the other bear behind him—quite a bit smaller—get his head between his hind legs and he pushed him down the hill. Use his shoulders to push him down the hill. Pushed him down quite a ways. That was the first time I ever see a bear do that.

And I keep saying to that lazy hunter, "Shoot!" That big bear was about twenty feet above us, on a high bank, looking down at us. We were down below him. "Shoot!" I said. He wouldn't shoot so I said, "Bill, shoot that bear for your friend. That's a good bear. Silver-tip grizzly bear."

And Bill lay down, rest the gun barrel on the side of the boat, and then he shot it. Hit that bear in the shoulder, high above the neck. Kind of a neck shot. And that bear started to come. He get mad at us. He was watching us all the time, now he was mad. Above us was a steep bank. Just a wall, like, twenty feet straight up. That bear made a couple of jumps down the hill, and come down at us. He was after us now. I try and start that motor so I could turn quick. Get out of there. But there was a bunch of sticks under water, sticking into the ground, and they were holding the front of the boat there. And that bear came, he jump through the air at us. That bugger was big, a thousand pounds of bear coming down at us. "Watch out, you guys, he's coming," I said.

You could feel the air coming down to the boat as that bear come close. Those three big American hunters all get scared, afraid the bear going to hit the near side of the boat. So they jumped to the other side of the boat. Them guys almost tip the boat over, trying to get away from the flying bear. Took a little water all right. But the boat didn't flip. That big grizzly bear missed the boat by a few inches. He hit the water. Water splash all on top of us. World's biggest belly-flop.

I could see that bear under the water, dark brown-black. "Grab him, grab him by the ear," I yell real loud at that lazy hunter. "Grab him by the head and shoot him." That lazy hunter could have shoot him all right, but he lose his mind, like. He can't do it.

Then that bear start trying to get in the boat. Look like it anyway. His claws scratch the wall outside the boat. Make a loud noise when he scratch that aluminum. I was scared. If that bear get his hand on top of the boat, he gonna flip us over. His hind legs sticking up too. Once in a while, his head come out of the water and blow.

I had some rope in the boat by my feet. I was still scared, I don't know what to do. I was afraid that bear gonna flip the boat, kill somebody, somebody drown, lose all our guns. "Tie the rope to one of the hind legs," I told him. "The only way to do it is to drown him. Tie it good. I'm gonna tow him to the beach on the other side."

We were in pretty deep water. Jim tied the rope to that bear's leg. Tied it up pretty good. I gave the other end of the rope to all them guys and then we towed that bear across. That big grizzly bear start drowning. I can see bubbles coming out to the top of the water. When we got to the other side I said, "Jump off and pull that bear up onto the bank." We try and pull him up but five of us can't lift him up out of the water. Just too heavy. We had to tip the boat over a bit, and roll that bear into the boat.

I started up the motor and told them, "I told you guys we gonna run out of gas. But if we get to the lake we'll be all right. I can't paddle this boat in the river. All this load is pretty heavy. But we not gonna lose anyone now. Nobody's gonna get drowned anyways. We are lucky we killed that bear and we are all okay."

It was night-time when we started heading down. We were about two miles from the lake. We were lucky we made it to the lake. When we got to the lake, I could only go pretty slow. Bear weighed a thousand pounds, and five of us weigh another thousand pounds. We got to the Third Narrows and the motor quit. Only got about two more miles to go. But it was a pretty good night. Not too dark yet. Not too windy. "Okay, you guys start paddling. You said you would paddle if we run out of gas. So paddle." That lazy hunter try to handle one paddle, and another guy handle the other paddle. But that lazy hunter was too weak, and the other was too strong, so we just keep going round in circles, not go anywhere. Jim and I had to take over.

I see a lot of bears in my life, a lot of bears on banks, too, but that was the only time I ever see a bear jump through the air.

An old Indian guy, Albert Pootlass, he tell me one day, "Clayton, you been killing too many grizzly bears. Better quit now. One of these days a grizzly bear's gonna kill you." I thought that was the day a grizzly bear was gonna kill me.

I had one hunter, he really likes to kill animals. Kills fish, kills clams, kills crabs, kills birds, kills bears, kills everything. He don't eat them dead animals, he just kills them. He likes to see dead animals, I guess. Alton Myhrvold.

Alton Myhrvold was a Hollywood city deputy attorney, lawyer guy. Head guy of the police in Hollywood. Him and Governor Brown, they were partners in the law. Make sure the people follow the laws. Alton was a good friend of mine, but I didn't like it when he kills all them animals. Alton hunt with me twice a year for six or seven years. I'm not really guiding him. I guide him the first time, then he just comes here to visit me and we go out in the inlet in my boat.

I remember the year Alton showed up just when I gonna take three hunters out on a grizzly bear hunt. Spring hunt. I don't remember the names of them three hunters but they were all big shots anyway—have big jobs. One guy owned a transport truck company. Owned big trucks, big as a train. Trucks that drive across the country. Trucks so heavy they can't use government bridges, he got to make his own bridges and make his own roads for them big transport trucks. Another guy make flour. He owned a flour company. The third guy, he builds big buildings like hospitals or city buildings.

Just when we get ready to leave, Alton came into Bella

Coola. He said to me, "I want to go with you, Clayton. I help you out on the hunting party. I'll do the cooking for you. But we got to do it quick. We get them guys their bears quick, then just you and me together, we'll go out hunting."

"Okay," I said. Alton likes to cook. He was a good cook. He was cook on this big steamboat one time. One of them big Love Boats. Alton was cooking on one of them. He learned how to cook on one of them Love Boats.

And we did get them three hunters their bears pretty quick. Took them down to South Bentinck, and it only take us a couple of days to get them hunters their bears. Three grizzly bears and three black bears.

You know, guns don't mean nothin' to Alton Myhrvold. He ruin a good gun on that trip but he don't care. He ruin that gun because he fire it after it gets wet in the barrel. It happen after one of them three hunters shot a bear in South Bentinck. Alton really wanted to go look at that dead grizzly bear right away. It was high tide and there's a slough running through the tideflat. Narrow but real deep. About six feet deep but only about three feet wide. They were on this side of the slough and that dead grizzly bear was on the other side. Alton, he want to get there quick so he try and jump across that three feet of water. Alton thought that it wasn't gonna be very deep. He jumped, he slipped, and down he went, right under the water. His twelve hundred dollar gun, .300 Wetherby, got all wet too. After he gets out, they hear me coming in my riverboat. Alton lift his head up and say to the hunter, "Clayton's coming, I'm gonna shoot my gun so he'll hear us and come over here." But Alton forget to blow out the water from the barrel of his twelve hundred dollar gun. He point that twelve hundred dollar gun up, pull the trigger. *Bang!* The end of the barrel balloon all up. Didn't blow up but almost did. I get there and see that gun. It's no good any more. He's got to throw away that twelve hundred dollar gun because he forget to blow the water out of the barrel.

But Alton tell me that he can get guns for free. I ask him,

"How you can get guns for free?" He say to me, "When guys fightin' in the city with guns, police takes the guns away from them. End of the year we get a boat and go across to the middle of the ocean and throw all them guns overboard. Before they throw them guns overboard, I pick out what I want. Get some use out of them guns." Alton used to bring me up guns too.

After we finished with them three hunters I told Alton, "There is one place I never touched. Never hunted before. But I see bears there in the summertime. Nootum and Restoration Bay, where the halibuts are." Good fishing country there.

"Well, we'll go there," Alton say to me.

Just when we leave Bella Coola dock we see a fisherman. He wave at me to come over. That fisherman ask me where I goin'.

"I'm goin' to Nootum, hunt bear there."

"I got a forty-pound sturgeon in my gill-net. I wonder if you want it. I give it to you if you want it. If you don't want it I'll give it so someone else," that fisherman said.

Alton say to me, "Take it. Sturgeon is the best fish in the world to eat."

I grab hold of that sturgeon and take it to the hold in the back of the boat. Then we keep on going to Restoration Bay.

We get to Restoration Bay and I see an eagle floppin' his wings in the water. Swimmin', you know, on the water. I tell Alton, "That eagle probably got a big fish. I bet it's a spring salmon. Too big for that eagle to fly with." I slow down and we watch that eagle. It swim to the beach. Drag a big spring salmon onto the beach.

"It's a big fish," Alton said. Alton get his gun to shoot that bald eagle.

I tell him, "You'll get me in big trouble if Fish and Wildlife find out you kill that eagle. Leave that eagle alone. Eagle hard to kill, you know, they cry like hell when you shoot 'em. I don't like to hear animals cry like that."

So Alton gets in my little rowboat. He row right up to that eagle. Then he try and chase that eagle away. First he throw

Big shot hunters

rocks at that eagle. But that eagle not want him to get close. That eagle open his mouth and he hiss and blow at Alton. After a while Alton did chase that eagle away and he steal his thirty-pound spring salmon. We throw it into the hold of my boat with that sturgeon.

Then Alton say to me, "I want crabs."

So we go jig for some small cods. We got eight or ten cods. Alton want to kill more but I say, "That's enough cods. We just gonna use them for bait in our crab traps." I show Alton how to bait three crab traps and put them in the water. After a while Alton go to check the traps. He come back with over thirty dead crabs. Way too many crabs. Allowed to keep only two crabs. But Alton wants to keep all them crabs so we throw them in the boat hold with the spring salmon he stole from the eagle, and the sturgeon.

Then Alton say to me, "Now I want clams."

I start him off. Show him where to dig for clams, show him how to dig clams with a manure fork—something like a pitchfork—then I leave him on the beach to dig for some more. Alton don't know how to stop killing them clams. He dig over four sacks of clams. One hundred pounds of clams each sack. Four hundred pounds of clams! "Gee, what you gonna do with all them clams?" I ask Alton.

"Oh, eat them," he say to me. I put them in the hold at the back of my boat. Now we got a forty-pound sturgeon, a thirty-pound spring salmon, thirty crabs, and four hundred pounds of clams.

Then we go to Nootum to hunt grizzly bear. Alton had one grizzly bear tag. First day he get his grizzly bear about a mile up the Nootum River. Big bear. A Boone and Crockett grizzly bear. On the way down to the boat I see a mink swimming in the water. Looks like a snake in the water. I say to Alton, "Look at that mink, looks like two-feet-long brown snake swimming in the water."

Alton stand back and get a good look at it. "That mink

would make a good scarf for my girlfriend in Hollywood. I'm gonna get him," he say to me. Alton ran after that mink and try to drown him underwater by stepping on his head. But that mink keep swimming out into the deep water, Alton slip in the deep water and went down on his face. Got all wet, just soakin' wet. Gun got wet too.

After Alton kill his Boone and Crockett grizzly bear in Nootum, I find out he don't eat fish or clams or crabs. I think, "Why didn't Alton tell me he don't eat fish or clams or crabs? He want to get that stuff, wants to kill it, but he don't want to eat it. How we gonna get rid of all this food?" I knew there was a big outfit in Kwatna, bunch of archaeologist diggin' in there. About twenty of them in there. Spend their days diggin' big holes down into the ground. Lookin' for things like combs, dead Indian bones and stuff like that. So we go in there. A bunch of young girls came out. The boss archaeologist was a woman too. That boss lady, she come out tie up my boat to a log.

I ask her, "We want to get rid of these clams and crabs. Do you want some?"

That boss lady say, "Sure we'll take the crabs, but we don't want the clams."

"What about the sturgeon and spring salmon?" I ask her.

"I don't want that," she said.

We give them the crabs, then I ask Alton to untie the boat. He untie the rope from the boom chain and he stand up on the boom log. Then Alton say to them girls, "We got to go now, we got to kill another bear tonight." Then he wave goodbye. When you wave like that on a boom log in the water, you lose your balance easy. Alton wave goodbye to the girls, lose his balance and slip and fall right into the water! Goes way down deep into the water. I don't think he was a very good swimmer. He stay underwater for a long time before he come up. When he comes up he paddles like hell to get to the boat. I helped him up.

Then we go to the Dean Channel. Just when we get to the

Big shot hunters

Channel we see a lot of them little black ducks. We call them Indian ducks. I say to Alton, "Look at all them ducks, must be a million of them there." After a couple of minutes, Alton took off. I was in the wheelhouse looking out the front of the boat. I take the boat right through the middle of them millions of ducks, cut right through the middle. Then I hear some gun shots, *bang, bang, bang.* Sound like three shots. Ducks start flying all around. I turn the boat around to see if he hit anything. I see dead ducks floating all over the place.

I yell at Alton, "Get in that rowboat and pick up them dead ducks. You're not gonna just kill them." He picked up twenty-seven dead ducks. I count them. There was more dead ducks out there too. I give Alton shit, "You Americans always wondering why you got nothing left in the United States. Look at all them dead ducks floating out there. Look at them twenty-seven dead ducks on the boat. You guys just kill everything. You can't eat twenty-seven ducks. One or two ducks good enough for the two of us. But you got to kill twenty-seven ducks! From now on all you gonna eat is ducks." I was mad. Alton kills too many animals. And he waste it all. I says, "Take the wheel, Alton."

I went in the back of the boat, and go to the back of boat, and I dump them four hundred pounds of rotten clams, that thirty-pound spring salmon Alton steal from that eagle, and that forty-pound sturgeon all into the water. Dump the whole works overboard. Then I take over the wheel and take the boat to Kimsquit.

When we get to Skowquiltz, I threw the anchor down. I went to the back of the boat. No ducks! Only two left out of twenty-seven. Alton sneaks out and threw the rest of the ducks overboard. I said, "What happened to all the ducks, Alton?"

"I don't know," he says to me.

"You throw them overboard. I know you did. You kill twenty-seven ducks but you don't want to eat twenty-seven ducks," I tell him. "If you stay here for one month you end up in jail for sure. You kill too much." Alton knows he breakin' the law too. He was a lawyer. Knows all about the law. I tell Alton, "Pluck them two ducks and cook them." But he never did. In the end I took them two ducks home to my wife and we ate them.

Alton got a black bear in Skowquiltz, right in the bay. We skin that bear. Then we go on to the head of the inlet to Kimsquit. On the way we see another black bear right on the beach. Walkin' right along the beach. Alton see that bear and say to me, "I want that bear. I need that bear for my friend in Hollywood."

I say to him, "We'll be here all day if you shoot that one."

Alton say to me, "It will take me only about six minutes to skin that black bear."

"Six minutes to skin a whole bear?" I ask.

"Yeah, that's all it takes. I can do it in six minutes," he said.

"Okay, go ahead shoot that bear. I'm not gonna go with you. You skin him yourself. I'm gonna rest on the big boat." So Alton shot that black bear, then he get in the rowboat and row up to the beach.

After a while I look at my time. Over an hour and half since Alton went in to the beach to skin that bear. Six minutes over long ago! I yell to Alton to hurry up. He bring back that black bear skin with the head and paws still on it. He tells me that he don't really know how to skin the ears, the head or the paws. I got to skin that bear in the end.

When we get to Kimsquit we check the garbage dump in the woods for bears. We see a wolverine there. Alton try and shoot that wolverine but he missed and it run like hell into the fog. Alton was mad, he really wanted to kill that wolverine.

Any crow or raven around Alton shoots at it with his big gun. He hit them all right. Nothing left at all, just feathers. Same thing with ducks or geese. Alton doesn't know how to just look at them, he's got to kill them. I tell him, "Don't shoot them ducks or geese in the body, hit them in the head." But he always hit them in the body. They blow up all to hell. I try and cut off the head, pull out the feathers and cook them, but not much left. Bird shit everywhere in the food. Not taste too good.

Alton killed quite a few seals, too, on that trip. Six, I think. Any seal swimming in the water, Alton will shoot it. We even see about six mountain goats high on the mountain, right near the top. Alton point his gun at them. "No, Alton, they are too far away."

So altogether Alton gets a forty-pound sturgeon, a thirty-pound spring salmon, thirty crabs, four hundred pounds of clams, over twenty-seven ducks, two black bears, and a Boone and Crockett grizzly bear. And he don't eat any of it. All he was allowed to kill was one grizzly bear. He just had one grizzly bear tag when he come visit me that year.

I find out later that Alton kills all them animals so that he can talk like a big shot at that Club Safari in Hollywood. Hunters from all over the world belong to that Club Safari. Millionaires who are business men, lawyers and doctors. I find out a lot of doctors belong to that Club Safari. I find out that a lot of rich doctors like to kill animals. Even the prince of Sweden goes to that Club Safari in Hollywood. I meet him when I go to that Club when I was in Hollywood. That prince of Sweden really wants to kill a grizzly bear with me but I never did take him out. When Alton takes me to that Club Safari in Hollywood, he tells all them rich hunters about the animals he kills here in Bella Coola. The other hunters hear that and want to come up here to hunt with me too.

Alton told me that some time around March, every year, they have a big meeting and talk to each others. Compare about what animals they kills. Figure out who killed the most animals that year, who killed the biggest and strongest animals in the country. Find out who got the biggest grizzly bear, biggest brown bear, biggest white bear, biggest moose, biggest elk—all kind of Boone and Crockett animals. The guy who killed the most or the biggest animal gets to win a trophy and money, too. I kid them guys at that Club Safari. "What about a mice? If you gut-shot a big mice and you track him down, find him and kill it, do you win money and a big trophy?" I ask.

They just laugh at me. "Yeah, maybe someday we will give trophies and money to hunters who gut-shot a big mice and track it down."

In that Club Safari house were all kinds of dead stuffed animal heads. Moose head, elk head, deer head, grizzly bear head, brown bear head, white bear head, cougar head, sheep head, mountain goat head—all kind of animal heads. They had all kind of stuffed birds, too, and one big stuffed snake on the ceiling. They even had man heads in there. Small little heads. Killed by those little small Amazon Indians who kill each others with blow-guns. They kill a guy, cut off the head, shrink the head and sew up the lips. Then sell them little heads to them Club Safari guys.

On the way back to Bella Coola from Kimsquit I went into that hot spring at Nascall. My grandson was there, Norman Hall. He's a well-educated guy. Went to college twice. Talks like hell, speaks English real good. College teaches him how to talk like a lawyer. When we pull into there, Norman recognize my boat and comes out to see me. "Granddad, where you going?" he ask. "Bella Coola," I tell him. "I'm going with you," he say to me. "Okay," I say, "come on over. Get your stuff. It won't be long before we head out."

Norman was living with hippies there. He join them hippies there. Hippies, they call them young people. A whole bunch of them were in there building a cabin. Norman was a Christian kid too. He reads the Bible, studies the Bible all the time. That's all he reads. Writes down what's in the Bible, thinks about what that means, and remembers it.

But Alton don't like my grandson. He go after Norman. He don't like hippies, and he don't like kids with long hair. He say to my grandson, "Longhairs like you break the law every half hour."

But Norman just look at him and say, "Some shorthairs like you break the law too."

I try and tell Alton, "Leave him alone. He's a good kid. That bugger might squeal on us. He knows you shot black bears with no tag, that you shot more than twenty-seven ducks, and you take thirty crabs and four hundred pounds of clams." When we get to the dock Norman tie up the boat, then he run up the wharf. "That kid's gonna run and get the police or game warden. You better apologize to him, Alton. You gonna get me in big trouble. I'm a guide. My job to make sure you don't kill too many animals. You killed way too many animals. I should have stopped you, but you keep going out all by yourself and killing things. What the hell you two trying to do anyway? Fightin' over long hair and short hair."

Then Alton yell to my grandson, "Hey, junior, come back here. I'm sorry. I want to apologize for what I said about longhair people. Where you going now, anyway?"

"I'm going home to my mother," he said. "I might stop for coffee on the way up."

Alton pulled out his wallet. Handed him a five dollar bill, "Here, go buy yourself a coffee."

After Alton go on that trip with me, I guess he thinks he's my partner. I guess he tell one guy in Hollywood that he's partner with me. I don't figure he's my partner. What I figure happened, Alton say it will cost them three thousand dollars to hunt with me. Then he keep fifteen hundred dollars and send me fifteen hundred dollars. When I hear the hunter pay three thousand dollars to hunt with me, I try and phone Alton to get the rest of the money. But Alton don't return my calls after that. You know, I never did see Alton Myhrvold after that.

The woman who wore blue lipstick
■□■□■□■□■□■□■□■□■□■□■□■□■□■□■□■□■

I had one hunter, Dr. Collin was his name. From Texas. He told me he shoot against the best shot in Texas and he do just as good as the best shot in Texas. For practice, he tell me he would cut little wood blocks, about two inch square, throw them up in the air and shoot 'em. One time he hit more than one thousand in a row. And he tell me that he can even hit smaller than that blocks. He can shoot a dime throwed up in the air.

I said, "I don't believe that you can shoot a dime in the air." So I get a dime, and he make me throw it in the air and he shoot it. He shoot it all right. He shoot them every time I throw 'em up. My wife keep some of them ten cent pieces he shot. He used a .22 rifle to do this.

And he told me, "My daughter can do even better."

"Your daughter?" I said. "How old is she?"

"She's about eighteen years old or something like that," he said.

"I don't believe it till I see it," I said.

"I'll bring her next year," he said.

His daughter's name was Carolyne. She could do better all right. She had a .22 gun with a wooden stock. She rest that wooden stock on her shoulder. I put a ten cent piece on the stock. Then she hit the barrel of the gun down on a fence and make that ten cent piece fly up in the air. Carolyne aim that .22 gun and shoot that ten cent piece out of the air. She hit it every time she tried that. That doctor must have spent a lot of money on shells so she could get to be such a good shot.

I took her out hunting bears. Carolyne had a good gun, .306 automatic. And I wasn't afraid to take her out because she was so deadly with a rifle. Before we go hunt bears I tell her where to shoot a bear. She was one of the only hunters I have that listen to me. I tell Carolyne, "If you can get through to their lungs they don't live very long. They die quick." She listened to me good. Carolyne wouldn't shoot a bear if she couldn't get the lungs.

First I took her to Kimsquit, we see a lot of grizzly bears but they were too far away. They always smell us first, running when we see them. When we were in Kimsquit I take her up the river. We walked up a creek. Deep water. Only way to cross that creek was over a big logjam. So we walked over that logjam. I walk ahead of Carolyne over that logjam. When I get to the other side I jump down and hit the ground again, and I was standing there looking for fresh grizzly bear tracks. I see some fresh grizzly bear tracks too. I had my back to Carolyne. She was walking over that logjam. Then I heard something make a sound, *"Woof, woof, woof."* It was a grizzly bear. There was a grizzly bear in that logjam and we didn't see it until we walk over him.

It was a hot day. That grizzly bear went in amongst them logs, down deep in the logjam. Nice and cool in there. Then he lay down and sleep. When we walk on top of that logjam we wake him up. When that bear was makin' that sound, *"Woof, woof, woof,"* that girl see the grizzly bear. I call to Carolyne, "You keep come this way. Come right here."

When that girl see that bear, she think he will chase her, so she run and jump right on my back. Wrap her arms around my neck but still holdin' onto her gun. She was pretty light but I was afraid of falling in the deep creek. I was still standing on the log. I told her, "Get off my back. Let go," I said. Lucky that bear just run away in front of us. It was a small grizzly bear, maybe three years old. We didn't get a bear in Kimsquit so we went up to the Skowquiltz River.

Carolyne got her first black bear at Skowquiltz. We went up that river with my skiff. I had a little skiff with an eleven-horsepower outboard motor. Real good for goin' up rivers. Quiet. I got a lot of bears with that skiff. There was a high bank and we see that black bear on top of a high bank. It was about twenty-five feet away. I point to him, "Take him, Carolyne." She got that bear. One shot. Right through the lungs.

Next we go to Kwatna. We went up the Kwatna River. I told her, "Let's just go look in the Oak Beck Creek. See if there is some good sign, then we can come back tomorrow morning." I walk ahead of her up the Kwatna River, takin' her to Oak Beck Creek. Tough going, lots of devil's club. Carolyne gettin' tired, she was goin' pretty slow after a while. Too much devil's club, I guess. I get to a point, near the Oak Beck Creek. I look down. I was right on top of one grizzly bear. I see it right away. I look back at that girl. That girl was coming pretty slow. I make a motion to her to come slow, point down to the grizzly bear about twenty feet away. That bear was eating the fish. Carolyne slow right down and sneak up to me.

Grizzly bear was right here. Right in front of us. Nice one. Nice silver-tip grizzly bear. "Better take him," I said. "Just a short ways to the boat." She came right along side of me. I said, "Go ahead, that bear doesn't know we are here."

Bang! Then two more shots right after that, *bang! bang!* She take three shots, all right through the lungs. All through the same place. The bear drop down, right now. Then she put another clip in that gun real quick. Aim again. "Carolyne, that bear is dead now," I said. "You don't have to shoot him any more. He is dead!"

The second black bear she get at Kwatna. Long shot. Maybe one hundred yards. Carolyne shot it in the same place. Right through the lungs. She was a good shot. A real good shot.

I always book my hunters just before Christmas. I line them up in my book. I figure out who is gonna be in the first bunch, second bunch, and third bunch. I remember one lady, she was nuts that one. Most women use red paint on their lips, this girl used blue paint on her lips. I try my best to get her a bear but it was real hard. I don't know where she come from. She wasn't even booked on the hunt at all.

It was the second bunch that gonna hunt that fall. Three guys. I get my brother Samson to guide for me. He was a good hunter too. And he said, "All right, I'll go with you." I told him I had three hunters coming in. I said, "You just do little hunting in your spare time, you go out with a hunter. Most of the time I want you to spend time in the kitchen." He said, "That's all right, I can hunt. You do the kitchen work, I'll do the hunting."

"No, no," I said. "I hunt the grizzly bear. You cook."

Samson said, "Okay." We had to talk about it before they come to hunt. Samson was a good hunter and a good cook. He's quiet, don't do much talkin'—lets me do all the talkin'.

We got my boat, forty-five-foot boat, tie it to the dock and wait for them three hunters to come. The plane came to the dock and we pick them up. Three American men. One big guy in the bunch. Used to be a boxer. He used to fight with Jack Dempsey in his young days, he told me. They were sitting around in my boat, drinking, and I was pumping fuel into the boat. I hear somebody yell.

"Hi, is Bob here?"

I look up and see this woman with the blue lips. I don't know this woman, never seen her before. She want to talk to one of the hunters. I went in the boat and told Bob, "There's a lady here with blue lips who want to talk to you."

"No," Bob said. He didn't want her to come. Bob had left

her behind, but she fly an airplane all the way to Bella Coola to catch up to him. She catch up all right.

"Go on, talk to her," I said.

She come in the boat. Look around. Ask me, "Who gonna do the cooking on the boat?" I point at my brother. Then she want to see what kind of cooking pots we have, what kind of food we have. Then she get a piece of paper and write down what we need, things that we didn't have on the boat and that we should get. "I'm gonna go to the store and get some more frying pans and cooking pots and food," she said. "I'm gonna do the cooking." I said, "Gee, I don't have a bunk for you." Only place I can find is a wide bunk above the engine. "One bunk is pretty wide on top of the engine. You could sleep double in there with one of the guys."

"Oh, yeah, that's good enough for me," she said. She like that. She can sleep with her boyfriend Bob up there. "Okay," I said.

My brother went to get the pots and extra food quick. Then I start the engine and we take off. They all wanted to get black bear. I know two places where I can get a black bear on the first day, always. Eucott Bay Hotsprings and Skowquiltz River. We went in to Eucott Bay. There was an easy black bear there, standing in a slough. I see that we can come through the timber, come out to the slough and get that black bear. I took Bob and his girlfriend, the woman who wore blue lipstick. The rest of the people in the boat watch. When we get close to that black bear that girl say she want to shoot that black bear.

"But you're not booked on this trip," I said. "I get Bob booked. He send me a deposit last winter."

But she bitched little bit behind me. I don't know what she said. Mad cause I wouldn't let her shoot that black bear. Her old man, Bob, walk ahead of me. I was in the middle and she was behind me. Then I start thinking I want to get rid of her. I think if she get a black bear I can forget about her. Don't have to take her out any more. She can stay in the camp.

I could see that Bob and his girlfriend were both out of wind. Tired out. So we sit down in that slough grass for a while. It was a hot day. I said, "Let's go and get this over with." We stand and see that black bear. I could have hit that bear myself. Was real close. Fifty feet away. Bob aim, gettin' ready to shoot that bear. Then that woman with the blue lipstick yell out loud, "Bob get this thing away from me. There is something flying around my head." There was a big bumblebee flying around her head. That woman make me laugh all right. That black bear take off. We lost that bear. That black bear go like hell into the heavy timber. We can't track him.

We went up to Kimsquit River next. In Kimsquit we get two black bears for the other two men, but none for Bob or his girlfriend. Bob spend so much time lookin' after his girlfriend he can't get a bear. He spend more time with her than he spend hunting bear.

We went to Kwatna River next. Below Oak Beck Creek is a real good coho fishing pool. Cast in there and you get coho right now. I told them guys, "Cast right there and let your hook drift down and you will get a coho." That girl say, "How do you get into this fuckin' river?" She had big gumboots on. I told her, "Don't go too far out in the river. If you walk out too far out, there is quicksand, like, and you will sink and go down."

She didn't listen to me. She go way out. Right at once I hear her scream, "Bob, help me!" She go down in that quicksand. She went up to her neck in that sand. Just her neck sticking out of the water. Her old man have to go in and get her out. Then she take all her clothes off and hang it up on the bushes to dry out. Walk around with no clothes on. Then she light a fire to help dry her clothes. Burned some of her clothes.

Later we saw three bear come down and cross the Kwatna River. A mother grizzly bear with small cubs. And she was coming down the river to fish. She was fishing in the river. Her yearling cubs start fishing in the river too. Them yearling cubs were pretty good size. One was almost as big as his mother. All them grizzlies was swimming around in the river with their heads sticking out. One of them yearlings was real nice. Had a white head on him. Bob wanted to shoot that bear. Aim his gun at that grizzly bear's head. I said, "Don't shoot that bear with a white head yet. If you hit him now, he will sink in the river and we will lose him. Wait till he gets up on the beach."

Bob didn't listen to me. He shot that bear and it sunk right where I said it would. Gee, I didn't want to lose that bear. Pretty bear. White silver-tip grizzly bear. I try to cut a pole and feel for that bear but I can't feel it. Must have gone down the big rapids below.

The mother run up the bank and stop right out in the open sidehill. She look at us. Just standin' there looking at us. Bob shot that bear too. Gut-shot. Lot of blood. He had a small gun. Always talk big shot, like, "One man, one bullet, one grizzly bear, one day." He had to reload his gun cause it only had one shell in it.

That bear stood there for quite a while, then it took off. That woman run up to us. She had a gun. She had her clothes on too. She not stop talkin'. Talk all the time, even in the woods when we hunting. She want to go with us to track down that wounded bear. But I don't want to take her up to follow that wounded bear. I think ways to fix her, ways to scare the shit out of her so she wouldn't want to come with us all the time. So we take the boat up the river, below a high rock bank. I show them the grizzly bear blood, and I tell them, "Your bear is up there on top of the bank. We got to go up there. But don't fall asleep, that bear might jump down on us. Come right in the boat." I told them about wounded grizzly bears that will dig a hole in the ground three feet deep, laying down there, and watch where they came from. Looking for people following them.

We start to go up that bank. Got a couple of hundred feet up when that woman start screaming, calling for Bob. "That bear's gonna get me. Help me." She went down to the boat. Bob and me go back up the bank. We left that woman with the blue lips in the boat. Then I hear a loud *bang* behind me. I turn around quick. I thought Bob shot that bear. I thought I must have walked by that bear.

"What did you shoot?" I ask.

"I shot at that tree," he said.

"Why did you shoot that tree for?" I ask.

"Oh, I just want to find out if my bullet can go through that tree," he said.

"Hell with this," I said. "Let's go back to the boat." You can't track a wounded grizzly bear like this.

We went down to our big boat. It was low tide and I can't run my skiff motor so I had to paddle now. Then I see another grizzly bear right in the middle of the Kwatna River on the tideflats. It was a nice grizzly bear, nice big one. I said, "There's your bear. Come to the front, Bob." I go slow, paddle slow in the current. That bear was looking for fish, he not see us or hear us coming down. Bob shoot real quick, empty his gun on him. Three shots. That bear took off running for the timber. He go in the woods. We found out later, twenty days later on another hunt, Bob had shot that grizzly through its paw, he shot that bear through its wrist, and he shot the bear right in its *googoo*, its penis. Cut its *googoo* right in half. I go look where that bear was standing. I see some blood. I follow that grizzly bear track. It was heading way up the mountain. It was getting dark, I couldn't go after it. Boy, I was having a hell of a time with Bob and that woman with the blue lips.

In the morning Bob wouldn't get up. I say, "Let's go look for your wounded bears. We got to look for two bears. Two wounded grizzly bears."

That big guy say, "Hell with them, Clayton, never mind about them. Go do it yourself. Let Bob sleep with that woman. That's his hunting grounds, right there in that tent." I went up but I never find them wounded grizzly bears.

We went back to Kimsquit after that. Too many fisheries guys around Kwatna so we go back to Kimsquit River. On the way we went up Skowquiltz in my little skiff boat.

Samson say, "I'll take them up. You stay and rest in the boat, Clayton." Samson row up the river. Bob and his girlfriend sittin' in the front of the skiff. Samson hear her say, "Bob, how am I going to handle this gun, how am I gonna load this gun, how am I gonna shoot a bear?" She doesn't know anything about guns. Bob said, "Lift this bolt action back, push it forward, push the bolt action down, aim and then pull the trigger." She pull the bolt action back, push it forward, push the bolt action down and point that gun right at Samson. It was loaded. She pointed that gun right at his heart. All she have to do is pull the trigger and then she would have shot my brother. She would have killed Samson right there. Samson turn that boat right around and went back to the boat. "The hunt is all over," he said. "I'm not guiding any more." I ask Samson, "What happen?" He said, "She tried to shoot me."

In the end she did shoot her own bear. We saw a black bear right on the beach. It was digging roots in the sidehill. So I row the skiff boat right up to that bear. That woman point her gun at that bear, almost touch that bear with the barrel. She can't miss. That bear almost rolled right into the boat. That's how close we were. About ten feet away. Pretty good shot. She was so happy. Jump all around. You'd think she was the best hunter of the whole works the way she talks after that.

That big boxer get tired of that woman with the blue lips. He always say to me, "Before the end of this hunting trip, I'm gonna lay her right over my knee and give her a big spanking."

That's what he gonna do. Maybe he did, I never hear from those guys after that. You know she never cooked at all on that trip. Samson did all the cooking.

The sasquatch
■□■□■□■□■□■□■□■□■□■□■□■□■□■□■□■

I was fishing in Kwatna all by myself, in August, nobody with me, and I came home on the weekend. I was getting pretty lonely, low on gas, and getting low on grub too. So I went home for a few days. Then I got a fresh start of grub to go back again. I told my wife, "I'm going back to Kwatna again." Early in the morning, Sunday, I took off from Bella Coola.

I was probably in my thirties. I had a little boat, about a thirty-foot boat with a single cylinder engine. I got to Jacobson Bay, about fifteen miles from Bella Coola when I saw something right out on low tide. I saw something on the edge of the water. It was kneeling down, like, and I could see his back humping up on the beach. It looked like he was lifting up rocks or maybe digging clams. But there were no clams there. I turned the boat right in toward him, I wanted to find out what it was. For a while there I thought it was a grizzly bear, kind of a light colour fur on the back of his neck, like a light brown, almost buckskin colour, fur. I nosed right in toward him to almost seventy-five yards to get a good look.

He stood up on his hind feet, straight up like a man, and I looked at it. He was looking at me. Gee, it don't look like a bear, it has arms like a human being, it has legs like a human being, and it got a head like us. I keep on going in toward him.

GRIZZLIES & WHITE GUYS

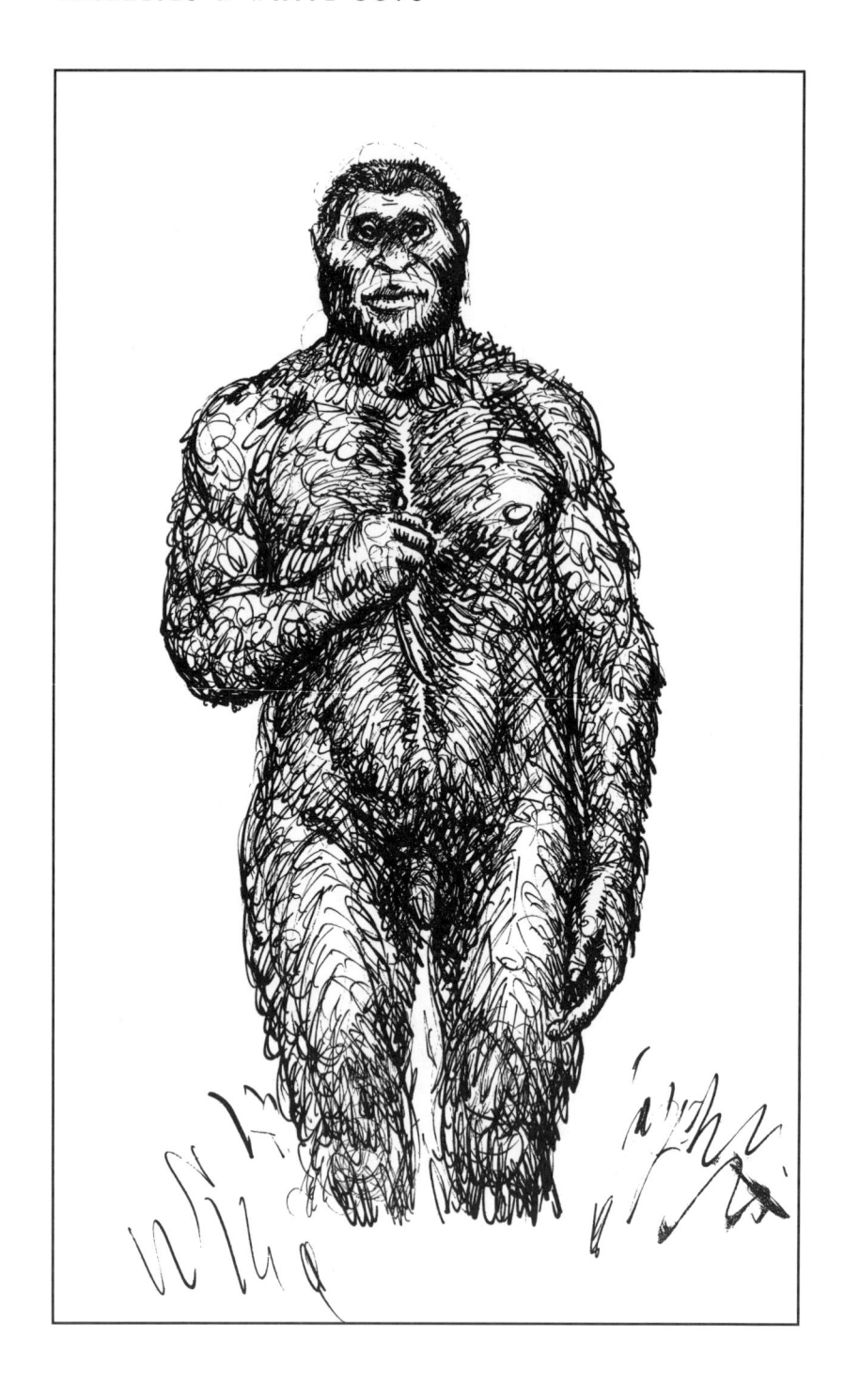

The sasquatch

He started to walk away from me, walking like a man on two legs. He was about eight feet high. He got to some drift logs, stopped and looked back at me. Looked over his shoulder to see me. Grizzly bear don't do that, I never see a grizzly bear run on its hind legs like that and I never see a grizzly bear look over its shoulder like that. I was right close to the beach now. He stepped up on those drift logs, and walked into the timber. Stepped on them logs like a man does. The area had been logged before, so the alder trees were short, about eight to ten feet high. I could see the tops moving as he was spreading them apart to go through. I watched as he went a little higher up the hill. The wind blew me in toward the beach, so I backed up the boat and keep on going to Kwatna Bay.

One evening, a year later, I was talking to George Olsen, who was the manager of Tallio cannery. I told him about what I had seen, a man-like animal with hair all over his body. George told me he seen the same animal, the same month and the same year as I had, but only on the other side of the bay. George and his crew watched from their boat as a man-like creature run across the river.

For many years after, I told that story to people. I told Paul Pollard, James Pollard's father, and he told me where they are. Where is the most sasquatch sign he ever see. Kitlope! I wanted to get into that country someday to see if that is true. One June, I took two Americans into Kitlope. They had both got their grizzly bear, and wanted to see if they could see a sasquatch. One of these Americans, we called him Cowboy, was crying all the time and sometimes use bad language. Mad at something. When we get to Kitlope I said, "What is your problem?"

He said, "My wife left me. She cheated me and she wanted lots of money from me. She wanted thirty thousand dollars from me and she got it. Then she took off. A few days later I got a letter saying she wants sixteen hundred dollars a month for the rest of her life. And she got it." That's what he was mad about.

There was an old house at Kitlope. Oil stove, cups, dishes, plates, and spoons were all in good shape. I light up the stove. I called the boys to come in, "It's all ready for us."

Cowboy was still kind of haywire, you know, he pulled out a bottle of Canadian Club Whisky and a carton of cigarettes and put it on the table. Cowboy started right away, drinkin' and smokin'. He got me nervous, like, after a while. I was laying down watching him. He was smoking lot of cigarettes, he'd just finish one and then light a new one again. He keep going like that. Then he'd get up and go to the kitchen and pour himself a drink again. I watched him all the time. I decided next time he goes I would follow him and have a drink and help him forget his problem. Then he went in, and I went and patted him on the shoulder.

"I'll drink a drink with you on this one."

He said, "Take a big one, you are way behind."

"Damn right," I said. "I'll take a big one so I can go to sleep."

Poured himself a drink and poured myself a drink. I drink that Canadian Club whisky and go back to bed. I had my gun right there beside my bed and a big flashlight, a six-volt flashlight. I lay down, Cowboy started in again smoking. I never say nothing, just lay there watching him. Tony, the other American was laying near the foot of my bed on the next bed. I was afraid Cowboy was going to burn a blanket, burn down the whole cabin.

Right at once something yelled through a little broken window, *"Haaaaaaa ohhhhhh."* He yelled right through that hole in the window.

I get up right away and grabbed hold of my gun. That's the big mistake I made. I should have grabbed hold of that flashlight and flashed right on his face to see what he looked like. I grabbed my gun and I tried to go out but I couldn't open the door because it had been raining too long in that country, I guess, and the door swell up so I couldn't open it. So I went out through the back door, and flashed the light at the broken window. He was gone already. He yelled again by the river, he howl again, *"Haaaaaa ha ha ha haaaa,"* like. I flash around, it gone now. I walk down to the river to see if I can see him, what it was, but I didn't see nothing. So I went back to bed.

Early in the morning I wake up Tony. "Let's go look for his tracks," I said. Yeah, it looked like we saw his tracks, all right, but not too good. He stopped too many places. He destroy his own footprints. The footprints look like our footprints, big, that's all.

The second sasquatch I saw was in Mud Bay, in Dean Channel. Mud Bay is about ten miles down from Brynildsen Bay. It is like a kind of a lagoon there, narrow entrance to go in there but lots of room once you are inside. I was looking for bears. I didn't want to go into the middle of the bay, so I went to shore and walked along the sand beach. I see a man-head, it look like, behind a tree. It was looking at me. The head was sticking out from behind a tree. I kneeled down and point my gun at him. Gee, he took off fast. He was about two hundred feet away. Not too big, about my size—five foot seven or eight. Had lots of hair all over his face. Almost look like a person but not a person. I didn't want to shoot him. So I walked up to where he was. And where he went in I followed him. I saw a tree, bark had been peeled off. I guess, he was eating the sap of a hemlock tree. I almost caught him eating that. I saw tracks, but not too good.

The third sasquatch I saw was in South Bentinck, right up the head of South Bentinck. Past Taleomey, right at the end. Asseek River. It was less than twenty years ago. I had a white hunter with me, an American guy from California. Maybe fifty years old. We were sitting down on a log, talkin' together, he told me he's bad luck. There was a dead black bear near us. We found that dead black bear the week before and it had been eaten up by a grizzly bear. That American hunter shoot and missed a wolf, then later he shoot and missed a grizzly bear that come to eat that dead black bear.

He told me, "I'm real bad luck. I missed that wolf. I missed that grizzly bear. I just lost my son in the Vietnam War." His son just got killed in the Vietnam War. That's what he told me. We were waiting for the grizzly bear who was eating that dead black bear to come back. We waited till it gettin' dark.

It was starting to get dark so I told this guy, "It's getting late, let's get out of here. We'll be back before daylight in the morning." Sometimes when it gets late, when it's gettin' dark, and you shoot and you can't see the sights on the gun too good, you will just nick the bear. You won't kill him, just wound that bear. It's hard to track a wounded grizzly bear at night. So we headed back to the boat and I walk ahead of him. We got into a big open flat, about quarter of a mile. It looked like there was a black bear eating in the grass. Look like it anyways.

I stopped, I told this fellow, "Black bear over there, let's go right close to him, let's go walk right up to him." We were on the dry land about a hundred and fifty yards from the water. "Black bears are stupid," I told him. "You can get right close to them. See how close you can walk up to him." So I started walking up to that black bear. "Just stay right behind me," I told that American guy. The "black bear" was about a quarter of a mile away when we first saw it. I made a big circle like toward the bear. When I got closer, not too far now, the hunter grabbed the collar of my shirt and pulled me back.

"Clayton," he said, "that's not a black bear, that's a sasquatch." He keep on saying, "It's a sasquatch."

I didn't say nothing, I started walking again. I said, "Stay right behind me." He was only about seventy-five yards away.

"Clayton," he said again, "that's not a black bear, that's a sasquatch."

I kneel down on the ground, I turned toward him, "What do you know about sasquatch?"

He says, "I come from North California, we get them in that country. In the big mountains that get snow on them.

Those mountains in Northern California which have glaciers on them. Some people hunt them," he said.

I said, "How do they look like?"

He said, "Well, you seeing one there now, that's how they look like!"

And I started walking again. I get pretty close, now. Then that "black bear" stand up on his both legs, and he look at me. I keep going closer. Gee, I was pretty close now. He started looking at me, make no noise or anything. I feel the barrel of a gun against my cheek. I pushed that hunter's gun away from my face. "Don't shoot him," I said.

That hunter whispered in my ear, "Look through your scope and see how he look like."

I turned the scope to 4X—wide and close—four times closer than naked eye. I looked through that scope, I look at his mouth. Little white thing in his mouth, look like rice. I look at his lips kind of turnin' in and turnin' out, the top and the bottom, too. I look at his face and his chest. The shape of his face is different than a human being face. Hair over face. Eyes were like us, but small. Ears small, too. Nose just like us, little bit flatter, that's all. Head kind of look small compared to body. Looks friendly, doesn't look like he's mad or has anything against us. Didn't snort or make sound like a grizzly bear. On the middle of his chest, looked like a line of no hair, hair split apart little bit in the middle. Skin is black where that hair split apart. It was a male, I think. I can't—no way I can—shoot him. I had a big gun too. Big gun, .308. I aim, had my finger on the trigger, point it right at the heart. One shot kill him dead, just like that. I couldn't shoot him. Like if a person stand over there, I shoot him, same thing. No way I can kill him.

My mother told me, "Don't ever kill sasquatch, don't shoot 'em. If you shoot 'em, you gonna lose your wife, or else your mother or your dad or else your brother or sister. It will give you bad luck if you shoot them, kill them. Leave them alone," she said. "If you see one, walk the other way, let them walk that-a-way." That's why I don't want to shoot one. My mother had seen them. She hear them too. A lot of Indian people seen them in the old days.

After we see it, we just leave it. That sasquatch went in the woods, went in the big timber. He took off fast. Looked like he used his hands when he took off first, like a hundred yards runner, looks like it. Pulling himself up with his arms, with his hands, looks like it. He never make a sound. Just ran into the heavy timber like a fast-moving shadow.

Next day we had a look again, around where that sasquatch was eating. We wonder to ourselves, "What was he eating?" He pull that grass, and right at the root of the grass is a little round seed. Look's like a little piece of rice. That white boy called it sweetgrass. That was what he was eating. That was the last sasquatch I saw, but I hear lots of stories about sasquatch. I was happy that American hunter from California saw a sasquatch. He was happy he saw a sasquatch.

I used to own a big boat. One time I took a basketball team to Ocean Falls, Bella Bella and Klemtu. Took about twenty-five boys on it. They hired me to do this. I have to be careful, don't travel in the bad weather or else you get in trouble, sink and lose that many boys. I was coming back from Klemtu, it was getting late, we get past Brynildsen Bay and we hit a strong wind blowing out from South Bentinck. I turn the boat around and go back to Brynildsen Bay. We going to wait till it is nice and take off to Bella Coola in the morning. The boys didn't like that, they wanted to go home that night. "No, I'm the boss," I said. There was too many of us in the boat. I hear sasquatch live in that bay area. Willie Hans got to the bow of boat and tied up the boat good. I cooked something to eat. We plan to leave early in the morning before the wind come up.

Art Saunders, he yelled at Willie Hans, "Sasquatch."

Willie Hans raised his head up high and said *"Baaaa qaaa, are you there?"*

Sasquatch answer right away, *"Haii haii haii."* Just like he call his name in our language. We call him *Boqs*. The thing answered right now. The whole works, jam in the door—they can't squeeze through the door fast enough. That was about fourteen years ago.

I also hear sasquatch in Skowquiltz River valley. Not too long ago, a hunter and his wife came in. I took him to South Bentinck. He was a poor shot, he can't hit nothing with his gun. Good gun too, twelve hundred dollar gun. I show him a black bear, *bang, bang,* he miss. Show him a grizzly bear, *bang, bang,* missed all the time. He can't hit anything. We talk about sasquatch one day.

"Ah, bullshit," he said. "No such thing as that in the world." He asked me how it look like.

I told him about the black one I saw in South Bentinck. Look like human being, body like human being.

He said, "It's all bullshit."

His wife get mad at him. "Don't call it bullshit," she said. "You never see one in your life that's why you don't believe? I bet you never see a wolf too." She was right, he never did see a wolf in the wild. I tried to get him a bear in South Bentinck, we did see a lot of bears but he can't hit them—missed all the time.

I told my son-in-law, "Let's go to Skowquiltz. It's easy to hunt there, easy hunting, lot of black bears there."

So we went to Skowquiltz River valley. It was getting late in the evening when we get there. Starting to get dark. I took this guy out and I sat down on a log, waiting for a bear to come out. I saw one right away, quick. A black bear, he wanted to cross the meadow in front of us.

"There's a black bear over there now, do you see it?" I asked him.

"Yeah, let's go look," he said. We went to a meadow waiting for the bear but he never did show. Lots of bear sign, ground all dug, but no bears. We went back to the same log and sat down again. A sound scared us. Real awful noise. Looks like a bluff up above, where the sound come from, *Awwwoooo wooo wooo*. That sasquatch was talking but I couldn't understand what he was saying. Real deep voice.

The hunter asked me, "What's going on over there?"

"You don't believe in sasquatch?" I said, "That's one now! You hearin' one now, you still don't believe it? That's what it is. Maybe lost each other, trying to call its mate, maybe it's his wife he's trying to call."

No answer though, just a big deep voice. Awful sounding voice. Scare me, usually I not scare in the woods. As long as I have my gun, I'm not afraid. But that voice sure scared me. I start thinkin' maybe it's a ghost or spirit or something like that. Cougar don't sound the same as sasquatch, I can tell the difference. Porcupine sounds like a woman crying sometimes, but that sasquatch cry is different than porcupine.

My brother saw a sasquatch. My brother Samson. Standing face to face, about a foot and half apart! He was on the tideflats here. He was working the boom there. Early shift in the morning, fire season, had to go across to the other side, the Old Townsite side, at about three o'clock in the morning. Samson meet that sasquatch right on the road. Samson stopped, the sasquatch stopped and they looked at each others. And Samson, he wouldn't tell anyone about it for a long time.

Sometimes I wonder what kind of animal is a sasquatch. Half man, half animal, I think. Just like a man but can't make fire, that's all. You know all the Indians up and down coast have the same name for sasquatch, *Bookwus* or *Boqs*. Many different languages, but same name for sasquatch. I think they live in caves in the winter, hibernate like a bear. I don't think they like fish. Sasquatch got strong smell, smell like a pig they say. I never smell it, never did in my life. But a lot of guys smell them. They see them and smell them. I saw the one in South Bentinck up close, but I never smell nothing on him. Maybe wind blowin' the other way.

The way a sasquatch finds out how far apart each others

is, is they pick up a stick and hit a tree with that stick. Makes a spooky noise. You will hear *bong* on one side of a valley, then *bong* when another one answer from the other side of the valley.

There are sasquatch hunters, quite a bunch of them. They try and get a sasquatch. Some sasquatch hunters come and see me. One guy say to me, "You tell me where I can get a picture of a sasquatch. If I can get it, I get 125,000 dollars."

"What you going to do with that picture?" I asked him. "Make millions of copies of it, and kids they will buy that and put it on their shirt," he said. He stay with me for awhile.

Look like there is a lot of money in that sasquatch hunting business. I want to join them someday. One day that sasquatch hunter, he need some money to buy grub to go back in the mountains. He was hunting back of Salloomt River valley. He want to buy oranges for bait. He claim that sasquatch likes apples and oranges. He going to scatter them all over his camp. He didn't have any money to buy this stuff he wanted. So he said, "Can I use your phone?"

"Yeah, okay," I said.

And he phoned a guy in Agassiz, who was hunting sasquatch too. He get through to the guy. I hear him say he needs over eight hundred dollars, he tells that guy to send the money to the Credit Union here. He get it just like that! Over a thousand bucks by the time he trade in his American money for Canadian money.

I think there is still a few sasquatch families around. Up the Talchako River, Kitlope River, Skowquiltz River, and in South Bentinck. They travel long ways, cover a lot of ground in a day. I think someday someone will get a sasquatch. I could have got one long ago if I wanted to kill one. I just couldn't kill it. I couldn't kill one for a million dollars. A sasquatch looks too much like a man.

About twenty years ago I met a guy whose name was Bob Mackie. From the United States. He was a young guy, about twenty-five years old. From Washington State. He likes to hunt and guide. I met him in Bella Coola. He wanted to come with me to learn how to guide. He said, "I don't want pay, just feed me, that's all." I told him he would have to get his assistant guide licence, and they were only sold at the head office in Williams Lake. The young fellow who wanted to learn to guide, wanted very much to come, but I just didn't need four guides.

I was getting ready to go on the last hunt of the fall that year. Obie Mack, Dusty and George Anderson were my guides. My nephew, son and son-in-law. We flew back to Owikeno Lake with two hunters. Dusty took one guy to the Washwash River valley, and George took the other guy to the Inziana River. They return that night to our base camp, they had seen lots of tracks and spoor but no bears. I told them to go back to the same place the next morning. I got up early that morning to make coffee so they could get an early start. I stayed in the camp.

They were gone just a short while and I heard an airplane, it sounded like it was going to land. It circled around and landed in the water, then coasted up to our camp. I put my gumboots on and went out to meet the plane. A guy waved at me, I pulled the plane by a rope as far as I could onto shore. There on the plane was the young fellow who wanted to guide, with a camera and a gun. He told me he had got his guiding licence, and all I had to do was sign my name and he would be able to guide for me.

Dusty and George both got grizzly bears that morning for the hunters they took out. Two bears that morning.

"It's all finish now," I said. "We go home now. Close up and you guys can go home now on the plane." It was around the end of October. We were at the Washwash cabin, Owikeno Lake, right up the head near the narrows.

They said, "All right."

Bob was going to come with me and get all the stuff and pack it into the cabin and help me close up for the year. Tents, stoves and stuff were about fifteen miles away. We got to pick all that up. After that we go home too. Bob like that, he want to come with me. Just the two of us and get all the stuff and pack it to the main cabin. The plane came in for George, Dusty and Obie. We packed some stuff in. George and Obie went home with the two hunters.

After the plane gone I told Bob Mackie, "Okay, let's go. We pack our stuff out of there." We camp out over night. He don't want no pay, this guy. He wants a grizzly bear for his pay. "Okay," I say, "we will hunt for a bear. I suppose you want a big one, hey?"

"Yeah," he said. "Grizzly bear anyway."

We pack our stuff and grub into the boat and we took off. I had a big boat, big flat-bottom skiff. Built like a little scow. A big motor on it. We can sleep in this boat if we have to. I run about another four more miles down the Owikeno Lake to the camp. I see something swimming in the water. I look at it, gee, it look like a bear. It was coming toward us. I slow the motor down, right down, idle slow. This thing was coming right straight for us. I look at it. Bob was looking too. I reverse that motor, back up so we just keep still. That thing still coming toward us. I see his ears. I look at it. Getting pretty close. About fifty feet away now.

Bob said, "It's a black bear."

"Yeah, maybe it's a black bear," I said.

Black head, little white around its nose. Bob Mackie picked up his gun.

"No, don't shoot him," I said. "Too much like work to drag him up to the beach."

We stand together and keep lookin' at it. That thing still coming toward us. And right at once, he hump up and dive down under the water.

"Black bear?" he said.

"No, it's not a black bear," I said. "Something different than a black bear. Black bear don't dive like that. Grizzly bear will stick his head in the water but not a black bear," I said.

I seen grizzly bear dive in with front part feeling for fish but black bear don't do that. He went right under and never come up again. We get out of there quick. I don't know what that was. It wasn't a bear, it wasn't a seal and it wasn't a sea-lion.

"Let's go," I said.

We go to the Neechanz River. I run up the river about a mile in the boat. We land, pack our grub and stuff. Got a little bit of wood for campfire at night. Cook something to eat. The next day Bob Mackie shot a bear. He got his bear, grizzly bear all right. Not very big but he was satisfied with it. Silver-tip. Nice silver-tip. We skin that bear as fast as we can skin him. Pack the tent and stuff in the boat and take off. Take this bear skin with us too. I told Bob, "If we see another grizzly bear, a big one, you take it too. I'll take the one you got." We didn't see any more bears. We went through the First Narrows, then the Second Narrows. Just as we pass the Second Narrows is the Third Narrows. There some pilings, they look like, log sticking up out of the water. I saw this thing stick its head out. I look at it. I pointed at it.

"Seal playing?" I said.

Bob pick up his gun right away. Bob Mackie had a powerful gun. .338 automatic. Real big bear gun.

"If it's a seal, shoot him," I said. "I don't like them seals in this country. They eat the fish, bust up the schools of coho. Lot of coho come up here. And those seals chase them, then the coho don't bite for a long time, don't bite any more. Too many seals in this country."

There are quite a few seals in that Owikeno Lake. We look at it close. It had its head up, way up. Had a long skinny neck. Not fat. Kind of bent over. Pretty dark black, it look like it. Pretty black, pretty dark. Small head too. I don't notice any ears. I can see its head sideways. Look like it had eyes, big eyes. Mouth closed, no teeth. Look like a snake, but had a different kind of head on it. From the head to shoulder I could see it. That thing had shoulders like an animal. Body of an animal,

The sasquatch

neck to head was quite long, about five feet. This young fellow aim, he was a deadly shot, he can't miss. And he aim and he look at me.

"Go ahead," I said. I stood beside him. He had .338 rifle, powerful gun. One shot can kill a grizzly bear real easy. He aim for quite a while. We were pretty close now. About a hundred feet from him. That gun went off, *bang!* and I kick the boat ahead toward where that thing went down. I think he hit him all right, can't miss. He went down when he shot. Head went in the water. I don't know if he killed it or if that thing just dive in the water. I think he kill it, hit its head.

That animal went down under the water and sunk. I kick ahead right where he went down underwater. I look for blood, or fat coming to the top of the water. When you shoot a seal or sea-lion in the water there will be blood or fat or bubbles coming up. But there was no blood. No fat. No bubbles. Maybe we were too close, bullet go through like pinhole, go right through that thing's head. Maybe the bullet hit a big bone inside. That lake water was kind of clear. I look where that thing went down to the bottom. I see a black thing down there, a big black thing. Just all black. I couldn't make a shape how he look like. Was big, bigger than the biggest grizzly bear. While I was looking that thing come alive, look like it. While we looking down there it started paddling, kicking ahead, like a big boat backing up and churning the water. The water was boiling, coming up. Look like he was taking off, away from us.

Then Bob said, "Go on, get going."

I put the boat motor in gear, and I open it up wide open out of there. We still had about six miles to go. Just past the Third Narrows, the lake opens up again.

Bob said, "Run the boat right up to the beach, I don't want to stay in the water any longer."

I had it going wide open. I ran the boat wide open to the cabin. I ran the boat up onto the shore by the cabin. We pack the stove and gear into the cabin. After that I said to Bob, "What was that you shot out there in the Narrows?"

"It was a dinosaur, they were around about a million years ago, but there shouldn't be any more around. You'll see a picture of it someday, you'll see it. You'll see the name of it—dinosaur. Maybe you see it on television," he said.

"How come I don't see teeth?" I ask.

He said, "There two kind of dinosaur. One dinosaur a flesh eater, eats meat, he kill animals; this one eat leaves like from a tree. That's the kind I shot, that's the kind we seen."

When we got back to Bella Coola we don't talk about what happen because we think people will laugh at us, say we bullshitting them.

I never heard if anyone else see that thing that year. I know the Rivers Inlet Indians from the Owikeno Village don't want to travel them narrows at night. When they come to our camp, they always want to take off before dark. Get out of there before too late. I hear stories that they are scared of them things. I talk to some relation of David Bernard, a Rivers Inlet Indian, after that. That guy told me David Bernard saw the same animal many years before we saw it.

Ways of the grizzly bear

If you are camping out in the woods all by yourself and you think there are bears all around, the best thing to do is make a fire. Them grizzly bear won't bother you then. They will come around all right if you have meat. Like if you have a goat or deer hangin' up. If there are two guys there, just take turns puttin' wood on the fire. One guy keep it going, other guy sleep for a while. Take turns like that. You can hear them grizzly bears walk around you but they won't bother you. If you don't have a fire, the bear sometimes will come right in and sniff around. Dogs are good. Bark will scare bear.

Grizzly bear have poor eyesight. Can't see you far away. I never see a grizzly bear with real good eyes. I saw one in Kimsquit about a hundred yards away, I guess. My hunter kicked a log and fell down. That grizzly bear heard us, look toward us and stood up on his hind feet. He look at me and then he took off just like that. About a hundred yards, and he saw us. So grizzly bear can see a hundred yards anyway. But I see lots of other grizzly bears from less than a hundred yards, they look at us. Not scared. Don't seem to see us.

Grizzly bear can smell real good, they smell better than

any animal in this country. One year in Kwatna I bury two fresh steelhead in the sand, four or five inch deep in the sand, and overnight a grizzly bear smell it and dig it out. I bury a grizzly bear head two feet deep in the bank of a river another time, six months later I go back and a grizzly bear just dig it up. Grizzly bear can hear all right but not too good. I think they hear about as good as a man.

Grizzly bear can run pretty fast. Run way faster than a man. Look like they can run as fast as a horse sometimes. I know they can run pretty fast. I was guiding for Tommy Walker up Stuie at his lodge one year. An old Indian guy from Anahim Lake came down with a bunch of horses. And he put them down below Stuie. One day he came up to me and told me he lost one horse. A grizzly bear chase his horse.

He said, "I need a good tracker. Can you track for me? That grizzly bear get my horse some place. I don't care if he kill my horse but I want to find out if that horse is dead or not. Then I don't have to look any more."

"Okay, I'll go with you," I said. And I went to track his horse.

I pick up the tracks. That grizzly bear chase that horse all right. There was a pool of water, and under the water was a cottonwood windfall. Cottonwood will sink underwater when it is wet. That grizzly bear chase that horse right into that water. What I think is that the horse run into the water and trip over that log. Then that grizzly bear got him. Drag that horse up to the dry land. Eat quite a bit of that horse's stomach. Then he dug a hole in the ground and cover that horse up. Bury that dead horse.

Some guys told me that bear can't stop if he runs downhill. He slides right by you if you dodge him on a steep hill. One day one of my American hunters shot a grizzly bear, he shot that bear's foot. That grizzly bear was crippled, he can't run too good. That bear went straight up the mountain. I followed him. That bear followed a creek, walk in the water. I don't know if he try to hide his tracks from me, or if it just feel better on his foot to walk in the water. He laid down about two or three times but he couldn't find a good place to lay down. No way he can find a good place to lie down. Then we come to a little flat valley. We could see that bear. That grizzly bear, he was layin' down and lookin' down at me coming up. When I spotted him, his ears were poking up a little bit. So I went and circled right around, came out above him and I see that grizzly was still looking down where I left that hunter who shot his foot. I went back and stood below the bear, on a little steep place. Smooth rocks around. I want to make sure that story is true, that grizzly bear can't get a man on a steep bank, can't stop going downhill.

So I went right in front of that grizzly bear. And I whistle at that bear. Raise my arms and wave my gun at him. "Right over here, you bugger," I said. Then he came down after me. I load my gun right away. I get behind a little hemlock tree. I look up from behind that tree. That bear try to stop, but he couldn't stop. He slow down all right, but slide down past me. He came back up to get me and I shot him. Kill him dead right there.

Grizzly bear can swim pretty good. I see them swim in Owikeno Lake, swimming across the lake. When you go after them in the water they will still fight like hell to get you. I went hunting one springtime with two men, two brothers. There is a small island that was covered with green grass. Tideflat grass had grown up quite high all over that island. I look and see that the grass was bent over and was moving side to side. There was a grizzly bear in that grass. So I head for the end of this island, but them two grizzly bear see us and jump off the island and start to swim for shore. I run the boat over there, go right in front of them bears. The smoke come out from the outboard motor and it go right in the grizzly bear face. That bear start to cough, he didn't like that outboard motor smoke. I tell them guys, "Don't shoot them grizzly bears. Where's your movie camera?"

Then one of them grizzly bear try and get in the boat. He really wanted to fight with us. I grabbed one oar and pushed his face, he bite that oar. Took a big chunk out of that oar. I kept doing that and after a while there was nothing left of the oar. That guy left his movie camera in the camp. He was crying every day after that because he didn't have his movie camera to film that bear eating my wood boat oar. We let them bears go.

Coast grizzly bear are bigger than Anahim Lake grizzly bears. Some Anahim Lake grizzly bear can be pretty big. Sneak up from the coast and go up-country, I guess. The biggest grizzly bear I ever guided for was over a thousand pounds. They estimated it was twelve hundred pounds. It was about eleven feet long from nose to tail. You can tell how big a grizzly bear is from its tracks. From the front paws, you measure how wide across it is in inches, then add one and that is how long the bear is in feet. If it's seven inch across the front paw, that bear will be eight feet long from the nose to the tail. On the hind feet, you look and see how many inches long. If it's more than twelve inches long on hind feet, you have a Boone and Crockett grizzly bear. I'm not sure how big the skin of a twelve-inch-long hind foot bear is, but I know it is a big grizzly bear.

I see a lot of different-coloured grizzly bears over the years. Brown, black, cinnamon, blonde, even white grizzly bear. I saw two white grizzly bears in Kwatna, and another white one in South Bentinck. I know Kermode black bear, these weren't Kermode bears, they were white grizzly bears. There was a family who live in Kwatna for about twenty years, the Sohanoviches. They raised pigs. Great big pigs. Some people claimed that some Kwatna grizzly bears mated with their pigs. That's why there were grizzly bears with fur that was the same colour as a pig in Kwatna! It's hard to believe, but I did see grizzly bears in Kwatna that were the same colour as a pig. A Hollywood guy killed one of them pig-coloured grizzly bears. I remember it smelled like a pig too.

GRIZZLIES & WHITE GUYS

Some grizzly bears are so black they look just like a black bear. But grizzly bears have different claws. A grizzly bear's claws are straight-like with just a little bit of hook on them; a black bear has got real hooked claws. That's why a black bear can climb a tree just like a squirrel. Grizzly bear can't really climb trees. Just a little bit, all right. Grizzly bear cubs have pretty curved claws but not when they grown up. Grizzly bear have a little bit of hook nose, but a black bear just have a straight long nose. A grizzly bear has a big muscle shoulder hump, and black bear don't have it. But I do see some black bears with that hump, and a brown colour like a grizzly bear, but they weren't a grizzly bear.

All the hunters like grizzly bears with silver-tip fur. But mostly the young bears have the silver tips. Three-year-old grizzly bear, that's the oldest silver-tip grizzly bear that I see. I have a real hard time see old grizzly bear with silver-tip fur. I see in the spring, after the bears come out of their dens, some grizzly bears with bald patches. No hair, just the skin. I try to find out from a lot of guys why some bears have these bald patches. Some guys say when the grizzly bear lay down in their den, the mice and rats will pull the hair off and make a nest out of it. Some other guys tell me that when they lay down, they lay down on one side and the hair rub off. Other guys tell me they get disease, skin get real itchy and scratch that hair off. But the hair grow back later in the spring and summer.

The grizzly bears hibernate around December. It seem to go by the coho spawn. If coho come late, they stay out late, too. Indians find them in the wintertime. Look for them where coho spawning grounds are. When the snow come, the bears come down from their den and they eat that coho. Go back to their den again, lay down, and when they get hungry they come down again and eat some more fish. Go up again to their den. You can follow their tracks right in the snow, right to their dens. There was a grizzly bear den in Skowquiltz, way up on a kind of a big slide of rocks. Big boulders. We were trapping in the valley bottom, in the snow, one year. We look way up and see a grizzly bear standing on top of the big boulders looking down at us. Right there, where we were, lot of coho spawn. Lots of cohoes in there. He'd come down and eat that coho. When his belly get full, he wanna go back and lay down in his den on top of that slide. Sleep in there for maybe two or three days and then come down again for more coho.

Some bears have their dens long ways away. In the fall there are lots of bears in the Atnarko River. Some go all the way up to the Itcha Mountains to hibernate. So many miles away they go to hibernate. I follow one set of grizzly bear tracks on horseback one year, and they go right up to them Itcha Mountains. It was around New Year's Day, one year. From the Atnarko River them tracks go all the way to the Itcha Mountains. Not too many bears do this though, go that far away to hibernate.

Josephine show me, up Atnarko River, two dens in one place. She show it to me. There was one hole there. The bear try and make a den and hit a rock, I guess. He quit, and make another hole there, about five or six feet apart. She thought a black bear or coyote use the first den. We never try and get it out. Mostly grizzly bear like to have a den near overhang rocks, cracks in the mountain rock, or caves in the mountain side. They can dig a hole like a fox, too, and they go in there. I see two dens like that up-country. They dig in the side of a little hill. Grizzly bear dens sometimes way up high on the timberline, but the most dens I see are by the bottom of the valley.

Bears like to use the same den every year. The bears will clean out their dens every year too. They break off tree limbs, pack them into their den and lay them down for the bed. Bears break branches down, they can't break branches up like a person or a sasquatch does. The bear will lay down on them limbs. Sleep on them limbs like a bed. The next year they take out them limbs and put new ones in there and lay on them. There is a den down in Kwatna. It is way down near tideflat. An old man told me about it so I went to look for it and I found it. I think that bear must have a hell of a time certain times of year. At certain time of year there is big tide. About twenty-five-feet tide. That grizzly bear sleeping in there, when that tide come up that high, gets wet when the water comes in. He has to wake up, come out, wait, then go back in when the den get dry again! I see where he try and chew the roots to try and make a bigger hole. He did this for so many years.

Sometimes bear will use other bear dens. Especially black bears will do this. My grandfather, he want to get meat for the winter. He found a black bear that winter. He followed that black bear in the snow to his den. A black bear don't care where he den. Will use hollow tree, go in there through a little hole in the bottom. The old man see where a black bear make a hollow den in a big cedar tree. My grandfather he go and chase that black bear out. The black bear come out in the snow. He go look for another den. That black bear walk and walk until he found another den. He try to go in but come out. There's another bear in there. My grandfather knows now where there is one hibernating bear. That black bear go on looking for another den. Same thing happen again, tried to go in a den but come out again because there was another bear in there. This happened four or five times. Once my grandfather knew where all the bear dens are, he go and kill a bear each month. December he kill the first bear and take it home for family to eat it. January he go and kill the second one. February go kill the third one. Do this till April or so. At that time fish start to come back up the river, he don't have to go look for any more black bear to eat. I think, four or five different dens my grandfather found, that's what my mother said. So my grandfather chased out the first bear and let it lead him to all the other dens.

In March the bears first come out of their hibernation. They come out for a few hours and eat a little bit, then they go back in again. They eat the tops of the willow brush. Kind of like a moose. The tips, they like to eat that. Get a little bit in their stomachs, I guess, and they go back in again. Then they come out again around April and they don't go back any more after that till next winter unless they are wounded. We wounded one grizzly bear up Kwatna one year. He climb right up the mountain, right to his den hole. I caught up to him next day way up the mountain, he was inside in his den home.

When they come out to stay they will eat roots of skunk cabbage and eat the greens of stinging nettle plants when it first grow. Anything that's new and green, them grizzly bears will eat that. They don't eat much devil's club. They will eat a lot of grass, like a horse, in the late spring and all summer. They will knock over alder trees and eat the tips of branches. They like huckleberries and blueberries. I never see them eat clover, but they will eat wild spearmint. They like plums and apples.

In the summertime they start to eat fish. Eat any kind of salmon. When there is a lot of salmon around, grizzly bear will sometimes just bite part of the head. Just eat the brains, look like it. They can kill a lot of salmon this way. Not only grizzly bear will do that, but wolf will do that too. Eat just the brains and leave the rest. If there is not too many fish, and sometimes when there are lot of fish the grizzly bear will eat all the fish. I see one grizzly bear in Kimsquit eat a dog salmon. I had the Maytag boys with me, brothers who own that washing machine company in the States. They got a Boone and Crockett grizzly bear. We sit down and watch that grizzly bear for quite a long time. We watched this bear catch a dog salmon, he take a bite out of the salmon head, then he peel that meat off the backbone from the tail to head—both sides. When he finish eat that meat from both sides of that fish, he start from the tail and eat the tail and bone all the way to the head. Then the head fall off. Eat the whole thing except the head. He leave the head go.

Grizzly bear will eat marmots. Dig them out of the ground. Grizzly bear try to eat squirrels but they can't get them. I see them eat mountain goats. They will steal dead animals from other animals like wolves or eagles. Eagles will knock them goat kids off the bluffs. They hit the ground and die. Grizzly bear smell that and go and eat that mountain goat. Grizzly will eat moose and caribou. I was in Precipice one year. I see a moose run into a big long meadow—about two hundred yards away—and start to run toward me. Another animal was running behind. It was a grizzly bear. When that moose come by me there was a lot of slime coming out of its mouth. It had been running for quite a while, I think. When that grizzly bear come past me, the same thing, it had lot of slime coming out of its mouth too. I don't know if that grizzly bear got that moose. I didn't stop him, I just let them both run past me.

Grizzly bear will eat eulachons too. There are so much eulachon fish in Kimsquit because nobody bother them. First week of May, I think. After them eulachons come up there, spawn and die, they will wash up on the shore. On the shore them eulachons get dried up and you can see lot of animals eat them. Black bear, grizzly bear, lynx, fox and birds.

Grizzly bears, they sometimes eat each others. They kill each others and eat each others. I took these guys up to Big Buck Hill. A lot of deer and a lot of berries up there. Mountain blueberries everywhere. We saw a big mother grizzly bear with a little baby cub. And a young grizzly about three years old was near them. That three-year-old grizzly came along and went after that little baby cub. He ran up quick, jump and grab it. And he started to pull the skin off the baby cub and started eating it! That little baby cub still kicking, screaming while that three-year-old grizzly rippin' the skin off him. Then that three-year-old grizzly bite the meat out of that screamin' grizzly bear kid. The mother was right there, right close, never even try to help her kid. That little grizzly bear still alive, and that three year old bear was eating it!

I told them guys, "Shoot, come on, kill that son-of-a-gun. That's all he does, I think, kill baby cubs. Not happy with enough of those berries, he want meat, he kill them little cubs," I said. I shoot too, and they shot. The whole works, four of us, shooting at that three-year-old grizzly bear. We hit him all right. I found a blood trail but couldn't catch up to him. He was too smart. He find a patch of short jack pines and crawl into them short jack pine trees. I seen him only once or twice, like a flash, then gone again.

I also seen grizzly bear cubs eat their mother after you shoot her and take her skin off. Cubs a year old or more will do that. I seen that a lot of times. Skin the bear, leave the meat there and the cubs start eatin' it right up, clean the meat right up before we go away. They will eat their mother right up! They don't waste nothin', them grizzly bears. Grizzly bears will eat each others right away if you shoot a bear close to another bear. It will eat that dead bear. Pack him away in the woods, bury him underneath the ground. Dig a hole in the ground and cover him up. Next day go back, pull him out and eat part of it. He keep doing that until he clean it right out.

I see how grizzly bear kill deer. They dig a hole right in the deer trail. They lay in the trail and wait for the deer to come. When a deer comes, they jump right there and grab it.

Sometimes a grizzly bear and a wolf, they will work together. Some really do work together. They partner up together in the fall. I see that in Owikeno Lake, in Kwatna and up here too. A grizzly bear can get a fish pretty easy in the fall. A wolf he can't get that fish in deep water. Too short of legs, I guess. That grizzly bear get that fish and feed that wolf. That wolf eat that fish. In the springtime, that grizzly bear come out of hibernation and is pretty hungry. He can't get a deer, but a wolf can get a deer. That wolf kill that deer, grizzly bear eat the deer after wolf kill it. I think they do it to help each other. Sometimes they stay together. Not wolf pack, just a big wolf and big grizzly bear together. Walk side by side. Working together in the woods. I seen that happening.

I also see grizzly bear not want to share fish with wolf. Was near a logjam, a grizzly bear pick up a coho. That wolf try to take a bite out of it, that coho fish. The bear not want to share it, too hungry, I guess. That grizzly bear slap that wolf, just slap him once. Looked like a dish towel flying through the air. That wolf not bother that bear any more. Let him eat by himself.

In Kwatna I seen a big sow grizzly pick up a salmon in the river. She packed that fish to a flat rock in the middle of the river. She put her hand on top of that fish and start to eat it. Her little baby young one, half swim, half drift in the river and get to the mother. He tried to eat that fish the mother was eating. The mother slap her baby, it fly about thirty feet in the air and hit the bank. Gee, a mean mother grizzly bear. The hunters want to shoot the mother. "No," I said. "Maybe she want to teach him how not to bother her when she eating."

Grizzlies are pretty smart. One time I had a hunter, long time ago, we were looking for moose. We were on Itcha Mountain. We found a grizzly bear track in the snow. Jack pine country. Old burn area. Real thick jack pine forest, about half a foot, foot apart between them jack pines. Jack pines were about ten feet high. That grizzly bear stay in that jack pine forest. He was hunting moose too. A moose try to cross that thick jack pine. His horn spread out about six feet wide across. The horns hook in that thick jack pine and he can't run. Too many jack pines, too thick. The grizzly bear would come behind and get him in that thick jack pine. He kill that moose, eat part of it. He dug a hole not too far from the dead moose. He used the dead moose for bait now. Any other animal come around, he get him. A black bear come around, smell that, and try and eat the moose. The grizzly jump that black bear and kill it. Eat part of it. Dug another hole alongside that moose and buried that black bear there. He got a moose and black bear so far. Then that grizzly bear took off for three days. Go way down, toward Chilcotin country, toward Redstone. Then he turn around and come back. When he get back he got another black bear, this time a brown one. Eat part of it, buried it again. Altogether, two black bear and a moose.

We got that grizzly. He lay there in a hole in the ground, stuck his head up waiting for us to get close. *Bang!* I shot it. Get him. Was supposed to be the biggest grizzly bear in the world but we used axe to cut the head off and chopped off part of the skull. Lost about inch and half, would have been twenty-seven and a half inch. Make it biggest bear in the world at that time.

A hunter said, "I give anybody who can find that chunk that was cut off that grizzly bear skull a hundred and fifty dollars. Go look for it."

"Not me," I said. "Inside a coyote stomach probably!"

One year some Americans gave me a name, call me Shit-foot. Whenever I see grizzly bear droppings I kick and smash it up and see what that bear's been eating. Them Americans call me Shit-foot when they see me do that. But I want to find out what them grizzly bear are eating because I'm a grizzly bear guide. I can find out where them grizzly bear are by read that droppings. If there are a lot of berries in that grizzly bear droppings, it will be poor hunting in the bottom of the valley. Have to go up the mountain after the bears. Better luck way up in the mountains to eat berries. But if all the droppings are of fish, it will be good hunting on the valley bottom. You don't have to go way up on the mountain.

The Fisheries tag fish. They want to find out where they go when they go way out in the ocean. Put a tag on their fin. I was hunting up the Machmell River, and I see some pretty fresh droppings. I kick it. A red fish tag come out. I washed it off and put it on my shirt. Them Americans want to take it away from me, but I said, "No, that's mine." That's the funniest thing I find in a bear's stomach. The funniest thing I saw in a wolf stomach was a baby grizzly bear paw. He eat the hand and swallow the whole thing. I gave it to the game warden.

I don't think grizzly bear eat birds. They will eat them black mussel shells but I never see them dig for clams.

In the spring, grizzly bears will bite trees, scratch trees and rub trees. Grizzly bear will scratch way up high on them trees. Like to do this in them cedar trees. I think they scratch up high to show other bears how big they are. One bear scratch way up high, then another come, if he think he is bigger he will try and reach higher and scratch above it. Seeing who is the biggest bear. I seen lots of sign like that. Grizzly bear will break the tops off of alder trees. Maybe they eat something at the tops of them alder trees. I never study it too hard. I don't know too much about that scratching and biting of trees.

Grizzly bear have a territory. Can be maybe three miles shortest. Bear will follow same trails all the time. Sometimes I try and tell hunters to wait for bears to walk their territory paths. There was a real big bear up Kimsquit, had sixteen-inch foot print on hind feet, about ten inch across front track. I think that bear would have been biggest Boone and Crockett grizzly bear in the world. Right on top anyway. We go after it for five years. A smaller bear got in his way one day and that big bear almost killed him. That smaller grizzly bear was all chewed up, could hardly walk. Pretty stiff when we saw it. I think that big grizzly bear caught that younger grizzly bear eating his fish and then beat the hell out him. I told the hunter, let's set up a camp here and wait for that big bear. But he wouldn't do it. He only want to hunt and track after that big Boone and Crockett bear. We never got him.

Grizzly bear like to bed or rest in sand. They like that best. A bear will make ten to twelve holes where he likes to lay down and rest. Some beds up to three feet deep in the sand. In the evening them bears go down and eat fish, and in the morning they go back there and make a new hole again in the same place. Every night he do this. Young ones go with their mother and do the same thing. Even though they like to make beds in sand best, I do see they make beds all over. Way up high, in their dens, in the sand, by the river. When it is real hot out they will like to rest under windfalls or in logjams near the river. They will rest under any kind of big tree.

When it's raining they will rest under a tree too. Grizzly bear, he doesn't like the rain. He goes right under them big trees, spruce trees or other kind of big tree, lay down there until the rain quits, then he come out. Then he will really move around look for fish. I don't understand it. The rain quits, no more rain, then the bear come out and jump in the water. Don't care for rain, but like to jump through the water to get fish. I don't know why they don't like rain. Cold, I guess. But I know it's no use to hunt when it's raining. Stay home. Don't go out there. You just spook 'em if you go out. They hiding and see you looking for them. Wait till the rain stops, wait till the sun comes out. Then the grizzly bear come out, then you go hunt them.

Grizzly bear make a lot of different noises. They will huff and blow when they know you are around. They roar when they fighting and mating, and when they charging close. They will bawl when they wounded. Awful noise, especially when it is a sow with babies around. Bears clack their teeth when they eating. Try to scare you away, I think.

It is pretty hard to tell, when a bear is charging, if it is just bluffing or if it is gonna get you. They will woof and puff and come right at you. Every jump they make, they make a noise. Don't move. Just get your gun ready. If they keep coming you shoot them. If you run, they will run like hell and get you.

I went across a high log one time. I had a hell of a time to get over it. Just as I going over it I saw a grizzly bear that was laying down. I jump back over to the other side. That big grizzly get up on its hind feet, put its hand on that log and look at me. I didn't want to shoot him. That bear start to come around after me then he took off. Lucky it ran away. I didn't have to shoot that grizzly bear.

Another time I had a bunch of fishermans with me at South Bentinck. Same kind of thing happened. There was a little kid, about ten years old, and he had a little dog. I see that little dog start smelling all over. I told the boy, "Your father is behind. Quite a ways behind. You better go and stay with your dad. We might run into a grizzly bear. Lot of tracks here. Call your dog with you too." He went back to his dad. I was quite a ways ahead. I see a bear, it had a fish in its mouth. A young grizzly. It looked down toward me. I had a gun, but it was an army rifle and all I had was hard-nosed shells. I turned off the trail and wait for them boys to catch up. I was watching that grizzly and it went in the timber. So I kept going and cut across another creek there. There was a big log there. I stand up and look over that log. And a big grizzly bear was there, just like that other time.

I jump back over to the other side. He did the same thing as that other bear. That grizzly bear get up on its hind feet, put its hand on top of that log and look at me. We look at each other, face to face, close like, about three feet apart. I lift my gun up and load it. Load it with hard-nose army shells. The butt end of the log wasn't too far away. That bear go down and start to come around the butt of the log to come and get me. Instead of run away like that other bear he keep coming for me. I get ready to shoot. I walk backwards, but got caught up in some old limbs and fell backwards. Right on my back. And that grizzly bear walk right over me!

Funny thing, that grizzly bear went in a circle and start to come at me again same way. This give me a real good chance to aim and shoot him right in the head. If he turn and come straight back to get me I wouldn't have a chance. But he come around in a circle and then come toward me. I almost touch his head with the barrel of the rifle, and I pull the trigger. That hard-nose bullet make a pinhole in the front and a pinhole in the back of his head. Killed him right now. Went right through his brain.

If a mad grizzly bear does get you down, sit real still. Don't fight him, or he'll bite you. He'll get more mad at you if you fight him. You can curl up for grizzly bear, cover your head and neck up. Just don't move till the bear is gone. But I don't sit still for black bear—I just fight 'em. I not scared of black bear.

The best place to shoot grizzly bear when you try and kill them is right through the lungs. That's the best place. Sometimes they fall right away, sometimes they run a little bit, then they die. You can see when you hit them through the lungs. Something like soap come out their nose, little bit of blood in that soap, like, then they drop to the ground. When you see that bloody soap from their nose, that grizzly bear is not going to get up. No way. You can shoot 'em in the head too. When you shoot them in the head, they kick like hell. He's dead right now. When you hit them in the heart they howl. Maybe two, three jumps then they howl. He's dead. When you hit 'em in the gut, gut-shoot a grizzly bear, it will bleed like hell, but will keep on going. A gut-shot grizzly bear will dig a hole in the ground and try and trap you. They lay down in that hole, just a little bit of his head sticking out of the ground and wait for you. That grizzly will look back where he come from. When you follow that blood, if you don't see him right away, that grizzly bear will get up and charge.

A wounded grizzly bear sometimes makes a loud howling noise. When it's gut-shot a grizzly bear will make that sound. *Oooowwww, huff, huuff,* and make blowin' sounds as it runs away.

I did gut-shot one grizzly bear in my life. I was haying up Anahim Lake many years ago. Something go wrong with the hay mow machine. I got to come to Bella Coola to get a part. So I come down on saddle horse, made a fast trip to Bella Coola. I get the hay mow machine part and I went back up to Anahim Lake. I was just above B.C. Wright's place, near park headquarters, when I heard some kind of funny noise. *Oooooohhh.* Like that. My horse look like it was spooked. Just ahead was a young guy and a young woman. Walking up the trail. They got packs on. I caught up to them. I know who they are when they stop and turn and look at me. Charles Snow and his wife, Josie.

I ask, "Where are you guys going?"

"We just taking a little hike, gonna camp out up there," Charles said.

"You guys in a bad place to camp out," I told them. Lot of grizzlies in that country in them days.

I went by them, heading on up to Anahim Lake. And I heard this funny noise again. *Ooooohhh*. I look ahead up the trail. I saw a white horse up there. With a harness on him. Another horse was there too. There was a funny looking harness and pack-saddle on that horse. It had a pack on it, big pack. Bob Ratcliff was there, standing and looking toward the horse. Then I saw a grizzly bear standing ahead of that old guy, standin' up on its hind legs in front of that horse. That grizzly bear was trying to slap that horse on the head. It was a sow with two cubs nearby. Bob Ratcliff, he didn't have no gun with him. I kept on going up. Went right along beside Bob Ratcliff. But as soon as that grizzly bear see me, she come toward me. She do the same thing, try to slap my horse on the head.

My horse stand up, stand up on his hind feet. I reach for my rifle, in the scabbard, and I pull it out of there. Just when I get my rifle out—I was still bent down, half off the saddle—my horse came down. Came down hard on its front legs. I slide right off the saddle, fall to the ground, almost right between that grizzly bear's legs. I hit the ground pretty hard too. I kneel down, load my gun quick, poke that barrel in that grizzly bear's stomach. I pulled the trigger and I shoot that bear right in the stomach. *Bang!* I stand up. And the bear move away, back up, and run down to the river with her two cubs. Howling *Oooww, huff, huff* and makin' blowin' sound as it runs away.

I told Bob, "Keep on going, go on, keep going. I catch up to you." I was worried about those two hikers walking up the trail. Afraid that bear would get that boy and that girl. So I waited for a while. I see them coming. I yell at them, "Bear went after us and I shot it in the stomach. Pretty mean right now. She's down there by the river. You can hear her howling at her cubs now." She was fightin' with her kids, sound like it. Howling too.

I got on my horse and went after Bob. We camp out in Precipice together. I asked, "You got no gun. How come you don't carry gun with you?"

"Oh, it's a nuisance, them bear never bother me!" he said.

"Sure," I said. "If that bear get that horse down you would have been in trouble."

Some bears are pretty tough. Take a long time to die. We shot one bear, eight shots through the same place. All lung shots. That bear still going. He lay down on his back on the mountain side. I say to the hunter with me, "Try and hit him in the heart this time." Killed him with that ninth shot. When a grizzly bear is wounded pretty bad, he'll go straight up the mountain. Not too hard to find him. When he wounded not too bad he will follow bear trails along the valley bottom. You will see blood but it's pretty hard to catch up to him.

I never eat bear meat. Too scared to eat it. But I did get trichinosis, I think they call it. The bear carry it in their blood. I got it in my liver, right now. Still in there. I get it from a grizzly bear. When I went to hospital in Santa Barbara Hospital, the doctor found it in my liver. Get it from smoking cigarette after skinning bear. I'd skin a bear and get blood all over my hands. I'd light a cigarette, and the blood on my hands get on the cigarettes, then on my lips. I swallow that little bit of blood, trichinosis in that blood, and then it get to my liver. It been in my liver a long time, but the doctor say I was so strong man, that germ, that trichinosis gets sealed, waxed in there. Like glued in there. It's supposed to be dead, can't cause no more damage.

The most grizzly bears I ever see in one place was nine. I saw nine grizzly bears together two different times. There were eight boars after one sow, like a bunch of dogs in heat. All the boars were following behind that sow just like a pack of dogs. Sometimes them grizzly bears will fight. If another boar try to butt in and take another boar's wife away, a grizzly bear will fight like hell. Sometimes they get wounded bad. Like an old .30-.30 bullet hole, you can see pus coming out of the ears, from around the eyes. From slapping each others, I guess. Necks all scarred up with pus coming out all over. From teeth marks. If there are just two boars and a sow, that sow will help the boar who she want to mate with. When the two boars start fightin' the sow will help her husband get rid of the boar she doesn't want to mate with.

Once a hunter and I were watchin' two boar grizzly bear fight. One young one and one old one. That young one lick that old one. Then the hunter I was with kicked an oar in the boat we were sitting in. Make noise, and the whole works take off—the two boars and the sow. We go downstream and we see that sow and young boar crossing the river. The hunter I was with was going crazy. He want to kill a grizzly bear so bad.

"Just sit down there," I said. "Have your gun ready. I'll do the paddling." By God, I see them two bears again, they were eating in the old Sohanovich garden. They were eating spearmint plants. That old lady planted them before. I don't know why she do that or what she do with them spearmint plants. But them grizzly bear eat that. I told that hunter to get the big boar. And he shot that young boar. We go to skin it. Then the sow circle around. I didn't see it. We were right behind a big rock about thirty yards from the dead bear when that sow came. She came toward us. I put my elbow right on that hunter's shoulder. I say to that hunter, "Stay down. Don't move." And I shot that sow right in the head. I think that sow was mad cause that hunter shot her husband. When that hunter see that sow coming at us, he pret' near get sick. Start to puke. After that he want to go home right away.

Sometimes the boar will fight with the sow. If a boar try to get on top and the sow not want him to, that's when the trouble come in. The boar try to get on top, the sow turn and fight, then that big boar will back up little bit and slap both sides of the sow near its back. Slap real hard. You can hear it far away. Make her bleed a bit. Next time he get on top, she give up, don't complain any more. I see that happen a few times. I think them sows are three and four years old when they first mate. They will have kids every three years or so. The most cubs I ever seen with a sow grizzly bear was four. Saw that once in South Bentinck. Four little ones. But I see lots of sows with three cubs.

It is pretty hard to tell boar from sow that is by herself. I can tell if that bear is fishing in the creek in shallow water. The male will have long hair hanging down where its *googoo*, its penis, is. Like a dog. When it's wet, that long hair kind a bunches up and sticks down. That's the boar. Easy to see. But when that boar walking around where it is dry, you can't always tell. When a bunch of grizzly bear are together, the bear with the biggest head usually the boar. But it's still hard to tell.

There is a bone right inside a grizzly bear's *googoo*, about ten inches long in full grown bear. It is always there. Up to twelve inches long. After a bear is killed I peel it off, out of the *googoo*, right away. Give it to the guy who got the bear. The hunters are always happy as can be to get that thing. When them hunters get home they clean it up, polish it up, paint the end red and write on it "cocktail mixer."

The grizzly that slept in my bed

In the olden days there used to be a big village in South Bentinck. Taleomey, they used to call it. The same number of people lived in that village in them days as live in Bella Coola Village now. One year, long ago, the biggest Taleomey chief sent out six hunters to try and hunt some mountain goats for the village. The chief wanted the boys to shoot as many goats as they could kill, smoke the meat, dry it and then pack it back down to the village. Then the chief would save it for the village people to eat in the wintertime.

So those six hunters went up into the mountains to get mountain goats. They were able to kill a lot of goats that summer. Each hunter killed six goats. It was getting late in the fall and they wanted to get out of there before it started to snow. But they were too late. One morning, one of the boys was yelling outside the tent to get the other boys to get up out of bed and see the snow on the ground. The whole works get out of bed. There was a lot of snow on the ground. They called a little meeting to figure out how they were going to get out of here.

One of the boys said, "Look, down there is a flat-bottomed valley that doesn't have too much snow. If we go back the way we came we will be bucking against snow and it will take a couple of days before we get out of here. We might get stuck."

One of the other boys said, "That flat-bottomed valley down there is dangerous, a dangerous place, that is *Numenta*, Grizzly Bear Valley. The grizzly bears come in there and hibernate every year. To sleep for the winter. Den holes all over that mountain. There is one clay bank there where the grizzly bear den holes are only about two feet apart. If we go down there grizzly bears are going to kill us for sure."

Another hunter said, "No, we have guns, we can shoot any grizzly bears that bother us."

But they were still a bit scared because three hunters had been killed in that valley in the past. Killed by grizzlies when they tried to go through Numenta. "Grizzly bears killed the whole works, and the same thing is going to happen to us if we go down there," another guy said.

But that valley looked so good, no snow to buck. "Okay," they agreed. "Let's go down." They made up their minds, they were going to go down there. They went down.

One guy got down to where the bears were, ahead of the rest. His pack came loose, and he lost some of the meat. He took off the pack, dropped it down and began to pile on the meat again and lace it onto the pack. Then the others who were behind, began to hear shouts from this hunter. Then they heard gun shots. That hunter was shooting bears. They could hear the bears howling. They ran down to see what was going on.

In those days they only had muzzle-loader guns. Muzzle-loader guns are slow to reload. Four guys hurried on down to help their friend. Soon all five men were fighting bears who wanted to get their smoked goat meat. The last hunter caught up to the others, and could see what was happening. One of the men yelled up to him, "Go back, go back over top of the mountain and tell our people that the grizzly bears killed five of the chief's hunters."

The last hunter took just enough meat in his hands, what he can eat to make it to the village. Left his pack and went back over the mountain. The grizzlies killed the whole works, five hunters were killed. The last hunter finally made it back to the South Bentinck village. When he got there he went straight to the biggest chief and told him the whole works dead, just him left, grizzly bears had killed the rest.

The chief went from house to house that night. Called all the young guys to go to a meeting that night. He got all the boys in the village to go to this meeting. He planned to go up and kill all them grizzly bears. But at daybreak, the chief went from house to house again and said, "We are not going up there, if we go up there them grizzly bears will kill us too. There are just too many grizzly bears in Numenta."

I asked Old Timothy Snow one day, "Is there really that many grizzlies in Numenta?"

Old Timothy Snow went up there just to prove if there is that many grizzly bears in that valley. He said it was true. "Grizzlies are like a bunch of cattle up there."

The way he described the country, it is really nice grizzly bear country, all right, with grass all around this big round valley. Good feed for grizzly bears there. The first time they went up there was in the summer and there was nothing—never saw a single bear. It was the wrong time of the year. The next time he went up they saw all the bears. They are up there just in the late fall and the spring. I talked to Old Timothy Snow, myself. I guess they come out of hibernation in spring and hang around there until they harden their feet. He said there was some great big grizzlies up there. Some had no hair, just skin patches on their bodies. The bears must come from all over—Bella Coola, Owikeno Lake, and they even think some come from Kimsquit. Grizzly bears from all over hibernate in there.

One day, when I stay with Old Chief Squinas up-country, somebody come visit. Old Chief Squinas said, "It's my friend, Chilcotin man from Redstone. He got nobody to look after him these days. No boys. He comes here every year. I take him up to the mountains. He trap groundhogs up there," he said. He meant marmots.

"Where you gonna take him?" I asked.

Old Chief Squinas said, "I go to Little Meadow. Then I turn toward that Little Rainbow Mountains. Near Hotnarko Mountain. A lot of groundhog up there."

Them groundhogs are just like man. Just like a man, they save food for the wintertime. All summer they pack leaves inside that hole. Way deep inside, they pile the leaves up and in the wintertime they eat all them leaves. That's how come groundhogs are fat all the time. This old man from Chilcotin would set traps for groundhogs. He set his traps in them groundhog holes. When he gets a groundhog in his trap, he kill it and skin it, and saves the meat. He uses the skins to make blankets. He would cut the meat in thin strips. Build a campfire and smoke that meat over the fire. When the wind blow, them thin strips of groundhog meat get dry and then that Chilcotin man put them away to take home with him. He's gonna eat that dried groundhog meat in the wintertime.

Old Chief Squinas took him up into the Little Rainbow Mountains. He used pack horses. Stayed overnight. Next day Old Chief Squinas get home. Chilcotin man going to stay up there one month, I think.

Squinas said, "That old man will be all right, he's got lots of grub." Not quite one month later, Old Chief Squinas called me to go with him this time. "We got to get that old man. We get him and bring him back. Time for him to go home now," he said.

As we came to the camp, Old Chief Squinas say, "Huh, that grizzly bear kill the old man."

I asked him, "How you know that grizzly bear killed him?" He said, "You see that big beaver house, like. That old man is underneath that beaver house now. That grizzly bear make a good job. Cover him up good."

There was a big, high dirt pile with sticks, grass and leaves.

The grizzly bear eat all the smoked groundhog and scratched the skins all up. We see that the old man had skinned about six groundhogs, stretched the hides square-like so he can sew it together and make a blanket out of it. Grizzly bear smell that smoked groundhog meat, I guess. I guess that old man try to chase him away. Grizzly bear kill that old man. That Old Chilcotin guy didn't have a gun. Easy for a grizzly bear to kill him. After the grizzly bear kill that guy, he eat all the groundhog meat. But we don't think he eat that man. We didn't see the man's bones around the camp.

Old Chief Squinas don't want to touch that dirt pile with sticks, grass, and leaves. He said, "That old Chilcotin man is underneath that pile, buried good, let him stay there. It's all right to leave him there."

That old man is still there yet, just below the treeline in the Little Rainbow Mountains. Not too far from Green River. I was putting up hay at Old Capoose's ranch around Anahim Lake. I was about twenty-two years old or so. I had a racehorse and three dogs. Two dogs of my own, and one belong to my friend.

I have to go down to Bella Coola. Have to make a special trip. I have to pick up a special thing for some farm machinery. It broke down at the ranch. I don't have to take no pack horses, I'll just ride my racehorse. Takes me just three days to get to Bella Coola on that racehorse, and three days to get back. Before I left, my wife Doll says she going to hunt moose or deer up in the mountains. So she want my good gun. I had two guns. The other was an ugly looking gun. Long barrel, clumsy, you know. Big shells on it. Old rifle.

Doll said, "You take that gun, I'll take the .30-.30. I'm going to hunt moose or deer up there."

"Okay, I'll take that ugly gun," I said. So I put it in my scabbard on my saddle horse and came down to Bella Coola.

I came down about five miles, I look back, I see that one dog is following me. One dog was coming after me. The other two dogs stayed behind. We call the dog following me Stubby. It got no tail, that dog. Just a little stub where the tail supposed to be. I try and yell at him, "Go back!" But he keep coming. I thought, "I guess it's all right, it's only one dog anyway."

I came down to Bella Coola. Came down for that special part for the farm machinery. I got it and headed back up again. I get to Atnarko River by the end of the day. Next day I head on up to the Precipice. I could see there were a lot of fish in the river now. Lot of humpies. When I get to Bert Matthews's gate, the gate was open. I went through that gate and that dog went in, he went in the woods. Stubby was going like hell right toward the river. Thick country, lot of brush. I hear that dog howl, *Ooooo,* and I look for that dog. By God, I saw him coming, with a big grizzly bear right behind him.

I pull that gun out. I managed to get it out all right, that long-barrel gun. That dog hit the trail and came right toward me. That grizzly bear running right behind him. Stubby the dog ran by me, then he turned and went back toward me. The grizzly bear still right behind him. I try and swing that gun toward him but that damn barrel was too long. I touch the neck of the horse with the barrel, I can't aim. The dog circle around and went back behind the horse. And that bear was right behind him. That dog go right between horse's legs. I try and hold the horse, I am gonna try to shoot that bear. I yell. That horse never run, never get scared. Just walk slow, like. When I get in the good ground, I try and run away and spur that horse. But that dog run in front of me again with the bear behind him. That dog keep circling around me with the bear just behind it. Funny feeling all right. Look like that bear look at me once in a while too. I'm right on a saddle, on top of the horse. But that bear not bother me, he just wants to get the dog.

When the dog run between the horse's legs, the bear try and follow. That bear go between the legs, and rub his back on the horse's belly. That horse not buck! I never think so much in such a short while. "What's gonna happen?" I wonder. I yell at that dog, I swear at it. The dog went up the woods a little bit, the bear went right behind him. Then I spur that racehorse, we go full gallop up that trail to get away from them. I got away.

It was good going above Bert Matthews's place, a good gravel trail. I go like hell on that racehorse. I get way up the trail, no more bears. Good going all the way. I get to Precipice that night. Gee, I had to ride a long way to get away from that bear country. Stubby, he catch up, came behind me.

There's a camping ground there in the Precipice, so I camp out there that night. I get out my sleeping bag, take off the saddle. Then I ride the horse bareback to the meadow. There is a meadow across the creek there. Lot of stakes in the ground there. So I tie that horse with a long rope so he could eat grass that night. I use about a forty-feet long rope. Tied that horse up to a stake in the ground. I walk back to the camp. Made coffee, had a little bit bread and made a toast. After that, I walk back to the horse to see if he was all right. Sometimes a horse will get tangled up in the rope if it's too long. Everything was okay so I walked back again, back to the camp. I fixed my sleeping bag and went to bed. It was still early yet, but I was tired. Had a long way to go tomorrow, I need a good rest.

Between twelve and one o'clock in the morning, I heard a loud sound, sounded like somebody dropping a bunch of lumber across the creek. Like someone was piling lumber on top of each others. I sit up. I rolled a cigarette, I smoke, I put that coffee pot closer to the fire to warm it up. I kneel down by the campfire, smoking, and I hear it again. Making a lot of noise. I try to lay down. I try to go to sleep. But the damn noise wouldn't quit. "There's no logging camp in here," I thought. "Where all that piling lumber come from, who's working across there?" I went and laid down, sleep little bit all right. Wake up and I hear it again. Pretty soon it's gonna be daylight. I listen, I sit up. It was still going on. I tried to go to sleep again but that noise keep me up.

Just before daybreak, I get up. I can see about seventy-five yards now. So I walk across the creek to the meadow where the noise come. Sound like it come from where my horse is. I walk down the trail, I get to the open meadow. I go slow. I see my horse there, it was all right. I walk toward the horse, I look behind to the edge of the meadow. I see two black things. Running at each others. I kneel down, I put my saddle gun—that ugly gun—down and I watch. It was getting daylight again, I could see them pretty good now. Getting lighter all the time.

Two bull moose fightin'. Every time the horns hit together it make a loud noise, sound like piling lumber. When them moose hit together, it sound just like dumping lumber on the ground. I didn't shoot the moose. They run away after I take the horse's rope, stand up straight, and walk toward them. They saw me and they took off.

When I was still up-country, Vinny Clayton would come and see me every weekend. Vinny not work on weekends. He cut hay for Andy Christensen during the week, take the weekends off. Andy was married to Vinny Clayton's sister.

He had a little boy. The little boy would come with Vinny when he visit me. They would walk over. They don't ride horses, they walk instead. I lay off on Saturday and Sunday too, sometimes, if I been workin' too hard that week. We would sit around and talk about duck hunting.

He come one weekend. I just get back from pack horse trip to Bella Coola. He want me to come with him, go down to the Dean River and shoot ducks.

"Okay," I said. He sit down by the fire. Sit down on a block of wood. He look at the smoked moose meat hanging there. I take the nicest meat, cut off some, stick a stick through it, put it in the campfire. I sit down beside Vinny. When that fat start drip on the ground, I give that moose meat to him. "Try that," I say.

He eat it. While he eat that he said, "Somebody talk about you, call you champion good runner in Bella Coola. How fast you run a hundred yards?"

"I can run a hundred yards in about ten seconds," I said. "About four minutes in the mile."

"Pretty good times. I run a hundred yards in ten seconds too," Vinny Clayton said. Vinny was about six foot four or six foot three inches tall. He tell me he used to be a good runner too in his young days. He didn't tell me how fast he run the mile, just tell me he run a hundred yards in about ten seconds. He tell me he used to be a boxer too.

"I try that but I'm not much good at it," I told him.

Then a guy come up to us on a saddle horse. His name is George Cahoose. He come from Ulkatcho. "Clayton," he said, "little black bear killed your sheep."

"Where?"

"Right on the road," he said.

And Vinny said, "Get your dogs, we'll go and get him. He'll never quit killing the sheep if you let him get started doing that."

"Okay, but how we gonna kill him?" I ask.

"Shoot him with a .22 in the eyeball," he said.

The grizzly that slept in my bed

All I had was a .22 rifle and all he had was a shotgun. And we had my two dogs, Dean and Buster. We walk, I walking ahead of him. Look for that bear. The kid try to come but I told Vinny, "Tell your boy to stay with my wife, with Doll. We'll come back here and you pick him up when you go home," I say. Lucky that kid didn't come.

Them dogs start growling and run ahead, one turn into a willow brush. Short and thick willow brush. He try to go in there. That's where that bear was, I guess. That bear killed the sheep and dragged them there, we find out later. I call them dogs, hit them on the shoulder with a little stick. "You stay behind." That's how I train my dogs. I don't want them to chase anything that I don't want them to chase. "Stay behind," I say to them dogs. And they stay behind, but they keep tryin' to run ahead so I hit 'em again. I guess they could smell that bear. We walked past that short and thick willow brush, and head down to shoot ducks in the river.

I hear Vinny, "Clayton, there's a big grizzly bear behind us!"

When I look back, I saw that bear. Big one all right. Full-grown grizzly bear. Coming like hell at us. Vinny was a little bit behind me. He started to run. And I started to run too. I threw my .22 down and I took off. Vinny still carry his gun, though. I run about fifty yards, I guess, I look back. By God, that bear's gaining. Getting pretty close to Vinny now. Them dog's turn around and face toward us. And I yell, "Get 'em, Dean! Get 'em Buster!"

And they went right there, they went after that grizzly bear. Buster, he bite and hang right on the neck of that grizzly bear. Dean, he bite and hang right on the stomach of that grizzly bear. They were both flopping, too, like a cloth. They turn that bear around, that bear run right through a log fence. He run right through, just split that log fence wide open, and he keep going away from us. Could hear them dogs barking at that grizzly far away. Them dogs saved us. We turn around and go back.

"We got no gun for that grizzly," I told Vinny. My grizzly gun's in my other camp, and his grizzly gun was in the ranch.

On the way back we stop and look in that short and thick willow brush. We found them three dead sheep. After that bear kill them sheep, he split their stomach open, gutted them. Gut them just like a human being does. Took the guts out. I guess he eat them guts. I don't see any guts around. He don't eat no meat out of them sheep yet.

We went back to that campfire again, this time we drink coffee and talk about that grizzly who killed them three sheep. We talk about how fast we can run from that big bear. Then I look and see a big bunch, whole string of people coming toward us. Coming from Bella Coola. The same bunch I lent my horses to before that. Dr. McLean, the head nurse, two more nurse and Teddy. I meet them at Burnt Bridge the week before. End of the old road. Let them use my pack horses. Teddy was the pack man for them. They were going up to Anahim Lake country to check up on the old people, like—Old Capoose, Cahoose, Charlie West, Captain Harry, Old Chief Thomas Squinas. They check up on the kids too. Look on their teeth, look way back down their throat, and give them shots too.

They had quite a bit of stuff to bring. About four pack horses' worth. The head nurse brought a mattress too, hospital mattress! I couldn't believe it. She didn't want to sleep on the ground without a spring mattress. "How we gonna pack this mattress?" she ask. "Only way to do it is to pack it right on top of the pack horse," I said. "You should bring a small mattress, not a big spring mattress, next time." They bring a truck load of new stuff, all shiny stuff. Coffee pots, kettles, cups and dishes. We just had some old bean cans for cups, and a old coffee-tin pot we found at the dump.

We make camp and they say, "Where's your pot?"

"Right there, coffee tin with wire over top," I said.

"Where's your coffee cup?" they ask.

"Them two empty bean cans," I said.

The grizzly that slept in my bed

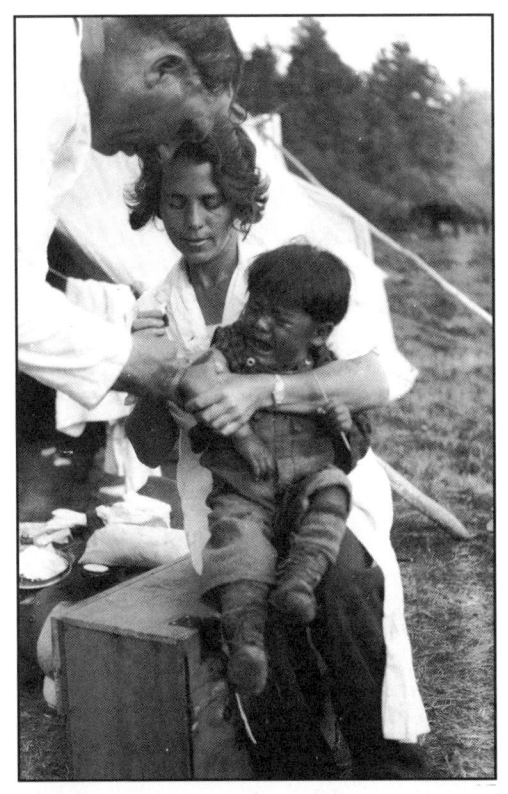

Doctor and nurse immunizing a Stick Indian boy, 1934

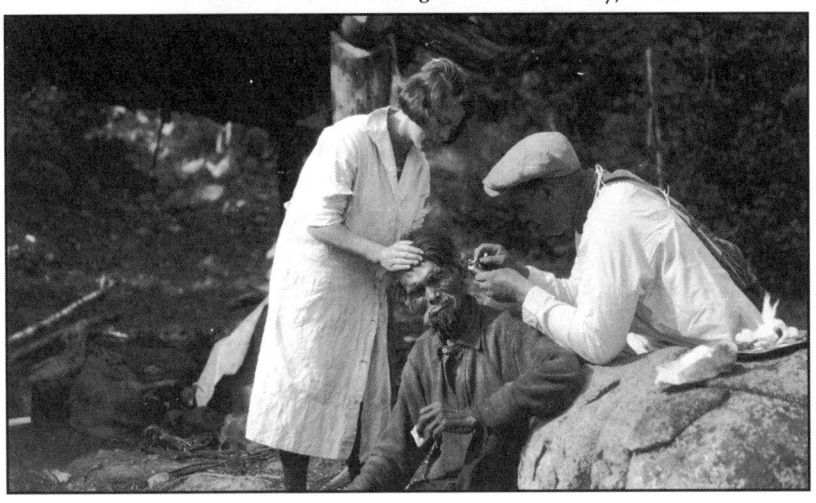

Doctor and nurse with old Olkatcho Indian, 1934

"Where your bed, your mattress?" they ask.

"Right there, that little thin horse blanket," I said.

They weren't used to the outdoors, I guess. But they did all right. They were a happy bunch. Scream, yell, laugh all the time like cowboys. They were scared of bears, though. But I say, "As long as you make a lot of noise the bears will stay away."

I help them for two days, then I take off back to Capoose's ranch. I let Teddy take them up to Anahim Lake. But they didn't show up for two days. I was starting to worry about them. Start to think maybe they lose the horses, maybe the horse run away on them. Maybe they don't stake them horses at night. Maybe they run into a yellow jacket nest, them yellow jackets bite them horses, and the horses run off. So I was glad to see them all all right. Took them over two days to catch up to me.

My nephew David Moody was there. He see that pack horse with the mattress. He sneak up to me, whisper in my ear, "They packed a hospital mattress all the way from Bella Coola! Why did they do that?"

They gonna return my pack horses, then go see the sick people. We told them, "Grizzly bear just killed three sheep. Better be careful."

And one of the nurses says, "Can I please go and see that bear?"

I said, "If you want to see that bear, you go ahead, go by yourself. I'm not going up there. You hear those dogs barking once in a while, go toward them. That bear see you, for sure he'll chase you. That grizzly bear's pretty mad now, we chase him out of his grub, then we sic them dogs on him. When he see you he gonna go right after you."

She stayed. They stay with us at Capoose ranch for one night. After they left, Doll—my wife—she said, "Put a bell on every one of them sheep. That's your job. You and Josephine can do that." So we put a bell on every one of them sheep. Next day we moved camp to the hay fields. Where we cut the hay.

There was a corral in there already so we put the sheep in it. There was hay already in the middle of the corral. Louis Squinas borrowed a .270 rifle from Vinny Clayton to kill that bear. Louis was living with Josephine, and he was helping us put up hay.

That night, that grizzly bear come in the corral. He came through the gate, knocked that gate down. I wasn't there, I was in Anahim Lake ten miles away that night. Louis was there, he heard that bear, so he jumped inside that hay corral. Louis had that loaded gun all ready. That grizzly bear chase the sheep, and them sheep run right into Louis's legs. He fell backwards onto one of them sheep, it packed him a little bit, then he fell to the ground. Another sheep step on his stomach, another sheep step on his chest, another sheep step on his face.

"About a thousand sheep run over me," he say. There was about a hundred head of sheep but Louis said it felt like a thousand sheep run over him. "Then the bear come next," Louis said. Louis stand up, looked but it was so dark he can't see much. "That grizzly bear stand right there in front of me, I didn't see it," he said. "And he put his nose right in my nose and he smell me. He smell me with his nose. I feel his whiskers."

"What did you do, you shoot him?" I ask.

"No, I pulled the trigger and the gun shoot straight up. Bullet went straight up between me and that grizzly bear. Lucky it didn't shoot my face. I reload that gun quick, pulled the trigger, but I shoot straight up again." He was so scared. Then he climb over the fence and run into his tent. That bear, he go through that gate again. There was a lot of noise when he pull down that log gate. Then that bad grizzly bear run away.

I came back early the next morning. I start off early from Anahim Lake. They told me about it when I got there. My wife was pretty scared. That night I wait in the corral for the grizzly bear to come again. He come. We got a milk cow, and she had a little calf. That grizzly bear stepping right over that cow's legs.

That cow never move, that grizzly bear wouldn't touch that cow. He just run back and forth outside the fence, he not want to come in. Stepping over the cow every time he get to the end of the corral. That grizzly want sheep, he didn't want to eat a cow. But he didn't come in the corral, I guess he smell me. The sheep, run back and forth, go to this end and they come back again. Bear chase the sheep back and forth. He kept doing it all night. You could hear them sheep bells ringing in the dark. I could see his black shape run back and forth, almost rub the outside of the corral fence. I stick my gun through the fence. I get ready to shoot both barrels, when he come back again. Then I hear Louis yell, "Get out of here, go on." Then the bear took off. I probably could have killed him if I shoot both shotgun barrels at same time.

It snowed that night. That morning I get my good gun, and my good horse. I'm gonna track that grizzly bear down. I circled around, circled around and hit the snow. But I didn't see no tracks. Must have a den right close some place. I don't find another single track. A big bear like that should leave lot of tracks. Dogs couldn't even find him either. I think that big grizzly went into his den. He never come back again.

One year I got nowhere to go and trap, so I went up Kwatna River. I liked that valley before they logged it. Crooked-Head Charlie had an extra cabin in Kwatna. "That's my cabin over there," he said, "and that's my trapline up there. I got a big trapline, got a lot of room. I can share it with you," he told me. "You can use my trapline and you stay with us. You can stay in my extra cabin. You can sleep in there, you don't have to sleep in your boat."

There were other family nearby. Paul Pollard, Jonathan Wilson family. They all want me to stay with them because I was pretty young and strong. Get meat for them, ducks for them, and help them out. They want anything, I can get it for them. I like to stay with them too. Old Man Jonathan and

Crooked-Head Charlie, they both got a lot of good stories. Old Paul Pollard, too, he got a lot of good stories. Night-time they tell me stories, stories about the olden days.

I go to see that extra empty cabin, and I went in there and look at it. Pretty good cabin. Only about a hundred feet from the other guys' cabins. Nice and dry inside. There used to be two boxes of fish eggs in there. Coho eggs. Them families were fishing before I get there. They get a lot of smoked fish and the ladies keep the eggs to make *mutsi;* stink eggs, we call it. Them eggs got a real strong smell.

They took the eggs out of the stomach of the fish. And they take the whole eggs, pile it side by side in the box. Cover it up and keep it there for quite a long time—two weeks maybe. After two weeks take it out and eat it. This kind of *mutsi* we call *anultz,* or Indian hamburger cheese.

A grizzly bear smell that *anultz,* I guess, break the window, come in, open and eat the whole two boxes of salmon eggs. When he finished eatin' that eggs he lay down on the bed. My bed. He'd been crawling through the window and sleepin' in that bed every night for about a month. When I see the wall, I see it been scratched. Claw marks. I guess that bear reach out and scratch the wall sometimes. I moved in there. Sleep in that bed. Where the bear was sleeping. Every night I hear him going around the cabin, wanting to come in and sleep in my bed. He smell me, I guess, didn't come in.

Every morning when I get up, this family call me to have breakfast with them. Have coffee with them. Crooked-Head Charlie usually come and see me. "Come on. Breakfast and coffee ready." He would ask, "Did that grizzly bear try and come back?"

"Yeah, he was around," I say. I can hear him outside every night. I hear that bear walk around the cabin all night long.

When I go trapping, I would go up the Kwatna River. Alone. Up about ten miles. No logging road in them days. I use a boat with an outboard motor for part of way, and I pole up some places. Shallow water. Then I walk up the rest of the way.

There was a cabin up there, no roof. Right at the mouth of Oak Beck Creek, up a little bit, left-hand side going up. No door, so I put sticks across the doorway. Any bear come around he got to knock it down, make a lot of noise, wake me up. That old cabin got no roof on it so I took my tent and make a roof. Out of my tent canvas. And I stay in there. There an old bed in there. I was okay. Comfortable enough.

The first night I heard two sasquatch. One yelling up the mountain, one yelling from the flat ground. Answering each others. I light the stove, put wood in there. Make smoke. I hope that when they smell that smoke they will go away. I was able to sleep all right after that. In the morning I wake up. I made coffee and I go outside. That morning there was snow on the ground. About six inches deep. I went and look for tracks. Try and find out where them yelling sasquatch were standing. I saw one wolf track, that's all I saw. I didn't go up the mountain though.

While I was away from that cabin at the tideflat, staying way up in the other cabin by Oak Beck Creek, that bear start to sleep in that tideflat cabin again. Those other guys down there see his tracks. Then those guys tell me he left. They say that grizzly bear probably go up to where I was. Followed me up, I guess.

I started to light my campfire outside the door of the Oak Beck cabin. I don't light the fire inside the cabin any more, because it made too much smoke in the cabin. So I cook in that campfire outside the cabin. I carried a lot of canned stuff to that cabin. Can beans, can meat, can salmon. That's what I pack all the time on trapline. That's what I eat when I'm camping up there. One morning I go outside. Where I light my campfire, that grizzly bear dug a deep hole. He dig a hole and lay down in there. Sleep in there. Keeps him warm, I guess. He keep doing that every night. I didn't like that bear to do that. Maybe too dark at night, I walk right on top of him if I go out to have a piss.

Then I worry when I come back late at night from trapline that I might walk into that bear. So I got to shoot my gun before I go near my cabin. Then I'm afraid that son-of-a-gun will break inside my cabin. So I dug a hole in there, corner of the cabin inside, and put all my can stuff in there. Cover it up good so he wouldn't smell it. One day I came in and there was cans all over the floor. That son-of-a-gun found my can goods. He bite a hole in the ends of all the cans, suck out the juice. Did it to all the cans. Even the coffee pot, he make holes in the bottom too. Bite a hole in my water pail too. Had a big pail, get holes in the bottom of that too. I got no grub then. I got nothing to eat now. Can't even make coffee too good, have to lay that coffee pot to one side to make coffee, because of the holes that bear bite into that pot.

After a few days I was just about crazy with hunger. Start thinkin' I'm gonna shoot that grizzly bear and eat that meat. That's what I was thinking. I look at the mountain for goat, but no goats. Supposed to be goats up there. But there was grizzly bear all over. Big trails full of grizzly bear tracks. Trails go way back the Oak Beck Creek. I start looking for a grizzly bear to shoot, a grizzly bear to eat.

I had a weak flashlight too. That son-of-a-gun grizzly bear scare me. When I try to get water and wood at night I got to be real careful, take my flashlight with me down to the creek. I know that that grizzly bear is around. I could smell him. I went down to the creek and try to get water. I flash my light into the water. I see little fish, size of eulachons, lots of them. Maybe five inches long. If I can get them, I'll be okay. So I sink my big water pail right on the bottom and I tie a string on the wire handle. Leave it there all night. Them little trouts, mountain trouts we call them, went inside that. I pull it up in the morning and there is some in there. Three or four mountain trouts. Now I get something to eat. I was gonna be okay.

That bear keep being real trouble for me. When I go up my trapline he go in my Oak Beck cabin or dig out the fire pit some more. Some days he go ahead of me on my trapline. He steal my bait and spring all my traps. He lay down sometimes, dig a hole where my trap is by tree, eat my bait, spring my trap. I was trapping marten. I only got a few marten. After a while I really want to kill that grizzly bear but I never got him, I never even see that bear.

That's how I learn about the grizzly bears up Kwatna. I only trap up Kwatna one year, but I hunt grizzly bear in there for so many years after that.

Molasses and the wolves

■□■□■□■□■□■□■□■□■□■□■□■□■□■□■□■□■

Four times I walked from South Bentinck to Bella Coola. Start from Noeick River and come out at the Snootli hatchery. I went once with my brother Samson, once with a guy we call Wahoo and all by myself twice after that.

It takes four days to walk from the mouth of Noeick River to Bella Coola. First night we camp in the cabin at the Noeick River tideflats. Second night we spend in a cabin six miles upstream where the Smitley River joins the Noeick River. Third night we camp about halfways between the cabin at Smitley and that big cave, near another cabin which was not quite finished. Near where the end of Clayton Falls Creek valley meets the Smitley River valley. That's where we would spend the third night. The fourth night we spend in a big cave at the back end of the Smitley River. From the cabin at Smitley to the big cave is more than ten miles. Takes a day to walk down from the big cave to Snootli Creek hatchery. Tough country up there all right. It's not an easy walk.

First trip, around 1945, there was bunch of us trapping up the Noeick River. John Schooner, Fred Schooner, Samson Schooner, Jim Kelly, Hank King, Samson my brother, and myself. Trapline belong to the Schooner boys. It's their trapline. They let us work on it with them. We take a boat from Bella Coola to the Noeick River. We start out from mouth of Noeick River. We camp out in a tent where the Smitley Creek comes into the Noeick. About six miles from the tideflats. On the north side of Smitley Creek. It was a rough year, lots of rain. We were trapping through to Nusatsum. Pretty tough. No game. Not much to eat. Fish down below all right, but where we camp out there was nothing.

We go out each day. Come back soakin' wet. We got to cross the two rivers every day, Noeick River and that Smitley River. Water right up past your chest. Come back wet to camp in that tent every night. No place to dry our clothes. Get up and put wet clothes back on. They don't get dry.

One morning I told them guys, "I'm gonna stay right here. I'm not going out today."

"What are you gonna do?"

"I'm gonna build a cabin here," I said. We got all the tools I need there. Saw, sledge hammer, wedges, axes, nails. We had everything there to build a cabin.

My brother, he said, "I'm not going too. I'm gonna stay and help Clayton."

Then one of the boys, I think it was Fred Schooner, said, "I'm gonna stay behind too, I'm not going out in the rain. I'll stay and help them build a cabin."

It was John Schooner's trapline. John said, "Okay, we'll stay." The whole works stay to build a cabin.

John Schooner ask me, "You ever build a cabin?"

"Oh, yeah," I said. "I build a cabin up at Anahim Lake. Build it out of logs. But here logs are lot bigger. We'll split them in half first. Put one half on one wall, put the other half on the other wall across." John Schooner said, "You just tell us what to do. We'll do it." I said, "Cut that spruce tree down beside that cedar tree."

They cut it down. They cut that big limbs off. Made

Molasses and the wolves

wedges from that limbs. Them spruce knot wedges are tough, just as strong as iron wedges. As hard as that steel. And they cut down more trees. Two guys split logs using spruce knot wedges and sledge hammers. Two guys clear the land and make it flat. By about three o'clock in the afternoon we almost get the walls up. Two other guys cut small logs for the rafters for the roof. They pack it over. And we get them up. We get cedar and make shakes for the roof. We keep a hole in the roof for the smoke of fire can go through. By about twelve o'clock at night we move in there. All finished! A good-sized cabin. About twelve by sixteen feet, I think it was.

We cut some of that thick fir bark. Pile it outside. Take our clothes off and hang them up inside. Make a fire. Start to get pretty warm inside. Dried our blankets. That fir bark is pretty warm wood. Makes the hottest fire. The next morning, I told my brother, "I'm not going up Nusatsum way. I'm going up toward Snootli Creek." So we went up Smitley Creek toward Snootli Creek. Just the same we get wet crossin' that Smitley River. Got no boat to cross. We have to walk in the water up to our neck. Come back at night the same way. But at night we can go into a nice dry cabin and dry out our clothes.

After a while we run out of grub. There was a big cabin down by the Noeick River tideflat. Down by South Bentinck. One guy tried to start a farm there. Old Man Jacobson, I think, his name was. He build a big house there.

We were talking to each others. "We should go back to the big cabin for awhile. Eat good, dry up, rest, and then come back again." Hank King smash his big toe. Broke it. I don't know how he did it. He couldn't walk very good.

I told my brother, "I'm going ahead down to the home cabin, to the tideflats, to our boats. By the time you get down there, I'll have the fire going and get the supper ready for you guys. You got to get that guy with a broken toe down to the cabin."

So I went ahead alone. I was all by myself. But I did have

a little dog with me. Small little dog. Just a young pup. Coho were coming up the river. November now. Trail to the tideflat cabin was right on top of the bank all the way. North side of the Noeick River. Nice trail. I get to the open and I saw a grizzly bear fishing. Great big grizzly bear. I keep walking on the trail. And he turn around and look at me. He just stood there for a while. Then he came toward me. I stop. I had a good gun with me. Automatic .350 Remington. But he kept coming, that bear came at me. I saw a tree right on the edge of the river. Lot of limbs. I can climb that with no trouble if he come after me. I yell at him, "Go on, beat it."

And he keep coming. I was standing on the bank above the river. The river eat away under the bank. You know how the bank sometimes stick way out and the river run underneath. I was standing right on the edge of that ledge. I put my pack down, put it down on the ground. I call that little dog. That little dog come alongside of me. And that bear come across the river and jump right up on that overhang bank. About five feet upstream from us. That little dog bark. That bear stop, hang on that overhang bank, and the whole thing break off into the river. That weight of that grizzly bear break that bank off. The bear drop back down to the riverbed. He went back to where he was fishing. He turn around and this time he run faster toward us. Going to jump right up on the bank. He just about made it, was getting up onto the bank when I shot him right in the chest.

After I shot him, I turn around and climb up that tree. That little doggie, he fight, he bark at that grizzly bear that I shot already. That grizzly bear was crippled. And I was up in the tree. My gun was down there on the ground. I stayed there for a while. Then I yell at that grizzly bear. He went in the woods. I know he crippled, I know because I hit him in the right place. After he went in the woods I came down and got my gun. I think to myself, "If he comes back I'm gonna shoot this time. I'll empty that gun on him. Finish him off." Then I heard that grizzly bear in the woods howl, *Wwwoooo*. Then it was all quiet. He was dead. I pick up my pack and I call that dog and we go down.

It was about a mile to go to the tideflat cabin. I start off again. I could see them coho spawning down there. Another grizzly bear there. This time I didn't want to shoot him so I yell. I yell at him. Then he took off. He came toward me all right but he not looking for trouble like that other grizzly bear. He went into that thick timber. I didn't shoot him. I went down to where he was fishing. I see a lot of nice coho.

I shot a coho. Try and shoot him in the head but I didn't kill him. Just stun him. He flip around till he get to the beach, like. Then I jump and grab him. Kick him out of the water. That's what the bear was after. I get a willow bush. Kind of big, like. I break the ends off and I pull it through the coho gills. Use it for a handle. I got nothing much to eat, I got to cook that. I carry that big coho. Female coho. Full of eggs. The eggs keep coming out of it, little bit at a time, all the way down to the cabin. Trail of eggs all the way down, like. There was a nail sticking out in the woodshed of the cabin and I hang that coho up on that nail. Let it hang there in the woodshed.

I get a big pot. I'm thinking all the time, "Them boys gonna come soon." I cut off the bottom half, tail part of that coho. Put the rest of the coho back in the woodshed. I'm gonna cook lots for the bunch of us. I peel potatoes and onions, and make coho fish stew. I sit down by the stove. Big stove. Drum stove. Heater stove. It was going good. I made the stew. It got dark but no boys yet.

I heard something in the woodshed. I thought it was them boys but I didn't go to look. I yell. Call for them. No one answered. I eat some coho stew. After a while I heard it again. I didn't bother to see what was makin' that noise. I was pretty tired and wet. I lay down and went off to sleep. In the morning I get up and look out there. Looked in the woodshed. That other half of the coho is gone. I follow eggs. I can see that there are grizzly bear tracks. Coho still had some eggs in it when that grizzly took it away. He pack it about a couple of hundred feet away from the cabin. I could follow a trail of eggs to where he eat that coho. Then I followed his tracks. He went back up the trail I came down. I went back to the tideflat cabin. Not too long after that, them boys came down. I told them about what happen to me. That I saw two grizzly bears. That I shot at one and he howl like hell in the woods. I say, "Let's go look for him."

My brother came with me. We went up. I track him from where he went into the woods after I shot him. We found that grizzly bear. He lie there dead. A real nice grizzly bear. Black silver-tip. Big one too. We didn't skin it. Left it there. Other grizzly bear will pack him away and eat him up.

We all stayed in that tideflat cabin for about three days. Every day those guys want more fish. I would go up to that same spot each day to get more coho. We had lots to eat now. We eat good. Eat smoke salmon every day.

Clayton and Samson at South Bentinck Arm, 1940

After three days we go back to that cabin again up Smitley Creek. When we get up to that cabin we leave some grub there. From there Samson and I would go to the other end of that trapline. Back end of Smitley Creek. Setting traps in that Smitley country. At the back end of the Smitley trapline was a cave. A big cave. We would stay in there. It's close to the back end of Snootli Creek. When we run out of grub we go back to that cabin up Smitley Creek. When we run out of grub there we go back down to that cabin on the tideflat. We keep doing this for weeks and weeks. We trapping mainly marten. Got some but not too good. Didn't make much money that year.

Pretty soon it was wintertime. Snow on the mountains. One night it snowed hard. We were in that cave way up Smitley Creek. We were running low on grub. Samson and I were getting pretty hungry. I know that from the cave it is shorter to Bella Coola than back to South Bentinck.

My brother, Samson, tell me, "Let's go to Bella Coola." We tried but the snow was too deep. We can't make it. We came back to that cave again. My brother say, "We still have a little bit of rice in the cave. We'll cook that."

We went back to that cave. There's nothing left, not one rice! Mice get in that sack, somehow get in there, chew a hole and pack it all away.

I say to Samson, "Let's try again tomorrow to get to Bella Coola."

I trap at the back of Snootli Creek before. I knew the country up there pretty good. I know that once we get into Snootli Valley we'll be okay. It was the divide I was afraid of. We had to go above the treeline, over the divide and down into the Snootli Creek valley.

Next day we tried again. No. Just too tough. I say to Samson, "Let's go back to that cave." We went back. We try to make skis. Some trees are bent like a ski. We find some that are just right. We cut them and whittle them into skis. Whittle them real thin. And make straps for them. Put 'em on. "If we can't ski on them, we can use it for snowshoes," I told Samson. We tried them snowshoes out. Middle of the day. No. We sort of play out. Got real tired. Go back to the cave.

It kind of rain little bit up there that day. Then it turn real cold that night. That cave was real cold. The cold north wind blow right into that cave. "Look, Samson, if we tough it out till the top of the snow freeze up, get cold from the north wind, we can walk down to Bella Coola like on a sidewalk," I said.

"We can try that," he said. Next day at night-time we take off. I check the snow. Still won't hold me. I still break through it. About ten o'clock that night, I try again. By God, it hold me.

"Come on, let's go," I said.

"Do you know where you going in the dark?" Samson asked me.

"Oh, yeah, I know where I going," I said. We tried them skis but it didn't work for me. I slide, hit some kind of crust, skis stop and I fall down head first. Lose my gun, have to dig all around in the night-time to find it. Sometimes I go too fast and I fall backwards. My brother have to help lift me up. Anyway, we got to about halfway across that snowfield, got to the top of the divide. We both played out.

Samson lay down. "Wait up. I can't walk any more. I'm play out. Maybe I get sick," he said.

It was late at night, black all around, few stars but no moon. I took his pack off. I took my pack off too. I usually pack a little canvas. Four by six. I use it for tents sometimes. Tie the corners, sit down inside when I get stuck, like. I spread that canvas and tell him to lay down on it. We had just passed a dead tree. Yellow cedar, I think. No limbs. It was sticking out from the snow like a pole. I saw that it looked dry. I went back to that dead yellow cedar tree. I chop it down and I pack it to Samson. I build a fire and I made coffee. I gave him coffee. After he drink that coffee, I ask him how he feel. "I feel all right," he said.

"You go to sleep," I said. I keep that fire going. He went

to sleep. In the morning I get up, make coffee again. That fire was way down below us, it melt down into the snow. I put the pot down on a rope, throw chips down there to build up the fire again. Make more hot coffee. We drink it. I always carry a rope too. Thin rope. I told Samson, "I tie the rope to the corner of that canvas, you lay down on it and I'll pull you down like a sled." So I tie the rope to the corners of that canvas, Samson sat in the middle of it, and I drag him down like a sleigh. We hit the timber. Lots of wood now. I'd camped there before. From Bella Coola, I trap there. I knew where we were. I build a big fire. Ate the last bit of food we had, little bit of smoked fish and a little bit of rice. I point down, "Down there is Bella Coola Valley now. That's Widsten's place down there."

Samson's mind build up, "Oh, we'll make it now." I packed what he had on his back and I put it in my pack sack. I told him to just walk behind me. I was all right. We went about two hours like that. Then Samson said, "Let me pack the stuff now. You take a rest for a while." I know he's okay then, he want to take over now. We made some more coffee and sugar. "Not too far now before we hit the Bella Coola highway," I told him. "I been here before." A friend of mine, John Cole, live near Widsten's. We made it to his house. He had a truck. I told him, "My partner's pretty tired. Can you take us down to Bella Coola? We'll fill up your gas tank some day." He took us down to Bella Coola. When we got to Bella Coola, Samson said, "I'll never go with you again, Clayton, you're too tough for me." He quit trapping after that. Sell all his traps.

I got to go by myself after that. Another guy came with me after that. Wahoo, we call him. Big guy. He can't take it. One trip and he quit too. We got up on the divide. He yell at me, "Clayton, where are you?" I say, "Wahoo." And all them little peaks up there make it echo. "Wahoo, Wahoo, Wahoo." He didn't like that hike either. I go alone after that. All by myself. I feel better that way. Don't have to worry if my partner can make it or not.

In the old days, the Indian people like to bury the dead under overhanging rocks. I know where there is two grave boxes, right close to the water. Just have to walk about a hundred feet and there is a grave box right there. I used to take hunters in to see them two different grave boxes.

Molasses is the one at the head of that inlet. An Indian guy named Molasses. The wolves killed him. He is still there in a grave box at the north end of an island, right at the mouth of the river. In an old Indian graveyard, in a big overhanging rock cave. Boxes all piled up in there. I took one guy in there, Martin. Martin had a big farm in the Bella Coola Valley. He dump over all them grave boxes looking for money. He found one fifty cent piece in there. I give him shit for that, "What the hell you doing, why are you robbing the dead people?" This guy has a big farm, and he sells so many head of butcher cattle every year to Ocean Falls. That should be good enough, he has no family, just him and his wife. Why he need to go around and try and rob the dead people? Rob them bones.

Molasses was an old man who lived in that village in the olden days. He lived all his life in that village. There weren't too many people living in the village when he was there because the Indian people were all dying off from smallpox and TB. Must have been not too long ago, because he got a white man name, Molasses. Probably a hundred years ago or so. Molasses was the oldest man in his family.

One day, Molasses went up the river in a canoe. Gonna set traps up that river. There was a slough near the high tide mark. I guess a seal came up with the tide and got caught in the slough. He can't get out. The wolves come hunting down to the tideflats. They saw that seal, and they kill that seal. Molasses see them wolves, he see what they were doing. He went over to that slough, scared away the wolves and dragged that seal to his canoe. Then he went on up the river. He got that seal in his canoe now. Wolves want that seal. The wolves follow him along the side of the river. He got to the spot where he is gonna set some traps. He tie his canoe to the grass along the riverbank. He pull grass bunches together and he wrap the rope around it. He ties his canoe up so it won't drift away when the tide comes up. He go to set his traps.

The wolves come down and chew that rope. The canoe drift away. Then they went after Molasses. They got him. No bite marks on Molasses, but his body was just like mush. Soft like there was water in the body. I think them wolves use their nose, hit him with their nose, until he die. The canoe drift down the river and the village people saw that canoe. "It's Molasses's canoe drifting down," they said. They wonder what happen to Molasses. Two or three boys get another canoe and pole up the river. They see them wolves still running a circle around Molasses up there. They look and see Molasses was dead already. They take Molasses, put him in the canoe, take him down to the village.

They figure out what happen by the tracks, grass, and seal in the canoe. At night they put Molasses on a bed, inside a long house. The wolves were still mad at Molasses so they came down to the village. You could hear them through the cracks of the longhouse, sniffing and smelling. Some Indian guys went outside and started shooting to try and scare those wolves away. The wolves never go away, just stay around all night. Them wolves never give up. Even come in the door after awhile. There was a hole in the middle of that longhouse where the smoke from the campfire goes out.

One old lady there, she told them Indian guys, "You tie a rope underneath his arms and pull him up on the roof. Then the wolfs won't want to come in here." They pulled Molasses up on top of the roof, fixed up a bed, and they lay him up on the roof.

Hot sun, sunny days all that week. Real hot, lot of sunshine. They think that's what cured his skin. His skin don't come off his body, just get dry. I look at it. His skin something like plastic now. Meat was all dried up. Looks like just skin over the bones. You can see his skin is still on the body, dried out, like a shirt and pants. He was on the roof for four days. After four days they took him down and buried him on the island in a cave.

I took a lot of guys in to look at Molasses. The hunters used to like to do that. They'd put skulls on top of the grave boxes and take pictures of that too. One day the archaeologist come talk to me. He wanted to find out where he can find more dead people. I tell him go see Molasses. I told them guys, take a picture of that bracelet band on Molasses's ankle. Molasses had a band on his ankle. I don't know what it was made of. Could be copper, could be gold, could be just the iron.

But I find out them archaeologists guys are bad. They dump out all them grave boxes and spread the bones all over just like Martin did. I think them archaeologists cut that ankle band off Molasses and took it. The archaeologists were there when I took some guys to take some pictures of that bracelet. When I went back again, it was gone. Archaeologists still there. So I think they took it. I wouldn't tell them archaeologists nothing after that, I wouldn't tell them about the masks, the coppers, or where any other Indian graves are.

I told that archaeologist, "You gonna get yourself bad luck if you keep stealin' from them dead people."

He said, "Maybe one of the kids do that, take Molasses's ankle band."

I said, "You should watch them kids closer."

Grizzly bears used to hibernate in that cave where Molasses's coffin is. Wintertime, I guess, them bears would go in there. I guess they don't like them grave boxes in there. Them grizzlies want to lay down where the box is. They would throw out two coffin boxes every year, and make holes where the boxes were. Two grizzly bears do that. Every year for so many years, they do that. They dump them boxes out every winter, and every spring I have to gather up all the bones, put them back in the coffin boxes, pick it up, and pack the box back up into that overhanging rock cave. Every year for so many years I have to do that. Molasses's head come off, but the body still in the skin stay together pretty good.

That other grave box near the shore is up that creek, in that channel. I told the archaeologist about that too. He found it, he told me he find it. The man in there, just bones, has a buckskin coat on him and he was all tied up in stinging nettle rope. Must be good rope, he is still tied up real good. I took an American guy in there. There was a little bowl in there, a bowl you eat with. He took that, he was gonna take it home with him.

"No," I said. "That's all that dead guy has got left, take it back. You gonna give us bad luck. Just take pictures, that should be good enough."

Wolves and wolverines are the hardest animals to trap. Wolverine especially can make fool of you. They will spring your trap and pull the bait or pull out the animal you trapped—you never get it. Go on to the next trap in your line and same thing.

Trap sprung, bait is gone, fur is gone and no wolverine or wolves. Makes you real mad.

Wolverines are bad animals. I kill, I shoot them when I see them. They get in your camp, they tear everything apart. Piss and shit all over. They piss in your bed, in your grub. Smell like hell. Shit all over the place. Even in the cabin. They get in there and tear everything up. Grizzly bear is even scared of wolverine. They fight over fish or animal kills. Wolverine, he won't give in. He keep coming back, wanna fight that grizzly bear. That grizzly bear took off! I seen that up-country. They were fighting over moose.

We used to see Old Man Hans in South Bentinck every weekend when I was a kid. My dad was handlogging about five miles away from there. Old Man Hans was trapping now.

My dad ask, "How you doing with your trappings?"

"No good," he said. He start swearing. "I set traps all the way up Noeick River and that wolverine, he take all the bait and spring my traps. I can't get nothing, I just go broke."

One Sunday we go again and we see Old Man Hans. "Did you get that wolverine?" we asked.

He said, "I get him, but he still make a fool of me. I did get him in a trap. I club him on the head with a stick, knock him out. Then I take the chain off the tree and I take him down to the canoe and throw him in there. Chain that wolverine in the canoe." He didn't kill it. Instead he tie that chain to the support bar which runs across the canoe. Tie the other end of the chain to the wolverine. He plan to let it wake up. He said, "Every time I think about the trouble he give me, I plan to beat him up."

He had a nice canoe. Real nice canoe. He used to come out in his canoe and get us when we anchor offshore in our boat, to bring us back to the beach. When Old Man Hans got back to his camp with his wolverine, he pull up his canoe. He plan to tie up the wolverine some place on land after he eat supper. He eat his supper, then he go down to the canoe to get the wolverine. He was afraid kids might get too close and the wolverine would bite them. When he got to the canoe there was two pieces of canoe left! That wolverine, he chew from the top of the canoe down to the water on both sides. Where it meet on the bottom, that canoe broke in half, right into two pieces. That wolverine was still there, so he shot that wolverine. Shot it dead.

I get chased by wolves one time. I was in Anahim Lake country. It was when I was living up there, married to my first wife. There were twenty to twenty-five wolves. I caught them trying to kill a moose, right close to my cabin at Anahim Lake. The moose was doing all right against those wolves but he made a mistake. He went out in the river, bottom real soft and muddy, and he tried to cross that. Close to the other side he sink down deep. His feet got stuck and he fall on the other side trying to get up the bank. He laid on the bank and the whole works get him. The wolves got him. Bite him on the ear and back.

I caught them eating that moose. They get mad at me because I sent my dog on them. One wolf kill my dog. She ripped a big cut on his back. Female wolf did that. I think they gonna try and kill me. They come around me, circle around me. They was yelling at me. I killed four of them before they go. Another guy came, Louis Squinas, and he shot two more. We got six wolves together. Then them wolves run away from us. We went home for a short time. Two hours later, I go back, moose was eaten up. Just the bones and a little piece of horns left. That's all that was left. Them wolves hang around there for two days after that, howling every night.

To kill deer and moose, wolves will bite a hole just above the hip, like. Tear it open and the guts come out. Then they pull that intestines right out. Then another wolf will bite the deer or moose in the throat and hold on tight. I hear them deer and moose screaming when wolves getting them. They will fight, try and kick them wolves with front legs and hind legs.

In Kwatna, I even see a wolf tear off a leg when the deer was still alive. That wolf went running up the hill with half a deer leg in its mouth. Them wolves, they really are a bad animal.

Once, I saw a moose standing in water. Five wolves get that moose cornered in a slough. Moose has long legs, he was not swimming, just stand there. Every time a wolf try and jump at him, that moose would open his toes up wide and push that wolf deep in the water or he would kick him with his hind leg. I get up and run toward them. Then the wolves and the moose took off, the whole works. That would have made a good movie.

The easiest animal to trap is marten. Use a steel trap, and put that trap by a tree. Sometimes we nail bait on the tree. When the marten come in and reach up to get the bait, the trap goes off and you get them. Trap fisher the same way in the same trap. The Kimsquit marten was real good to trap. Them marten worth a lot of money because they have black colour fur. Skowquiltz marten were black too. They used to pay a hundred dollars a skin for them Kimsquit and Skowquiltz marten.

Beaver are pretty easy to trap. Put the trap in four inches of water by the dam. Attach it by a long chain. Tear the dam a little bit. Let it leak out. The beaver will go and put sticks there to stop the leak. Tie about ten to fourteen pounds to the trap. When the beaver get trapped, he will swim out in the deeper water and pull that trap into the deep water. The heavy trap will keep him underwater, drown him.

Wolverine and wolves are the hardest animal to trap. They can make a fool of you. We get lynx and bobcat too. There are lynx and bobcat up-country. Wherever rabbits are you can find lynx and bobcat. Trap them, snare them, or chase lynx and bobcat with saddle horse in the deep snow. Any old horse or old cow, gonna die, you shoot 'em. Cut off one leg and tie a rope on the ankle. Then pull it behind a saddle horse. Pull it all through the woods, between jack pines. Keep going, sometimes for couple hundred yards. Where you drag that heavy

Molasses and the wolves

leg, it presses down the snow. Leaves a blood trail. Any kind of animal, like a fox, coyote, lynx, wolf or bobcat that smell that blood trail will follow it. Easy walking for them on the packed snow too. Then you put a snare between two jack pine trees, close together. That animal goes through them two jack pine trees, sniffing that blood trail, and gets caught in any snare. Sometimes we tie the snare to a spring-pole which flips up when the animal gets caught in snare. The snared animal is hanging in the air after that. If you want to snare fox and wolf and coyote, you can't use rope, got to use special wire because they will bite through rope.

We used to chase fox, wolf, coyote, lynx and bobcat on horseback when I was up-country. Mostly fox and coyote. Wait till snow was about three feet deep. Then you ride through the timber on horse, lookin' for fresh fox or wolf or coyote track. When you see fresh tracks you follow them. When the fox or wolf or coyote hear you coming they start jumping in the snow. When you see them jumping tracks, okay, time to spur your horse hard. You know that the fox or wolf or coyote not too far away. He can't make it too fast in that deep snow. You get beside that fox or wolf or coyote and you club him while riding the horse. Sometimes the fox or wolf or coyote try and bite the horse on the leg or on the nose. In a good year we kill more than ten fox, and ten coyote. But can't kill wolves that way. Wolves too smart. They run ahead fast, take a rest and wait for you to catch up, then they run ahead again.

John Hall always wanted me to go with him up the Skowquiltz River to trap. There was grizzly bears in that country and he was afraid of grizzly bears. So he called me to go. I said, "Okay, I'll go with you." And they called my brother Samson to go too. He said, "Okay." This was November. "When are we going on the trapline?" I asked. John Hall and Samson said they would go as soon as they get enough wood for their wives. Both of them got no wood yet! "Okay, you guys go cut wood, I'm taking off today."

I had my own boat so I went up and stayed in the longhouse at the mouth of the Skowquiltz River. I had a little boat too, so I rowed around in it. Hunting ducks and geese. Goats too up there but I never go after them. Them buggers never show up after a few days. I wonder, "What the hell going on? Why don't they come?" So I count out my traps. I go upstream and get some coho for bait. Then I put the traps, the bait, my sleeping bag and a little grub and took off upstream. I think, "Hell with them guys. If they want to stay in Bella Coola, let them stay there. I gonna go set traps up river."

I did see a lot of bears, but no grizzly, all black bears. I keep on going upstream. It started to rain hard, half snow and half rain. I get just soakin' wet. But I keep on setting traps. I got to a waterfall and I decided to camp out there. Under a big overhanging tree. It was real wet, raining hard. I start a campfire. That big tree, it bend out over the fire, and then goes straight up.

I took my logging boots off and hang them up on a limb of that big overhanging tree. I took my shirt and underwear off too. Hang it all up on them limbs. I put wet wood on top of that fire, get it going good. I didn't have no tent, so I get in my sleeping bag and I get underneath that bent tree. Get in out of the rain, beside the fire. I guess I went off to sleep right there. My logging boots get burned on the bottom. Gee, brand new logging boots too. That wet wood got dry after awhile, and the fire get real big. And my shirt and my underwear burn too!

In the morning I get spare clothes from my pack sack, some long underwear. But I didn't have any extra boots. My boots, the bottoms were all curled up, dried up and burnt. I try and get my feet in them boots. Too small, them boots were all curled up. But I knew I had to get back to the camp. So I moved that fire close to that creek, and then I put them boots in the fire. They get soft little bit. I could put my feet in them, but then my feet started to burn so I jumped in the water quick. I stand in the water till the boots shape up to my feet. By God, they look all right after that.

I get my pack and I went back toward that cabin down at the tideflat. I went about a mile and the sole come off one boot. I can feel the rocks on my feet but I keep on going. Then the other side, the sole come off too. Then I hear someone yelling lots. I yell, "Hey, hey, over here."

John Hall said, "I'm not going to pick Clayton up. Let him walk. That damn wolf." He used to say I was like a wolf. They were coming down in a canoe. They were hunting goat. They passed me. I thought they were going to pick me up. I need help. No boots. My feet get hurt on them sharp rocks. I see them go by me.

So I took off, I run down. I was way ahead of them when I get in that longhouse on the tideflat. I build a big fire. Took my clothes off and get changed. I get two martens on the way down. A hundred dollars each, pay for our expenses right there.

When my brother come, I throw them marten at him. "You guys don't do nothing at all. Lazy guys. Stay in Bella Coola, stay in the cabin all the time. Skin them marten," I said. "I work hard enough to get them marten for you guys. I'm not going to do this any more, I got no more shoes. Look at them. Used to be brand new logging boots, all worn out now!"

We used to get forty dollars a cougar, bounty money. The government paying forty dollars a bounty for cougar skins or cougar ears because they say cougars kill anything. They say that them cougar will kill the deers, just suck the blood out and then leave the deer there dead.

Thomas Squinas and I went after cougar one year. A lot of deer in that one valley, lot of deer in there and lot of cougar. That valley is just a few miles east from Anahim Lake. Bunch of sidehills, lot of grass there. Right up the head of that stream. Big deer there, mule deer, big ones. We would chase them cougar with dogs in there. Thomas had two cougar dogs. We would look for cougar tracks and when we find some, then we send the dogs after the cougar. "Go on, go get him," we say. Them dogs took off. Then we follow them dogs and cougar.

I remember one day we chased a big cougar to a hole under one big rock. That cougar went underneath that big boulder. Outside that rock the snow was all brown. That cougar been in and out of that hole. We see fresh cougar's tracks go in there and then the dogs try and go in after it. By God, we saw that cougar come back out of the hole. The dogs go after it. I follow the tracks down to the top of a ridge. The cougar tracks keep going down. I call the dogs to come back. I went back to where Thomas was. Thomas, he crawl underneath into that hole under that big rock. I hear him swearing in there. He was swearing in English. I hear something in there yellin'—*Wwwweeessssss, wwwweeeesssss, wwwwweeeessss*—like. Then I stand there and see something fly out of that cave. Little baby cougar. Thomas throw it out. Then he throw out another one. Three of them altogether. Three baby cougars. Hundred and twenty dollars worth of cougars, forty dollars for each cougar kitten. Thomas came back out of that hole. I look at his hand. He had buckskin gloves on. "Them son-of-a-guns try and bite my hands," he said. There was no blood so I guess them cougar kids didn't bite through. Then Thomas, he kill them all with the butt of his gun. Killed them little baby cougars.

"The mother's gone," I said, "going down this way." I call them dogs. "Go get him," I said.

Them dogs went, went after the mother. And we run behind, running on foot. We didn't ride horse, down there. We went on foot. I hear them dogs barking down below. The cougar jump in a tree. We see that cougar up there. She climb a tree. Thomas shoot that cougar. Missed. She came down, drop to the ground and them dogs jump her right away. That cougar rip one of them dogs' stomach right open. Her claws are kind of like a knife. Guts come right out. Was the best dog we got too. The leader.

Thomas killed that cougar, then grab that dog and carry

him. Thomas pret' near cry. He pack that dog to the camp. Thomas had thread and needle with him. He sew that dog's stomach, push his guts in and sew it up. Used black thread. That dog lived! That dog live, but he was no good after that. Was scared of everything after. I killed altogether maybe twenty cougars in them days with other guys. Used dogs mostly. I knew one white guy from Kleena Kleene Valley, down toward the coast, who killed so many cougars he bought himself a new car. Lot of cougar money.

In the old days, Fisheries try and pay me five dollars a day just to kill grizzly bears. All year round. Out of season or open season. Just go around and kill them. The government want me to shoot grizzly bears and then leave them there. Leave them to rot. I was pretty young yet. The Fisheries guy who asked me to do that was a pretty young guy too. He was scared of grizzly bears. He used to go see the country with me. Places like Kwatna. I like to guide him around places like that. He would count how many fish go up the rivers. I never did it. Never killed grizzly bears for the hell of it.

I talked to Richard Carpenter, the Indian skipper from Bella Bella. I asked him, "Is it the right thing to do just to kill 'em and leave them there?" Save the fish, more fish, but no bears. He said, "No don't do it." Instead of that I went guiding. Make more money that way!

I remember when I was a kid, the policeman came down to the wharf. I was about seven years old then. I see eagles sitting down on the trees. They eat the salmon heads that drop off in the cannery, the heads we throw away outside. Them eagles like to eat them fish heads. The police told us, "The government want you to kill them eagles, chop the head off, take it down to the police station. You get one dollar for every eagle head you bring to me." The government not like eagles because they say that eagles knock too many young mountain goats off the bluffs and kill them. Some of the boys did hunt them bald eagles all right. I didn't. The government had this bounty on eagles for a long time, maybe twenty years. White guys and Indian guys kill them. Nobody make big money. Five or six heads, five bucks or six bucks at a time. Some white guys up valley would kill more, fill up potato sacks with eagle heads.

Wolf bounties were not till after the eagle head bounty, I think. Twenty or forty dollars a wolf. Wolf bounty start around 1925, I think. I kill wolf. I don't like wolf. Kill them down here and up-country, too. Most I kill was four in one day. The best way to kill wolf is to poison it. The government pay Tommy Squinas to kill all the wolves in the country around Anahim Lake. The government give him poison to do that. Tommy find out that the best way to poison wolf is to find an old moose. Just barely alive. Still kicking its legs little bit. Put that poison in the blood vein of the moose. Heart still working, blood spread that poison all in the meat. Tommy Squinas did that. He killed over nine wolves in one bunch and one coyote, when he put that poison in the blood vein of a moose that was just alive. One night catch. Tommy sent me a picture of that.

The Ulkatcho people didn't want Tommy going around the country doing that, they claim he was poisoning all the animals that eat moose. Like marten, fox, fisher and birds like crows. Dead animals all over the place. So Tommy quit doing that. They hired a white guy from the Williams Lake country to do that poisoning after that.

There was a bounty on Dolly Varden trouts too. Skeena River country, I think, but not here.

Old Chief Squinas

There was a chief in Anahim Lake. Old Chief Squinas. Tommy Squinas's father. Old Chief Squinas had a nice-looking daughter. A young fella, a half-breed boy—Alexis—really wanted his daughter. Alexis had grey eyes, white skin, and he looked like a white boy. He did marry the chief's daughter.

It was springtime. Spring salmon coming up the Bella Coola River now. Old Chief Squinas say to that boy, his son-in-law, "Spring salmon coming up the Bella Coola River now, let's go to Stuie. We take the whole family down there. Take the nets, catch spring salmons and we smoke fish."

Alexis say, "Okay," and he get the horses. They all go to Stuie, where the Indian smokehouse camp is today. That's the place that belong to Old Chief Squinas. He build a nice long smokehouse in there at one time. A bunch of other Indians from Anahim Lake would come down to Stuie, stay with him every year, and net and smoke fish too.

So Squinas and his family went down there in May, I guess. Bears are out in May, they are startin' to go all over the country now. Some go down to Stuie. After Old Chief Squinas and his family set up camp at Stuie, he went to that young guy again, "Alexis, we want meat. You go across the Atnarko River to that island. Lot of deer there, grass grows quick on that island across the other side. I'll take you across on the canoe and you can go hunt for deer or other game over there."

After Old Chief Squinas took Alexis across the Atnarko River, he crossed back over and then he drive their horses across to Alexis. That young fella got the horses and he walk them to that island. He walk the horses. Old Chief Squinas was right. There was a lot of grass in there. Lot of feed for horses. Alexis, he hang his saddle, ropes and bridle in a tree on that island. Turn the horses loose. He walked by the saddle, look back at the horses. Everything seemed all right.

He started look around for deer. Saw two deers right away. He shot one of them deer. Then he got a rope, saddled a horse, tie one end of the rope to the saddle and the other end to the deer. Then he make that horse pull the deer up to a tree. Alexis hang that deer up and gutted it.

After he gut that deer, it was still too heavy for him to pack all the way to the canoe. "Too far for me to pack," he thinks to himself. He went to get a gentle horse, three-year-old mare. But that gentle mare still doesn't know bridle or hackamore. A gentle wild horse who don't know nothing about saddle. Alexis made a hackamore out of rope. He was going to put a saddle on that gentle wild mare, then put the deer on her and lead her to the canoe. He ride that mare bareback, go to get his saddle but when he got back to the deer, a grizzly bear come and was eating the guts.

That bear went after him. He ride bareback out of there, wrap his hand around the mane hair on the neck of that gentle wild mare, and he make that horse go about sixty mile an hour—make her run like hell. "I hang on for life," he said. That horse was runnin' fast. There is an old spruce tree, dead long ago. One long limb hang way down. That horse went underneath that branch. The branch caught Alexis right in the stomach, and then the limb bend way over. That limb spring Alexis right off that horse, he pull the hair right off the horse mane, and he flew to the ground. He landed on his back right between the grizzly bear's front legs. Landed right between the legs! He get up and started to run for a spruce tree which had branches hanging way down. He made it to that tree, and he climbed the tree with the bear right behind him. He went up so high that the bear can't reach him. The bear stand up, all right, but he didn't climb the tree.

Alexis was up there looking down at that grizzly bear. The grizzly bear was going around the tree, looking up at Alexis. This young half-breed boy remembered an old Indian story. If a bear gets you in a tree, pee on him. Alexis look down at the bear, the grizzly bear look up at him. That young guy opened his pants and pissed on the bear. That bear not run away. Alexis think to himself, "Those damn Indians tell a lie to me!" He look down, the bear still looking up at him. So Alexis took his pants down and shit on that grizzly bear this time. Shit on him! Smell like hell but that son-of-a-gun still won't go away.

Grizzly bear still there at the bottom of the tree, looking up at him. Alexis went up to the very top of the tree and yelled for help. Old Chief Squinas wasn't too far across the river, but the wind blow like hell, so Squinas couldn't hear him. Alexis tried to yell again. Bear still there. He went down about halfway. Lots of moss there. He pulled the moss and threw it at the bear. That bear not going anywhere, he just stay there. Alexis stayed in that tree for a long time, lot of hours. It was getting late in the afternoon, now. Alexis get worried. He don't want to have to sleep in that tree overnight.

Alexis pulled some moss off the tree, make a ball out of that moss. He try and throw it at the bear again. Again, that bear, he don't care. Alexis got some more moss and he think, "I'm gonna burn that bear." He will light that moss, throw it down to that bear's back, burn his hair, then maybe he'll run away. So Alexis tried it. He light a match, moss catch on fire. He throw it down right for that bear. The wind was blowing like hell. The wind blew that fire back into the tree, and burn the moss below. The tree started to burn below him! The wind spread the fire all over the tree on the bottom.

Alexis start to think, "That fire going to kill me, burn me alive. But if I go down there that grizzly bear's gonna get me." Alexis climbed to the top of that tree. Tree started burning up pretty good. Alexis decided he didn't want to burn alive, rather let that bear kill him. He was way up the tree, and he jump down to the ground. The whole tree was burning way up to the top. Alexis got to the ground and look for that bear. No bear! Then he started to run. He run for the canoe now. He got to the river, but the canoe was on the other side. Old Chief Squinas had rowed back over and tied up the canoe on the other side of the Atnarko River. Alexis looked back, no bear still, it was gone. He thought to himself, "Those damn Indians bullshit me. I piss and shit on that bear and he wouldn't go away." He yell and howl and Old Chief Squinas came down to pick him up.

Old Chief Squinas say, "What the matter? That tree over there is burning like hell."

The young guy told him, "Grizzly bear chase me up that tree."

The old man went to get his gun. He really wanted to get that deer meat. So he went back over to that island. When he got to the deer, he have to drag that deer back himself. The horses had all run away.

After this, that young fella took off. Alexis went back up-country. He don't want to stay there. Too many grizzly bears. But the Old Chief Squinas stayed down there. There was lots of fish and lots of wild berries down there. Raspberries, real good raspberries. His wife went to pick berries there every day. One day Old Chief Squinas decided that he want to make raspberry homebrew. So he took some of the old lady's raspberries and he cook it little bit in the fire. He had a three-gallon crock. He put that raspberry water into his crock, and he put yeast cake and sugar in there too. Then he dug a hole in the ground, put a blanket in there to keep his crock warm, put the crock of homebrew in there and buried it. Waited one week. He tried to drink it, it was good. Alcohol taste strong now. Better than the wine you buy in the store!

There was quite a bunch of them Anahim Lake Indians there now. They would all sit around the campfire and talk about things. One guy ask Old Chief Squinas, "Give me a drink of your homebrew, Squinas. I'll make you another. Lots of berries around." But Old Squinas wouldn't give nobody a drink, he drink all by himself. For two or three days he'd drink a little bit every day. One of them Anahim Lake Indian people get mad at him cause he don't give them a drink. So he came down and tell the policeman here in Bella Coola that Old Chief Squinas was drinking homebrew every day up at Stuie.

The policeman went up there and find Old Chief Squinas. "Squinas, you making homebrew here?"

He said, "No, no, I not making homebrew."

The policeman look, but that crock was underneath the dirt so he can't find it. The policeman left.

After Old Chief Squinas drink all his three-gallon crock of homebrew there were still lots of berries around. Old Squinas took some more of that old lady's berries again and make homebrew again. This time Old Chief Squinas took that crock down the Atnarko River quite a ways, about two hundred yards from the camp. There was springwater there. He dug a hole in the ground near that springwater and buried that homebrew crock. A week after he go to taste that homebrew. It was ready to drink. Each day he took a small little bucket—holds maybe three or four cups of wild raspberry homebrew—and fills it up and goes back to camp to drink it.

One morning he go back to get some more homebrew from his crock. He went slow into that springwater place. He heard somebody sleeping in there, snoring and softly snorting. Old Chief Squinas kneel down and look through the bushes. He see a big thing laying down there. Not a man. Got hair on him! He went slow up close to look. Grizzly bear! That grizzly bear drink almost the whole three gallons of homebrew and pass out there, right beside the crock. He look inside his crock. It was all dry. That bear lick everything inside. He grab that grizzly bear on his head, grab his ear, "Damn you, shit-head."

That bear just keep snoring. Squinas went home. No homebrew. That bear had cleaned him right out.

After I went up-country, before I got married to my first wife, I stayed with Old Chief Squinas. Around 1929 or 1930. He asked me what I'm doing up there. "Oh, nothing much," I said. "I got grub and pack horse." He said, "You can stay with me if you like." He could speak our language. Bella Coola Indian language. "You can stay with me," he say to me. So I stayed with that old man that first winter up-country. Cut a lot of wood for him. Haul hay for him. Old Chief Squinas was pretty old now. Thomas Squinas was his son. He live a couple of miles north from the old man's house.

I used to go see Thomas. Young guy, he was a couple of years older than me. Thomas is still alive, still going strong. He had a gramophone. He order a Jimmy Roger record, and he just got it. Cowboy songs. Thomas call me to come over and listen to them cowboy songs. I was sitting down over there listening to them cowboy songs on his gramophone when I look through the window, and I see two saddle horses going by. One old guy had a white cloth around his head. Look like it had blood on it.

"Thomas, look out there," I said.

"My dad," he said, "must have fall off the horse." Old Chief Squinas used to make homebrew at Christensen's every week. Old Man Christensen and Old Chief Squinas like to make homebrew every week. Thomas said, "My old man probably go over there and get drunk like hell. He must have fall off his horse on the way back home."

Thomas turn over the record and we listen to another cowboy song. Then we heard a horse galloping our way. Stopped right outside the cabin. Balonique, her name was. Balonique was Thomas's sister. She was real excited. She speak their own language to Thomas. Thomas tell me, "A moose almost kill my dad. He cut the old man's face wide open and his chest has all busted ribs too." That's what Balonique told Thomas. We got on horses, and we all went to see Old Chief Squinas.

I talked to Old Chief Squinas in my language, "What happen?"

He told me, "I see that moose. I get off my horse and shot it. Must have hit his horns. It fell down right away. I walk up to him. Take my knife out of my pocket. Going to cut his throat and bleed him. As soon as I try to cut him, that moose get up and went after me. I run into some jack pines. I get behind one good-sized jack pine. That moose pushed the jack pine over, knocked me down and he stepped on me. He open his toes and he stomp on me lots of times. That toe something like a knife, cut my face, broke my ribs too." Then Old Chief Squinas said to me, "I'm all right. I'm okay." Old Man Squinas had a bottle of whisky. I don't know where he get it from. He drink little bit out of it and feel better again.

There was a little boy with Old Chief Squinas at the time that moose stomped him. That kid was only about seven years old. Little Thomas we call him. The chief's grandson. When the moose was jumping on top of the old man's body, the kid scream out.

I asked that boy after, "Tell me the whole story."

"I scream as hard as I can," he said, "and then that moose come after me. I run into a hole in the ground. Black bear hole. I crawl in. Hit my head on the bottom end. I turn around gonna look out. The moose was digging, almost cover the hole."

The boy backed down the hole when the dirt start to come down on him. He backed up deep in the hole. He went backwards. He could hear real good underneath there. He could hear the moose take off, galloping away. He came out. He see the two horses were still there. They never run away. He could see Old Chief Squinas on the ground.

Little Thomas got the old man's horse. Lead that horse to the old man. Put the horse alongside him. "Pappa, here's your horse," he said. And he took Old Chief Squinas's scarf and wrapped it around that cut on that old man's head. Blood go right through that towel. Old Chief Squinas lost lot of blood. "Pappa, get on your horse," he said. The old man, he hear that kid and got on his horse. The boy get on his horse and lead him home.

That's how Chief Squinas died. He lived for about a month and then he died. I help take care of him, all the best I can. I don't know why he didn't want go down to Bella Coola to see doctor. He was an old man when he died. Must have been in his late eighties. After he died I stayed in his place for a while, then I met my first wife and went to live with her.

Nobody seemed to know much about them bones in that Poison Lake. Poison Lake is about ten miles up the Dean River from Anahim Lake. You can see those bones under the water, on the bottom of the lake. A lot of guys talk about it, Ulkatcho Indians, but nobody seems to know how they get there. Nobody see anything.

Some guys say the water is poison. If a moose drink in there he die. Or deer drink, he die right there too. Other people think something lives in that lake, comes out and kill animals. Maybe caribou fall through the ice one spring. There used to be a lot of caribou in that country. One guy walked out onto that lake in the winter, he looked down through clear ice and see bones, two feet thick right across the lake. I just don't know how them bones get there. No one know how them bones get there.

One day while I was hunting moose I run into it, that Poison Lake. Hot day, real hot day, in late August. I get off my horse and drink the water. My horse drink the water too. Water never bother me, never bother the horse. When I get on my horse to go, I look in the lake and I see them bones. All kinds of bones on the bottom. A big pile of bones, maybe one or two feet thick. I took my shoes off, try to walk out there to get a piece of bone. I wanted to find out how old them bones are. Show it to some guys, make them guess how old they are. I took my clothes off, and I went out and I dived down. I look for a good bone, and got a shoulderblade. Look pretty fresh, so I grab it, and I come out. I put my clothes back on, get on my horse and went home.

I tied that shoulderblade bone up on the limb of a tree in my hay camp at Blaney Meadow. Guys come around and look at it. "How old?" I ask. Some guys say about a year old, some say about two weeks old, some say a month old, some say ten years old. Nobody really know how old it is.

A year after, I went up to the foot of the Itcha Mountain. There's little lake in there. I was hunting muskrat up there with my nephew. Muskrat pretty good price that year—seven dollars a skin, I think it was. I run out of shells, shotgun shells. I told my nephew, "I got traps there at Poison Lake, mink traps in there. I stored them there last fall. Let's go and get it." This was in March, maybe April. Snow was gone on the sidehill where the sun shines but the ice was still on the lake. Just under the water. About four inch of water on top of the ice. We were about fifty yards from the lake, and we smell something, real strong smell. Smell like kelp from the ocean.

My nephew say, "You smell it?"

"Yeah, I smell it," I say.

"What is it?" he asked me.

"Maybe old bull moose ready to die," I said. "They get pretty strong smell in the spring."

We keep walking down to the lake. Get to where the traps are. Kind of a flat beach there, near all them big rocks there. My nephew jump down and stand beside me. I hear something, something making a swishing sound. Make a sound like rustling of last year's leaves. My nephew says, "Look at your feet." I look down. I was standing on top of three snakes. Small ones. They were trying to get away. I lift my leg, let them go. I look behind me. Holy smoke! Talk about a pile of snakes. About two and half feet deep. All coiled up. All over, wherever you look. Millions and millions of snakes. Smell too! I try to go down, walk on that ice to get away from them snakes. But there was snakes swimming in the water. Then I climb up onto the sidehill, the sand hill there. I had to walk through them snakes to get up onto the sidehill, away from those snakes. I look down. Seemed like there were millions and millions of snakes there.

Someday I like to go back there. But I can't remember if it was in March or April. It was muskrat season, that's what I remember. I'd like to take a movie of all them snakes. I never seen so many snakes in one place at one time. Millions and millions of snakes. Must be where all the snakes go to hibernate in the winter.

Fishing stories

One day the government give the timber in Kimsquit to Crown Zellerbach. Quite a while ago. I was married to Cora. This was before I had my logging company. The company hire pret' near all the Indians in the village. Guys who are able to work and fall timber. Lots of work to do. To cut all the wood above the old Kimsquit village. Right close to the ocean.

I asked for a falling job. They hire me. No power saw in those days. We pull a saw back and forth. Both ends of that sawblade has a handle. Eight feet long. One guy on each side of that sawblade. We pull that sawblade back and forth all day long. Cutting down big trees. Monday till Saturday. You got to file that saw on Sunday.

One weekend I told one guy, "Let's walk up the valley. See what we can find up there."

This guy Hank say, "Okay, let's go."

I told him we young yet, we can go up there and back same day. Far as we can go, figure out how far it take us to get back here. It was toward the end of March. We filed our sawblades Saturday night, and we started walkin' up the Dean River early Sunday morning.

I didn't know the country, but we found a pretty good old horse trail. We followed that horse trail, and we go down along the riverbank too. River was pretty low. We went up about twelve miles that day. We get to where the Dean River and Sakumtha River meet. There was a cabin there. In our Indian language *Sakumtha* means place where you cross. That Sakumtha River goes up to the Big Ootsa country.

Lot of steelhead there in them days. Gee, pools were black like there were eulachons in there. Couldn't see the bottom, that's how thick they are. I grab a rock and I throw it and they open up. You can see the bottom of the river. Them steelhead get away from where that rock drops down to the bottom. Then they close up again. Black bottom again. That's how thick the steelhead were.

There used to be lots of steelhead and trouts in the old days. Not as many now. Too many fishermans from all over. They kill them all off. Steelhead from here should be for Bella Coola people only. Vancouver bunch, Williams Lake bunch, Kamloops bunch, Quesnel bunch, Chilcotin bunch, they all come here to get steelhead and salmon. Not enough fish for all them guys. Fish and Wildlife should know that!

We were hungry and decided to stop at that cabin. There was a woodstove in it. I look around for wood first. There was some wood there all right. Inside cabin and dry, that's what I was looking for. And I found that kindling. All ready too. Nice, small pieces of wood to light in the stove. I cut some wood shavings. I told the guy, "Go downriver to get water. Use that little bucket there. We'll boil up some water. I'll make some coffee and some bannock." He went down to get the water.

I get some paper. I put that paper, shavings and kindling in the stove. I go to light it. Gee, I look down there. Funny thing happen to me. Something like somebody in my head tell me to look closer in there. I look closer. I see a shiny thing, right in the ashes. I pick it up. Box of dynamite caps! One hundred dynamite caps in there. I feel around, another box. Another hundred. Two hundred dynamite caps in that woodstove. If two hundred caps blow up, would have killed me. Just as good as one box of dynamite. I guess some guys, they leave the caps in the stove to keep it dry. I put them caps away and I light that stove. Short while, that stove was red hot. Nice dry wood burn good. We make our coffee, and our bannock. After that I went out and look around. I count seventeen boxes of dynamite beside the cabin. Seventy grain each stick. Would have blown up the whole mountain if the caps and dynamite all go off.

I work on makin' road one time. I know little about powder monkeying from doing that. Tallio Point. Blowing out stumps for logging road. Last World War. An old man teach me how to do it. How to blow up that dynamite. I told Hank, "I'm gonna put those two box of caps right amongst that seventeen boxes of dynamite and blow the whole thing up. Somebody going to get killed if we leave it behind like that."

"No, don't do that," Hank said. "The whole mountain will fall down. Could kill someone down below. Sidehill slide, plug the river up, and that dam let go and flood the whole village and kill people."

So I just blow that box of caps alone. I blow the whole works of caps. Leave the dynamite sticks alone. I put one cap right in the middle of the whole works, all the other caps, with a whole roll of fuse. I put them on the top of a stump. I light that fuse. By the time we gone about two hours it blow up. Just the caps, make a lot of noise. That guy jump up, and he run yelling "What's that?" He looking up at the mountain. He thought the mountain was gonna slide down on us.

I found out later five guys were mining copper up there. They blows holes in the mountains to find out if there is any better copper deeper inside.

The old people believed sturgeon live in Charlotte Lake. Joshua Moody and Alexander Clellamin used to trap all the way to Lomesome Lake, even right up to that big lake called Charlotte Lake. Used to be a good trapline. They tell me that they see a real big fish there, almost big as a whale.

GRIZZLIES & WHITE GUYS

I think it was a sturgeon. I know about sturgeon. When I was a little boy I see the Indian people get them sturgeon in the Fraser River. There were all kinds of sturgeon in Agassiz in the Fraser River. Big ones too. Sturgeon can grow up to thirty feet long. Way bigger than a halibut. Built like a salmon, built like a shark. Weigh way more than four hundred pounds.

I ask an old guy, "How do you get them sturgeon?"

"Go to the Chinese store and buy a whole chicken, put a big hook in it, tie it to a rope and throw it in the water. They will swallow that and you get 'em!" he said.

In the olden days the Agassiz Indians spear them big sturgeon with real long poles. The Indian people cut them sturgeon up and dry the meat by the sun. It taste all right. I ate some. I was just a kid. I don't remember too much about the taste of sturgeon.

I was only about twelve years old. I was with my mother. My dad had died. And a few months after she took us down there to Agassiz. My mother got to work to feed us. Good country down there to pick fruit. Lots of grapes. Lots of hops. There were big fields of hops in Agassiz. Three of us, me and my brother Alfred and my mother went picking hops. Hops is for beer. They are round, soft, and you grab a handful and put them in a basket. When you fill that basket, you dump them hops in a big box. When the box is full, some guys come in, take your box and give you another one to fill up.

We didn't make any money. Boxes were five feet wide by ten feet long. We got to fill that for three dollars. Some white guy pay us three dollars for a big box of hops. We didn't stay too long. Take two days sometimes to fill a box. Take three of us two days to fill the box for only three dollars. Some white guys would come by and steal your hops and fill their own boxes. We never go back there.

I don't think there is sturgeon in the Bella Coola River. But we do get them in the ocean, out in the inlet. Gill-net them little ones. About the size of a steelhead. But we never get them in the river. Maybe some guys do, I don't know. Maybe some guys get them and never tell.

There was an old man who used to live up-country. Joshua Moody was his name. He used to take me up to Burnt Bridge and Stuie every year. We stay up there for two months. Set nets in the river. Pick berries too. Get berries, mash it up, dry them into berry cakes about half-inch thick or more. In the wintertime dip that berry cake pieces in the water and in sugar. Taste real good. Loganberries were real good for berry cakes.

What I like best is them soapberries. Lots in Anahim Lake country, some around Stuie. They are a red berry. Lots in one bush. Lots of them. You get a big garbage sack. Put that garbage bag right over the bush. Bend the bush right over and hit that bag with a stick. The berries come out into that garbage sack. The Bella Bellas were really crazy about them berries. You squash them berries and whip them up. Taste like ice cream. Lots of white people eat them too.

Joshua tell me a lot of stories about Stuie country when we stay up there. Joshua told us there is big trouts in Lonesome Lake. Big Dolly Vardens, I think they call them. They even eat spring salmons! Joshua tell us, them big Dolly Vardens live right in that Lonesome Lake. They stay there almost all the time.

Dolly Varden like to eat fish. Like to eat little fry of spring salmon, and humpies and other fish when they hatch out in the spring. We used to catch them Dolly Vardens and cut them open and count how many fries were in 'em. The most I count, I count sixty fries in one Dolly Varden. My nephew had a Dolly Varden bigger than a steelhead, he had ninety-six fry in its stomach. The biggest Dolly Varden I ever get was up at the Burnt Bridge about fifteen to twenty years ago. You put two steelheads together, it was as big as that! Over twenty pounds. I caught it on a fishing rod.

Joshua Moody say that the biggest Dolly Vardens live in Lonesome Lake.

"How big do they grow, them Dolly Varden?" I ask.

He didn't say how big them Dolly Varden get but he did tell me that they could swallow a twenty-five pound spring salmon. "Just like nothing," he said.

We don't believe it. One day Sam Moody ask Old Man Edwards if that is true. "Do Dolly Varden swallow spring salmon in Lonesome Lake?"

"Yeah, it's true," he said.

A few years ago, when I first started to guide on Owikeno Lake, I took a Japanese guy out to get a grizzly bear. James Mullin was my assistant guide for that trip. He was a white guy from Vancouver that used to be a moose, deer and caribou guide. Then one day he decided he want to be a grizzly bear guide too. He came and talked to me, then I got him a licence to guide for me.

This hunt was in October. I took them up that Sheemahant River. We saw a lot of bears that trip. Counted fifty-two bears in three days, I think it was. I find one good place to rest and camp up the Sheemahant River. Nice grass, and the sun shines right out in front of you. Bear tracks all over. We made a camp there. I had a little radio. I put up the tent. James, he like to cook. He cut up some bacon and started to fry that bacon over the campfire.

That Japanese guy go out fishing. I tell him to use a T-Spoon lure. He got a coho right away. I cut it for him. That coho meat's kind of white. I tell him to go try again. He go back, cast out, and he get a big trout. I don't know what kind of trout. Maybe ten pounds. Rainbow, I guess. And I cut that for him too. White meat too. So I told him to go try again. He went down there again. Then I heard that Japanese guy yell, "I got another one, it's a big one." And I look, and he got a sockeye. Bright silver. Look like it just came from the

Fishing stories

ocean. "That's what we looking for," I said. "Hang onto that." I clubbed that sockeye, then I cut the head off right away. I cut it open from the back, cleaned off that meat good. I barbecue that sockeye in the campfire, the whole fish. On a big fire. James Mullin was cooking beans now, he plan to have fried bacon and beans. When that barbecued sockeye start to smell good, I put a little brown sugar and salt on it. I wait till it get nice and brown. I turn it, keep turning it till it is just right.

James, he smell it. He pinched a thin part of the cooked sockeye. Break a piece and he eat it. "Boy, it's good," he said. And that Japanese guy came and he ate some too. Then James grab his frying pan of beans and he dump it all over the ground. Spill the whole works. He decided he'd rather eat that fish than eat them beans. "Let the bears eat up the beans," he said. I told him, "You make coffee, I'll hook up that little radio. We gonna listen to weather. Find out if it will rain or sunshine tomorrow." I hook that radio wire to an antenna on a tree quite a ways away. We listen. Gonna be good weather. Late that night the radio fall down on the bed, James Mullin's bed. I didn't have that antenna wire high enough. A grizzle bear smell them beans, I guess, come around our tent and got the radio antenna wire caught on his neck. He pull that radio over. "They eating your beans, James," I said. James went out. "Go on, beat it." The bear went away. James said he could hear the bear running away.

T-Spoon worked good in that river, and in a lot of other rivers around here. Coho, spring salmon, steelheads, doesn't matter how muddy, I can get them on a T-Spoon lure. Silver one side of the blade, brass on the other side. T-Spoon lure was my favourite lure over the years, I use it for years and years.

I was sitting at home one day and a strange pickup truck stopped outside. I went out to meet them and it was George Ape and his son from Williams Lake. They worked in the mill in Williams Lake in them days. They asked me if I could take them out to the halibut grounds to get halibut, and they wanted to get some crabs and prawns too. Want me to guide them. I told them I could do that. We went out in the boat and stopped at Namu first to pick up some jiggers. We bought some extra 125-pound test line, it's deep out there. Need lots of line.

I always used to ask around. Ask the guys where is the good halibut fishing holes. "Where do them big halibuts live?" I ask them. And they would tell me where. Whenever I go where they say I stop and try it. Sure enough, I get them halibut every time. So I took George Ape to one of these spots the guys told me about.

I turned off the motor, and as we were drifting along I told George, "Right there in that big hole is where the halibut are hanging around." It was a little bay in the mountainside where there were a lot of herring and black cod. Halibut like to feed on herring and black cod. He threw his line in the water. I think that jigger was still going down when that big halibut get it. It never touched the bottom. George pulled up and yelled, "I think I get one already." George tried to pull it up and said, "No, I think I got the bottom." I grab hold of the line and pulled it. It pull back. I said, "No, I think you got a big halibut." So he try to reel it up but he couldn't do it. His son Bob tried to help his father and they both tried to pull it up but couldn't get it up. Crazy Horse, my grandson, he pulled it up for him. He was about eighteen years old at that time. He was strong, though, that boy. All muscles. Work hard all the time. Hammering, carpenter work. He took a look and said, "It's a real big halibut. I can see the head but I can't see the tail of that big halibut. I think the tail is still on the bottom of the ocean yet!"

I was in the bow of the boat and I could see the head of the halibut. He come up a little ways from the boat, about fifty feet away. So I picked up the .350 magnum handgun that we had with us and I shot that big halibut. One bullet right through the head. The fish went down again, and the others take turns to pull him up again. But this time he come up a hundred feet away. When I saw its head come a little above the water again, I shot and hit 'im again. That big guy, Bob, he couldn't pull it. He try to pull real hard. Crazy Horse feel his muscles, "There's nothing wrong with you, you're not weak, just lazy, that's all." He tease him. Three of them taking turns to reel it in. They were having a good time doing that.

I told the boys to go out in the small rowboat. My boat was too high to pull that big halibut up into. So they all got into my little rowboat. They pulled again on the line and that halibut must of swam a little because he came up in a different place. I shot him a third time with my .350 magnum handgun. They were pretty sure that this time that big halibut was dead. We all pulled his body over to the boat and with the two grapple hooks that we had, we dragged his body on board the big boat. He weighed three hundred forty-two pounds.

After we got that big halibut in the boat, George Ape came inside the boat and he talk to me. He look and see how far I shoot to hit that halibut in the head every time. He was a short guy. About five foot one, with few chin whiskers. Japanese guy. He look way up to me, make me feel like I'm six foot tall. Ask me where I learn to shoot so good. "Home Guard training," I tell him. "I learn to shoot like that when I was a Home Guard Ranger."

Them Fish and Wildlife guys

Sometimes I think the government is crooked. One year I take them Fish and Wildlife guys out. Went with Mitchell. He used to be head guy of Fish and Wildlife in Williams Lake. He died in a helicopter crash few years later. Some other guys from Fish and Wildlife went too. They hire me, paid me three hundred and fifty dollars a day. For ten days.

They hire a helicopter too. To go up all the rivers lookin' around for grizzly bear and salmons. Count how many bears we see up the creeks. I got to go in the helicopter too. Every day, from morning to night. We go in every valley. See if any salmon go up there, see if any bears in there or moose or goats. Come back out and go in the next one. Just keep going like that. All day for ten days. All the way from Kimsquit to Smith Inlet. I like it. I like helicopters. Can see a lot of country with helicopter.

Them Fish and Wildlife guys sleep on my boat at night, put the helicopter on the beach. Go fishing then. In Restoration Bay we hit a school of spring salmon. Big school of salmon. I jig with a buzz bomb. Buzz bomb is a good jigger. Any fish on the bottom will take that buzz bomb. Look like herring, I guess, look like a sick herring that's gonna die. Halibut take that, they wanna eat herrings. Salmon like coho and springs take them too. I got a coho on, he fight like hell. And I lost that buzz bomb. Those Fish and Wildlife guys ask me, what kind of lure you use to get that big coho that broke the line? "Buzz bomb," I said. Two guys get in that helicopter and fly to Bella Coola or Ocean Falls to get buzz bombs. Helicopter bring back them buzz bombs. And the Fish and Wildlife guys change to buzz bomb. Gee, every cast they get a spring salmon. They weigh them. Thirty-eight pounds. Twenty-five pounds. One got one forty-three pounds. Got about eight springs, two each for four guys. They keep all them spring salmon they catch.

Mitchell bring his kid too. His kid was about eight years old, I guess. That kid, he try to cast, backlashed, and his line got all tangled up. I try and help him untangle it. I told him, "Let it go down. Let the line sink. Much easier to untangle it that way." The kid, he listen to me. His father was in a little rowboat away from us. I guess when that buzz bomb hit the bottom, when that kid was working on untangling the line, he move that buzz bomb around. A big halibut grab it.

The kid just pull up and said, "I don't think it's a spring salmon." "Could be," I said. But that fish pull steady, that's halibut. I tell him, "Get on that other little boat with your dad. Then reel it in." He get down there in the boat. Pull and pulling until he get sore in the chest by the end of that fishing rod there. His father grab hold of his kid's rod.

"Clayton," he said, "I think it's a halibut."

I said, "There is halibut anyplace, all over here. Halibut can go in shallow water." There was only about twenty-five feet of water there. "I seen them in ten feet of water in Bella Bella," I told him. "I'm sure it's a halibut." Line about twelve-pound test only. I have to talk to them, "Don't fight it too much you will break the line." I yell at that Mitchell, the head guy in Fish and Wildlife, "Give that fishing rod to your son. That's his fish.

That's not yours." I know that kid wouldn't break that line. He's not strong enough to break it.

Mitchell look down and see it, "It's a big halibut. Maybe a hundred pounds."

I said, "I'm gonna shoot him."

That head guy said, "Yeah, we better shoot him. Or else we gonna lose him."

I had a small little gun. That halibut came along side of the boat. Mitchell, he grab ahold of my handgun, and he aim to shoot that halibut's head. He hold on to the line and point the gun inward. I said, "You gonna shoot your leg. That bullet's gonna go through the head of that halibut, go through the aluminum boat, right into your leg." Mitchell didn't think of that. So he pointed the gun the other way and shot that halibut. Then we got that halibut in the boat.

I'll tell you how crooked them government guys are. We took my boat to Kwatna and them government guys killed twenty-seven coho. About three of those guys fishing. Allowed only two salmon each a day in those days. They keep all twenty-seven coho, pack them into the helicopter and fly them all the way to Williams Lake in the helicopter to get rid of them. Must be expensive to do that. The helicopter brought back four new guys. I told Mitchell, "We got no bed for these four new guys." Those guys got enough coho, they want halibut now. We got eight halibut for those four guys. Two each. Allowed one each in those days. They put them halibut in the helicopter and flew back to Williams Lake.

I say, "I think you get your limit! If a game warden come around here you gonna get in trouble. Breakin' the law. You take too many fish. If the game warden come around he gonna pinch us all. Lock us up in jail."

Mitchell just laugh at me. That's why I say, sometimes I think government people are crooked.

Crooked-Head Charlie. We called him Crooked-Head Charlie. Indian guy. He came from Kwatna. Kwatna Indian, I think. His head was crooked to the side all the time. He can't straighten it. I asked my mother, "What the matter with Charlie, his head crooked all the time?" She said, "One side of his mother's tits haywire, not good." She could feed him only with the good tit. Charlie had to keep his head to the one side all the time, feed on just the one side. And his head never come back. Stayed like that all the time. That's how come his head was crooked like that.

He was a real good guy. Everybody liked him. He works hard too. He would turn them sailing fishboats into gas boats. Buy them old sailing boats and change them. Cut the stern off and make it wider, and put a crook on it and a post. Then put a motor into them old sailboats. He was doing that for so many years. Made a good job for himself.

Crooked-Head Charlie was crippled too. Hurt so many times. Hurt his hand. Cut his hand pretty bad. Big scarred-up cut. He was filing that prop, file it so that the prop is sharp as a knife now. Somehow he slipped, cut his hand. He can use it, but looked bit crippled. He get blowed up with dynamite one time too. Just the caps blow up on him. So many years after some brass come out of his head. He feel it one day, cut a little hole, get some tweezers and pull it out. Years after. Tough guy. Short but he's stout. But what a nice guy. Kind of funny too.

Crooked-Head Charlie told me he been hurt so many times, that he got a bad heart, and that he get short-winded when he just do a little work. Walk too fast, get out of wind right now. Walk up the gangplank at the float, he's just make it to the top, then look like he was gonna die. All puff out.

One year just after I came back to Bella Coola from Anahim Lake I see Crooked-Head Charlie walking toward me. It was in May. I was still married to Doll. He came up to me, "I wait for you all winter, Clayton. I want to let you know I want a grizzly bear gallbladder. I can't write to tell you to come down. So I wait for you to come back to Bella Coola and help me. I need your help. Bears come out and eat grass like horses at Kwatna this time of year. Now, right now, let's go to Kwatna and get a bear. I'm a sick man, I need that grizzly bear gallbladder right away. My boat is all ready. I got gas and grub. Please help me, Clayton."

So I went out there with Crooked-Head Charlie. Just a few minutes after we get to Kwatna, some grizzly bears come out onto the tideflat. We saw three grizzly bear all in one bunch. Two were eating grass head to head. Their head just close together. And a big one right behind them. He's just as long as the two. That's the one I shot for Crooked-Head Charlie. After I killed that big grizzly bear for Crooked-Head Charlie, he cut open that grizzly bear and took out the gallbladder from the liver all by himself. He was holding the outlet tube where the gallbladder juice come out. He hang onto that. He show that grizzly bear gallbladder to me. "I get it now, my medicine," he said. And he started to laugh. He was laughing. He get better, like, before he even drink that gallbladder juice.

We go down to the boat. Crooked-Head Charlie got a kettle on the stove. There was hot water in it, ready for coffee or tea or anything. Crooked-Head Charlie get a cup and he pour some hot water into that cup. He squeeze some of that grizzly bear gallbladder juice right into that cup. He stir it up, cool it off a little bit, and then he drink it all. Looked like piss water to me. Same colour anyway. I don't know how he can drink it. After he drink it he start to laugh. He grab my hand and he shake it. "Thank you Clayton," he said, "you saved my life." He laugh again. Usually when Crooked-Head Charlie laughs hard he runs out of wind, but not this time. This time he laugh and laugh and not run out of wind!

After that he was really happy. Laughing all the time. Every time he get sick he drink some more of that grizzly bear gallbladder juice. I just get the one gallbladder for him, but he trapped in Kwatna country and late in the fall a lot of grizzly bear are around there eating salmon. I think he got his own grizzly bear gallbladder after that. Or his brother-in-law got it for him there in Kwatna. He lived a few years after and then he died. I think he would have died sooner without that gallbladder juice.

One day a Chinese guy came up from Vancouver. He was looking for me in the village. That's what he told me. He came in the back door of my house. Him and his daughter. She was eighteen or nineteen years old, I guess. He was about fifty-five or more years old. He can't speak English. We had a hard time to understand each others. His daughter help him talk to me. I took them both into the kitchen. He wanted bear gallbladders. He said, "I'll give you thirty-five dollars for grizzly bear gallbladder." He write that down. Thirty-five dollars. He don't know the English name but his daughter did. She said, "My dad wants gallbladders—black bear or grizzly bear."

He also tell me he want sea-lion *googoos,* penises. I had a hard time understanding that he wanted the *googoo* of a sea-lion. First he try and draw on a piece of paper what it looks like. Then he speak Chinese to his daughter. He try and get her to tell me what that sea-lion *googoo* is called in English but she wouldn't say it. I figured out what he wanted. He said he would pay one hundred bucks for that! One hundred dollars for a sea-lion *googoo.* I just tell him I would try but I never did. That Chinese girl phone me later from Vancouver. Ask if I get any gallbladders or sea-lion *googoo* but I didn't have any for them.

I did try to save bear gallbladders one year. Before I took the hunters out that year I bought steaks, stew meat, bacon and meat and put it in the ice box in my boat. I had ice in there. That ice keeps the food cool. On that trip we get black bears right away. I saved their gallbladders. That Chinese guy told me to keep any bear gallbladders I get in a cold place so I put them in the ice cooler in my boat. Then we got four grizzly bear. I save their gallbladder too. Put them in the ice cooler too. Same place. But I found out it was pretty hard to keep them gallbladders without making a big mess. One day, I open that cooler to get some meat to cook. But that gallbladder juice leaked right through some bags to that meat. "Oh, what the hell," I think, I threw them all in the water. I found out later I threw away so many hundred dollars when I do that.

I forget how much money that taxidermist in Williams Lake say I lost when I throw them eight bear gallbladders in the water. Maybe sixteen hundred dollars worth of gallbladders! I visited him after that hunt. Some guys shot a bear in the mountain around Williams Lake, right close to their car, they threw it into the car and drove it right to the taxidermist's house. "I want you to skin and tan that hide," one of them say. The taxidermist say, "Okay, I'll do that for you. Will cost you twenty dollars for me to skin and tan that bear hide." He didn't say nothing about the gallbladder. He skin that bear, I help him skin that black bear. He cut it open, take that gallbladder. Next day, a Chinaman come. The taxidermist had three gallbladders to give him. The taxidermist got six hundred dollars for three gallbladders! Got only sixty dollars for skinning those three bears.

Another Chinese guy and a Japanese guy came into Bella Coola after that. I was all by myself, alone in the house. And they came in. I never meet them before. That Japanese guy speak real good English. They were looking for things to buy. They buy anything! Smoke fish. Want smoke fish in the worst way. Mines like gold mines or copper mines. Hotsprings. Want to buy all these things. "What about bear skins?" I ask. "We buy that too," he said. "We will buy anything." They even wanted to buy my grizzly bear guiding area. I told them, "I don't hunt bear any more. I'm gonna sell out. I can't get no more bears." They told me, "Hang on to your grizzly bear guiding license for a while, don't sell it right now. We'll take it over."

"But he give me some money, down payment money already," I said.

"Give his money back," they say. "There's a lot of Japanese and Chinese guys that want to shoot grizzly bear and eat grizzly bear parts." Then we get to talking about bear gallbladders. I tell them about this guy from Vancouver who offer me thirty-five dollars for one gallbladder, and I tell about that guy in Williams Lake who pays two hundred dollars for a bear gallbladder. They tell me if you get hold of the guy in Hong Kong, the backbone of the gallbladder business, he will give you a thousand dollars for one bear gallbladder!

I ask that Japanese guy what they do with gallbladders, "Make it into pills for medicine bottle?"

"No," he said, "hang it above a stove and let it dry. Dry till it get hard. Grind it up. Then get half a cup of warm water and you cut off a small piece of gallbladder. Put it in that cup of warm water and stir it up. When that ground-up gallbladder meat dissolves, when it's gone, you can drink it."

"Oh, no," I said, "I don't think I can drink that piss water. Why don't they make it into pills? Make it easy to swallow, so you don't have to taste it." I never hear from them any more. They say they were gonna come back. But they never did.

One day I ask Brenda Nygaard, since she works at the hospital, "What they do with them gallbladders? Why does that guy in Hong Kong pay so much money for a bear gallbladder? One thousand dollars for one gallbladder. For lousy piss water." She know more than me about those gallbladder. She tried to tell me that them Chinese, they want to keep up their own sex. That's what she told me. I still don't know what she mean by that. Next time I see her alone by herself, I gonna ask her what she mean by drinking that bear gallbladder will help keep up sex. How does it work? Is it for the man or the woman? When that Chinaman get too old and can't raise no hard-on, does he take that gallbladder and get a hard-on like an eighteen-year-old boy? I just don't know. I think I'm gonna try that gallbladder medicine one day. If I get a hard-on like them Chinaman I'll sell lots. Sell it to those bald-headed old guys in the United States who are always looking for nice-looking womans. I'll sell it to them. Make big money!

GRIZZLIES & WHITE GUYS

I think Fish and Wildlife is gonna cut out hunting for grizzly bear altogether now because too many guys kill bears just for gallbladders. Lot of guys been doing that, shoot that grizzly bear, cut out the gallbladder and take the claws. Sell the gallbladder for two hundred bucks, and sell each claw for about twenty-five dollars.

I had a few grizzly bear claws. I give it to my grandson in Vancouver. He says he can sell them in Vancouver for twenty-five bucks each. I met one guy in Owikeno Lake who had a bunch of grizzly bear claws. He was a Fisheries guy. He tell me he found a dead bear. Took all the claws. He tell me, "You know how much those claw necklaces cost in Vancouver? Eighty-five dollars! They drill a hole through one end of a claw. Put a fancy chain through there. Make it into a necklace and then sell it for eighty-five dollars."

"What about the teeth?" I ask him.

"No, not teeth," he said. "Just the claws."

I seen some dead bears around Owikeno Lake, look like someone shooting them grizzly bears and just cutting the claws off and taking the gallbladder. Leave the rest of the bear to rot, leaving it for the other bears to eat up. I hear some white guys were doing that. Maybe even that Fisheries guy was doing it. I don't really know. All I know is that when I was younger, Fisheries guys didn't like grizzly bears. Fisheries even offered me a job to kill any grizzly bear I see, all year round. They were gonna pay me five dollars a day to do this. In them days they think the bears were killing too many fish. I didn't do it.

I don't like the way the Fish and Wildlife study them bears. Fish and Wildlife sticks a needle right into the bear's hip, bear falls asleep, then they put an ear tag on, radio collar, and tattoo their lips. Then they let that grizzly bear go. They want to find out how far them grizzly bears go. They snare the foot to catch the bear and sometimes that snare wire cuts right in. Right through his skin. Can kill the bear, you know.

I kill one grizzly that got his foot caught in a snare. This was just before my stroke. Right across from Robin's Nest, near Noosgulch bridge. I had to put him out of his sickness. That snare wire was cut right in through the wrist joint. Almost cut the leg right off that grizzly bear. I could see he needed help. I remembered a story from the old peoples. When a bear smile at you, he needs help. Well that bear was smiling at me. I try and chase him into the heavy timber, but he wouldn't go. I talk to him, "Go on, go hide yourself. Get away from the mushroom pickers." But he walk behind an old dead log, he want to stay near the shore. It look like the snare wire was wrap around his neck too. He was dragging that snare wire around. Keep on smiling at me, ten to fifteen feet away. Holding his hand up like he want me to help him. But I can't help him, can't take it off, he might bite me. He can't fight, he can't get food. So I killed him.

I took the hide, that hand and the head to Vancouver to the taxidermist. They skin the paw, say it was rotten. Meat was black and rotten and there was little worms growing inside the skin. Worst thing they ever saw. They said it was wolf snare wire. Someone used snare wire that was too small to use for a grizzly bear. I don't know why Fish and Wildlife needs to collar them bears. Them grizzly bears go a long ways. Fish and Wildlife should know that. There was one grizzly bear who walk into the kitchen in a South Bentinck logging camp. And the cook had a box of apples in the kitchen. That bear walk right into the kitchen and start to eat that apples in the box. When he get enough he goes. But he keep coming back so they phone the Fish and Wildlife to take that bear away from the camp or shoot him. Some Fish and Wildlife guys took a trap in there. That grizzly bear went in the trap and the cage door dropped. They took him out to an island twenty miles away. The next day he was back in the cook house kitchen.

Ever since I was old enough to remember things, guys fish with gill-netters and trollers. Mostly with gill-netters. No engines

Clayton beside the Kwatna River, 1938

when I first go fishing. Two guys in one boat. One guy rowing, one guy setting net. Every morning a fish packer boat would come around and pick up any fish we had. Every Sunday morning, tugboat tow us out. We go out as far as Labouchere Channel, about thirty miles from Bella Coola. Friday he tow us in again. Sometimes we sail back to Bella Coola from Labouchere Channel. Later they turn them sailing fishboats into gas boat. Cut the stern off and they put in an engine. They use one cylinder, five horsepower engine in the beginning. After a while motors get bigger—two cylinders, ten horsepower. Then three cylinders, then the four cylinders. After a while the car engines come in, over one hundred horsepower. Then they get them big diesel engines. You should see some of them speedy boats now out in the inlet. Gill-netters that go like hell, go to Vancouver in one day!

Later seine boats came. Now there is hundreds and hundreds of seine boats. Lot of seine boats now, and they take a lot of fish. I'm afraid them seiners take too much fish. Salmon and herring. I think the herring seiners are the worst. Them herring seiners make up to a million dollars in fifteen minutes' work. They put a big net in the water. By the time they pull the bottom of the net together, takes only fifteen minutes. And they get tons and tons of herring. One guy tell me he get seventy tons in one set! Then they sell the roe to the Japs, and make fertilizer out of the heads and bodies. Them herring seiners kill everything that gets caught in the net. Big salmons, young salmon, sea-trouts, cods, and millions and millions of herrings.

When the herring is all gone in the salt water them fishermen will be sorry. There will be no more salmon for commercial fishermen, no more salmon for the Indian people. Salmon feed on herrings. All the big fish feed on herrings. Spring salmon, coho, and even codfish and halibut, they all feed on herrings. Why does the government want to clean all the herrings out of the coast?

When I was a kid there wasn't much logging on. Guys cut cedar logs for their houses, and some guys cut wood for the canneries. Each cannery needed about three hundred cords of wood a year to cook the fish. That's not many logs. That was the only logging they did when I was a kid. Cutting trees for the canneries. Then the white men started to cut more and more trees down. Now they can cut down all the trees in a valley in just a few years. They do that to big valleys too!

I don't like it when they log the whole valley. They didn't used to do that in the old days. Too much. Too fast. Something bad going to happen, I don't know what's gonna happen, but it's gonna happen. I kind of believe that after they log like that the whole land moves downhill, kind of like slow-moving water. When they cut all the timber there is nothing to hold the ground any more. No roots. Then the whole earth moves.

I pret' near lost my boy and George Anderson in Owikeno Lake one year. The logging company is cutting all the timber in Owikeno Lake. Not leaving much. We were hunting one side valley in Machmell. We put up a camp in there. I told Dusty, my son, and George Anderson, "You leave that little blue boat by that stump over there and then we'll take just one boat up the river." So they did. They tied that boat to some big roots coming out of the ground from that big stump. We headed up the river. It started to rain hard. Started to flood. So I said, "Let's get out of here. Go back to our cabin in Washwash. Higher ground there."

Dusty walked down the Machmell River, and George went with him to get that little blue boat. I picked up the hunters and got our stuff together. Then we headed downstream. After a while we see Dusty and George. They were trying to reach the boat. But the stump and boat and the land was moving out into the lake. Keep going out into the lake. Like a slow-moving landslide. When George and Dusty got to the boat, the boat and stump sunk into Owikeno Lake. George and Dusty get there and hang onto the rope. When I get there, we cut the rope and save that boat.

Up-country they cutting the whole thing up too. I talk to a guy from up-country. I told him something's gonna happen, something bad. He tell me already one lake up there dried right up after they cut all the timber around it. They have machines now up-country which cut a hundred truckloads of trees a day. That one machine can clip the trees and take the branches right off. Big claws wrap around the trunk, move up and clip all the branches off. Then them claws go down and clips the whole tree. Another arm comes and grabs the log and carries it into a pile. Then they load the whole works into a truck. One hundred loads a day. Way way too many trees.

After they log like that you can't trap animals. We tried but not much luck. We tried in South Bentinck. Used to be a real good trapline. But they logged the whole valley, both sides. Fur animals go someplace else. Kimsquit, the same thing. That Kimsquit River valley is gonna get in big trouble. I look at it a few years ago from a plane. I fly through there. Nothing but riverbed there now. Big wide riverbed. Nothing but rocks. No trees, no brush grow beside the river like in the old days. Way different now than in the old days. Big trees are all gone on the bottom valley, and trees are gone up to two thousand feet on the sidehills on both sides of the river. Them loggers are cleaning the trees right out of Kimsquit. Leaving just bare dirt and rocks.

When you cut all the big trees from the river it is bad for the animals. Grizzly bears need them big trees. They sleep underneath that. I remember counting over fifty grizzly bears on the riverbank along the Sheemahant River one year, in just two or three days. While we were going up and down that river in a riverboat we see that many grizzly bears. Two years after everything was all cut. They cut all the trees down. We don't see any more bears by the river after that. Nothing. Only far up on the sidehills and creeks we can get them. Other birds and animals need them big trees to live too. They make nests, eat, hide in them big trees. Them forestry guys should know that. I guess they don't care about the birds and animals.

I think that greedy logging is no good for the fish too. When there is no big trees by the river, spawning fish don't like that. When there is no tree shadow on the river, the fish quit going up the river. They don't like to move upriver in the bright sunshine. When it rains real hard after they log like that, no moss and trees to suck up the water. Water just go right down the hill, take all the dirt and turn the creeks brown and muddy. That mud kills the spawning fish eggs and the little fish. They should do just a little bit of logging every year. Not fifty million feet of timber in every valley in one year. It's just too much. I hope they don't log the Skowquiltz. Lucky to get three million feet of logs out of that country. Leave it to the sasquatches. I hope they don't log the Kitlope too. There's not much logs in there either. Leave them rivers alone. That Kitlope is mountain goat, grizzly bear, moose, and black bear country. Lot of black bears in there. Skowquiltz, Koeye and Kitlope Rivers. Those are some of the last ones.

Any grizzly bear and salmon river or creek around, them

loggers go in there and get the trees. Ashlulm, Aseek, Bella Coola, Cascade, Chuckwalla, Clyak, Dean, Eucott Bay, Frenchman Creek, Genesee, Inziana, Jenny Bay, Johnstone, Kilbella, Kimsquit, Kwatna, Larso Bay, Machmell, Milton, Namu, Necleetsconnay, Neechanz, Nicknaqueet, Nieumiamus, Noeick, Nooseseck, Nootum, Quatlena, Sheemahant, Taleomey, Tzeo, Wannock, and the Washwash River. They all been logged.

Why does the government have to kill so many trees and kill them so fast? Trees been there hundreds and hundred of years, why them white guys want to cut them all down in less than fifty years? What is the rush? Why are those white guys so damn greedy? Why does the government want to do that to all the grizzly bear and salmon river valleys?

Indians don't do nothin', can't do nothin', we just sit and watch the white men do that to the land.

Index

A

Abuntlet Lake, 27, 34, 38
Alert Bay, 9, 20–22, 38
Alexis (Old Chief Squinas's son-in-law), 201–204
Alexis Creek, 27
American Sportsman television program, 57–59, 62, 67
Anahim Lake, 9–10, 22, 25–27, 31, 33–34, 36, 38–39, 41, 141, 143, 155–156, 164, 170, 172–173, 180, 193, 197, 200–201, 205, 209, 215, 223
Anahim Peak, 25, 34
Anderson, George, 72, 80–81, 134–135, 231
Ape, George, 217–219
Aseek River, 234
Ashlulm, 234
Asseek River, 47, 127
Atnarko River, 28, 39–40, 49–51, 145, 165, 201–202, 204–205

B

Behind Meadow, 24, 34
Belarko, 50
Bella Bella, 9, 14, 17, 20, 41, 47, 130, 199, 215, 221
Bella Coola, 9, 13–17, 26–34, 36–39, 41, 44, 49–50, 52, 57–58, 66–67, 71–72, 80, 96–98, 100–101, 104, 106, 111–112, 118, 123, 130, 134, 138, 155, 160, 162, 164–165, 168, 170, 172, 179–180, 185–188, 196–197, 201, 205–206, 208, 214, 221, 223, 226, 230, 234
Bella Coola River, 47
Bentinck Arm, South, 42, 105, 127, 130–133, 143, 154, 159–160, 162, 179, 181, 184–185, 192, 229, 232
Bernard, David, 139
Big Buck Hill, 148
Blaney Meadow, 34, 209
Boo-Boo, 81–84
Boone and Crockett awards, 47, 53, 81, 83, 92, 98–99, 107–108, 111, 143, 147, 152
Bowser family, 22
Branford, Reed, 43
Brooks, Joe, 57
Brown, Jerry, Governor of California, 60–61, 104
Brynildsen Bay, 127, 130
Butcher, Walter, 57

C

Cahoose, George, 168
Cahoose, Tommy, 56
Calvert Island, 41
Capoose, Anton, 25–29, 31, 38
Capoose, Doll, 23, 25, 27–34, 37–38, 41, 164, 169, 172, 200, 223
Capoose, Rosalie (nee Sandyman), 24
Carpenter, Richard, 199
Cascade, 47, 234
Chilcotin, 9, 11, 150, 163–164
Chilcotin Indians, 10
Chinook language, 14, 19–20
Christensen, Andy and Dorothy, 33–34, 36, 167
Chuckwalla River, 47, 234
Clayton, John, 14–18, 36
Clayton, Vinny, 34, 167–168, 173
Clellamin, Alexander, 20, 213
Cless Pocket, 34
Club Safari, 69–70, 111–112
Clyak, 234
Cole, John, 187
Collin, Carolyne, 114–117
Crooked Jaw (Indian agent Foughner), 33, 36
Crooked-Head Charlie, 174–175, 222–224
Crown Zellerbach (logging company), 43, 211

D

Dean River, 23, 42, 47, 168, 208, 211–212, 234
Dempsey, Jack, 117
Dorsey, Lester and family, 22–23
Draney, George, 43

E

Edgar, Herb, 42
Edgar, Joe, 74
Edwards, Ralph, 216
Eucott Bay, 47, 118, 234

F

Felix (farm hand), 31–32
Fish and Wildlife Ministry, 47, 58, 106, 220–221, 228–229
Fort Rupert, 14–17
Frenchman Creek, 234

G

Genesee, 234
George, Dan, 62
Gibson, Phyllis, 19
Gilbert, Ned, 61–62
Graff, Pat, 92
Green Bay, 44
Green River, 164
Grizzly Bear Valley, 161

H

Hall, John, 195, 197
Hall, Norman, 112
Hans, Old Man, 192
Hans, Willie, 130
Harry, Captain, 170
Heckman, Maxie, 28–29, 40
Hollywood, 10, 58, 60–61, 63, 66–67, 69–70, 104, 111, 113
Hotnarko Mountain, 163
Hunt, Tommy, 17

I

Inziana River, 47, 81, 134, 234
Itcha Mountains, 24, 34, 145

Index

J
Jacobson Bay, 123
Jamos (farm hand), 31
Jason, Rick, 58, 67
Jenny Bay, 234
Johnstone Creek, 234

K
Kelly, Jim, 179
Kilbella River, 47, 234
Kimsquit River, 47, 234
King Island, 47
King, Connie and Jane, 36
King, Hank, 179, 181, 211, 213
Kitlope, 125–126, 133, 233
Kleena Kleene, 199
Klemtu, 130
Koeye River, 47
Kwatna River, 42, 44, 47–50, 52, 57–58, 85, 87, 108, 116–117, 119, 121–123, 125, 141, 143, 145, 147, 149–150, 174–175, 178, 194, 199, 222, 224–225, 230, 234

L
Labouchere Channel, 44, 230
Larso Bay, 234
Little Meadow, 163
Lonesome Lake, 215–216

M
Machmell River, 47, 151, 231–232, 234
Mack, Alfred, 17, 21, 214
Mack, Cora, 41, 43, 211
Mack, Donald, 17
Mack, Doris, 41
Mack, Dusty, 41, 98–99, 134–135, 231–232
Mack, Eliza (Clayton's daughter), 34, 37–38, 41
Mack, Eliza (Clayton's sister), 17
Mack, Minnie, 17
Mack, Obie, 134–135
Mack, Orden, 13, 17
Mack, Samson, 15–17, 117, 122, 132, 179, 184–188, 195
Mack, Wanda, 41
Mack, Willie, 14–16, 18
Mackie, Bob, 133–136
Martin, Mungo, 17
Mastrangel, 85–87
Matthews, Bert, 165–166
McLean, Dr., 170
Mesachie Nose, 11
Mitchum, Robert, 67
Molasses (mummified body in grave box), 188–191
Moody, David, 172
Moody, Joshua, 20, 213–215
Morrison Meadow, 35
Moses Inlet, 47
Mosher Creek, 53
Mud Bay, 127
Mullin, Jim, 97, 100, 216
Mussel Inlet, 41
Myhrvold, Alton, 60, 104–113

N
N'anikda, 14–16
Nascall Bay, 47
Necleetsconnay River, 234
Neechanz River, 136, 234
Nicknaqueet, 234
Nieumiamus Creek, 234
Nimpo Lake, 35
Noeick River, 47, 179–182, 192, 234
Nooseseck River, 234

Noosgulch Mountain, 13, 17, 229
Noosgulch Village, 13
Nootum River, 47, 106–108, 234
Numenta, 161–162
Nusatsum River, 180–181
Nusatsum, Mount, 13, 180–181
Nuxalk nation and language, 9–10, 19–20
Nygaard, Brenda, 227

O
Ocean Falls, 43, 130, 188, 221
Olsen, George, 125
Orden, Elizabeth, 17
Ounpuu, Hanna, 92, 97
Owikeno Lake, 11, 47, 63, 83, 93–94, 97, 134–136, 138, 142, 149, 216, 228, 231–232
Owikeno Village, 138

P
Poison Cove, 41
Poison Lake, 208–209
Poison Lakes, 34
Pollard, James, 125
Pollard, Paul, 125, 174–175
Pootlass, Albert, 104
Port Hardy, 14, 17
Precipice, 37, 148, 157, 165–166

Q
Q'uit, 14–16
Quatlena River, 234
Quesnel, 24

R
Ratcliff, Bob, 156
Redstone, 150, 162
Restoration Bay, 20, 106, 220
Rivers Inlet, 9, 20, 80, 138–139
Robin's Nest, 229
Robson, Bert, 39–40
Robson, Josephine (nee Capoose), 23–30, 32–34, 38–42, 145, 172–173

S
Salloomt River, 133
Samson, Mary, 13, 16–17
Sasquatch, 125, 127–133
Saunders, Art, 130
Saunders, Joe, 50
Schooner, Fred, 179–180
Schooner, John, 179–180
Schooner, Samson, 179
Sheemahant River, 47, 97–100, 216, 233–234
Shilling family, 22
Shutts, Walter, 56–57
Skeena River, 200
Skowquiltz River, 47, 76, 109–110, 116, 118, 122, 131, 133, 144, 194–196, 233
Smith Inlet, 220
Smitley River, 179–181, 185
Snootli hatchery, 179, 181, 185
Snow, Charles and Josie, 156
Snow, Timothy, 162
Sohanovich homestead, 143, 158
Squinas, Balonique, 207
Squinas, Louis, 29, 38–39, 173–174, 193
Squinas, Old Chief Thomas, 22–23, 162–164, 170, 201–208
Squinas, Thomas, 22, 207
Squinas, Thomas (Tommy), 22, 56, 197–201, 206–207
Stuie Lodge, 43, 49–50, 52–53, 55, 141, 215

Index

Sulin, Sam, 35
Swallop Creek, 47

T
Talchako River, 133
Taleomey River, 47, 127, 160, 234
Tallio Point, 213
Tanya Lakes, 49
Taylor, Elizabeth, 67
Teddy (Bella Coola Indian constable), 33–36, 170, 172
Thomas, Father (Catholic priest), 23, 29, 207
Tweedsmuir Park, 37
Tzeo River, 47, 63, 98, 234

U
Ulalitsuk, 14
Ulkatcho, 27, 31–32, 168, 200, 209

Union Steamships, 26, 52

W
Wahoo (trapper), 179, 188
Walker, Tommy, 43, 47, 49–52, 54–55, 141
Walkus, Thomas, 17
Wannock River, 234
Washwash River, 47, 63–64, 80–81, 83, 94, 96, 134, 232, 234
West, Charlie, 170
Wilderness Airline (Bella Coola), 58–59, 80
Williams Lake, 33, 35, 60, 67, 92–93, 134, 200, 217, 220, 222, 226–227
Wilson, Old Man Jonathan, 174–175
Wright, B.C., 155